DAILY BIBLE READINGS THAT CONNECT WITH YOUR LIFE

ENGAGE 365

—— VOLUME TWO ——

GET TO KNOW GOD'S PEOPLE

Engage 365: Get to Know God's People
© The Good Book Company, 2023

Published by:
The Good Book Company

thegoodbook
COMPANY

thegoodbook.com | thegoodbook.co.uk
thegoodbook.com.au | thegoodbook.co.nz | thegoodbook.co.in

Unless indicated, all Scripture references are taken from the Holy Bible, New International Version. Copyright © 2011 Biblica, Inc. Used by permission.

A CIP catalogue record for this book is available from the British Library.

The notes for this volume of Engage 365 have been edited by Alison Mitchell and Sarah Hughes. Based on Engage notes mainly written by Martin Cole, with extra material from Cassie Martin, Roger Fawcett, Chris Jennings, Carl Laferton, Jim Overton, Jill Silverthorne, Fiona Simmons, Sarah Smart, Adrian Taylor-Weekes, Tim Thornborough and Helen Thorne.

ISBN: 9781784988821 | Printed in India

Design by André Parker

Contents

-- -- -- -- -- -- -- -- --

INTRODUCTION

Time to engage

1 Set a time when you can read the Bible every day.

2 Find a place where you can be quiet and think.

3 Grab your Bible and a pen.

4 Ask God to help you understand what you read.

5 Read the day's verses with *Engage 365,* taking time to think about it.

6 Pray about what you have read.

BIBLE STUFF

We use the NIV Bible version, so you might find it's the best one to use with *Engage 365*. But any modern Bible version will be fine.

If the notes say, "Read Matthew 1 v 1–17", look up Matthew in the contents page at the front of your Bible. It'll tell you which page Matthew starts on. Find chapter 1 of Matthew and then verse 1 of chapter 1. (The verse numbers are the tiny ones.) Then start reading. Simple.

GET GOING

Each day's page throws you into the Bible, to get you handling, questioning and exploring God's message to you — encouraging you to act on it and talk to God more in prayer. And there's space along the side of each page to jot down what our great God is showing you.

And whenever you start a new book of the Bible, or a new section within it, there'll be a page introducing that book or section.

ENGAGE 365 CHART

There are many ways you can use *Engage 365*. If you'd like to read the Bible for a year, starting in January, the chart below gives dates to follow. Or you can start on any date you like by beginning with Day 1. Or just search for a Bible book you'd like to explore and jump right in. However you use it, *Engage 365* will help you to dig into God's great word for yourself.

DAY	PAGE	DATE	BIBLE PASSAGE	DAY	PAGE	DATE	BIBLE PASSAGE
1	13–14	Jan 1	**MATTHEW** 1 v 1–17	24	38	Jan 24	Romans 4 v 9–17
2	15	Jan 2	Matthew 1 v 18–25	25	39	Jan 25	Romans 4 v 18–25
3	16	Jan 3	Matthew 2 v 1–12	26	40	Jan 26	Romans 5 v 1–2
4	17	Jan 4	Matthew 2 v 13–23	27	41	Jan 27	Romans 5 v 3–5
5	18	Jan 5	Matthew 3 v 1–12	28	42	Jan 28	Romans 5 v 6–11
6	19	Jan 6	Matthew 3 v 13–17	29	43–44	Jan 29	**JOSHUA** 1 v 1–5
7	20	Jan 7	Matthew 4 v 1–11	30	45	Jan 30	Joshua 1 v 6–18
8	21	Jan 8	Matthew 4 v 12–17	31	46	Jan 31	Joshua 2 v 1–24
9	22	Jan 9	Matthew 4 v 18–25	32	47	Feb 1	Joshua 3 v 1–17
10	23	Jan 10	Matthew 5 v 1–5	33	48	Feb 2	Joshua 4 v 1–24
11	24	Jan 11	Matthew 5 v 6–12	34	49	Feb 3	Joshua 5 v 1–8
12	25–26	Jan 12	**ROMANS** 1 v 1–7	35	50	Feb 4	Joshua 5 v 13 – 6 v 14
13	27	Jan 13	Romans 1 v 8–17	36	51	Feb 5	Joshua 6 v 15–27
14	28	Jan 14	Romans 1 v 18–23	37	52	Feb 6	Joshua 7 v 1–26
15	29	Jan 15	Romans 1 v 24–32	38	53	Feb 7	Joshua 8 v 1–29
16	30	Jan 16	Romans 2 v 1–11	39	54	Feb 8	Joshua 8 v 30–35
17	31	Jan 17	Romans 2 v 12–16	40	55	Feb 9	Joshua 9 v 1–27
18	32	Jan 18	Romans 2 v 17–29	41	56	Feb 10	**ROMANS** 5 v 12–14
19	33	Jan 19	Romans 3 v 1–8	42	57	Feb 11	Romans 5 v 15–21
20	34	Jan 20	Romans 3 v 9–20	43	58	Feb 12	Romans 6 v 1–7
21	35	Jan 21	Romans 3 v 21–26	44	59	Feb 13	Romans 6 v 8–14
22	36	Jan 22	Romans 3 v 27–31	45	60	Feb 14	Romans 6 v 15 23
23	37	Jan 23	Romans 4 v 1–8	46	61	Feb 15	Romans 7 v 1–6

DAY	PAGE	DATE	BIBLE PASSAGE
47	62	Feb 16	Romans 7 v 7–13
48	63	Feb 17	Romans 7 v 14–25
49	64	Feb 18	Romans 8 v 1–8
50	65	Feb 19	Romans 8 v 9–17
51	66	Feb 20	Romans 8 v 18–27
52	67	Feb 21	Romans 8 v 28–30
53	68	Feb 22	Romans 8 v 31–39
54	69	Feb 23	**MATTHEW** 5 v 13–16
55	70	Feb 24	Matthew 5 v 17–20
56	71	Feb 25	Matthew 5 v 21–26
57	72	Feb 26	Matthew 5 v 27–32
58	73	Feb 27	Matthew 5 v 33–42
59	74	Feb 28	Matthew 5 v 43–38
60	75	Mar 1	Matthew 6 v 1–4
61	76	Mar 2	Matthew 6 v 5–15
62	77	Mar 3	Matthew 6 v 16–24
63	78	Mar 4	Matthew 6 v 25–34
64	79	Mar 5	Matthew 7 v 1–6
65	80	Mar 6	Matthew 7 v 7–12
66	81	Mar 7	Matthew 7 v 13–14
67	82	Mar 8	Matthew 7 v 15–20
68	83	Mar 9	Matthew 7 v 21–23
69	84	Mar 10	Matthew 7 v 24–29
70	85	Mar 11	**JOSHUA** 10 v 1–15
71	86	Mar 12	Joshua 10 v 16–27
72	87	Mar 13	Joshua 11 v 1–23
73	88	Mar 14	Joshua 13 v 1–33
74	89	Mar 15	Joshua 14 v 6–15
75	90	Mar 16	Joshua 20 – 21
76	91	Mar 17	Joshua 22 v 1–34
77	92	Mar 18	Joshua 23 v 1–16
78	93	Mar 19	Joshua 24 v 1–15

DAY	PAGE	DATE	BIBLE PASSAGE
79	94	Mar 20	Joshua 24 v 16–33
80	95–96	Mar 21	**DANIEL** 1 v 1–7
81	97	Mar 22	Daniel 1 v 8–21
82	98	Mar 23	Daniel 2 v 1–23
83	99	Mar 24	Daniel 2 v 24–49
84	100	Mar 25	Daniel 3 v 1–30
85	101	Mar 26	Daniel 4 v 1–37
86	102	Mar 27	Daniel 5 v 1–31
87	103	Mar 28	Daniel 6 v 1–28
88	104	Mar 29	**PSALM** 24
89	105	Mar 30	Psalm 25
90	106	Mar 31	Psalm 26
91	107–108	Apr 1	**ROMANS** 9 v 1–13
92	109	Apr 2	Romans 9 v 14–33
93	110	Apr 3	Romans 10 v 1–13
94	111	Apr 4	Romans 10 v 14–21
95	112	Apr 5	Romans 11 v 1–10
96	113	Apr 6	Romans 11 v 11–24
97	114	Apr 7	Romans 11 v 25–36
98	115	Apr 8	Romans 12 v 1–8
99	116	Apr 9	Romans 12 v 9–21
100	117–118	Apr 10	**MATTHEW** 8 v 1–17
101	119	Apr 11	Matthew 8 v 18–22
102	120	Apr 12	Matthew 8 v 23–27
103	121	Apr 13	Matthew 8 v 28–34
104	122	Apr 14	Matthew 9 v 1–8
105	123	Apr 15	Matthew 9 v 9–17
106	124	Apr 16	Matthew 9 v 18–34
107	125	Apr 17	Matthew 9 v 35 – 10 v 15
108	126	Apr 18	Matthew 10 v 16–31
109	127	Apr 19	Matthew 10 v 32–42
110	128	Apr 20	Matthew 11 v 1–19

DAY	PAGE	DATE	BIBLE PASSAGE	DAY	PAGE	DATE	BIBLE PASSAGE
111	129–130	Apr 21	**JUDGES** 1 v 1–15	143	162	May 23	Romans 15 v 1–13
112	131	Apr 22	Judges 1 v 16–36	144	163	May 24	Romans 15 v 14–33
113	132	Apr 23	Judges 2 v 1–23	145	164	May 25	Romans 16 v 1–16
114	133	Apr 24	Judges 3 v 7–11	146	165	May 26	Romans 16 v 17–27
115	134	Apr 25	Judges 3 v 12–30	147	166	May 27	**MATTHEW** 11 v 20–30
116	135	Apr 26	Judges 4 v 1–24	148	167	May 28	Matthew 12 v 1–14
117	136	Apr 27	Judges 5 v 1–31	149	168	May 29	Matthew 12 v 22–37
118	137	Apr 28	Judges 6 v 1–10	150	169	May 30	Matthew 12 v 38–50
119	138	Apr 29	Judges 6 v 11–24	151	170	May 31	Matthew 13 v 1–17
120	139	Apr 30	Judges 6 v 25–32	152	171	Jun 1	Matthew 13 v 1–23
121	140	May 1	Judges 6 v 33–40	153	172	Jun 2	Matthew 13 v 24–43
122	141	May 2	Judges 7 v 1–25	154	173	Jun 3	Matthew 13 v 31–35
123	142	May 3	Judges 8 v 1–21	155	174	Jun 4	Matthew 13 v 44–52
124	143	May 4	Judges 8 v 22–35	156	175	Jun 5	Matthew 13 v 53–58
125	144	May 5	Judges 9 v 1–21	157	176	Jun 6	Matthew 14 v 1–12
126	145	May 6	Judges 9 v 22–57	158	177	Jun 7	Matthew 14 v 13–21
127	146	May 7	**DANIEL** 7 v 1–8	159	178	Jun 8	Matthew 14 v 22–36
128	147	May 8	Daniel 7 v 9–14	160	179	Jun 9	**JUDGES** 10 v 1–16
129	148	May 9	Daniel 7 v 15–28	161	180	Jun 10	Judges 10 v 17 – 11 v 28
130	149	May 10	Daniel 8 v 1–14	162	181	Jun 11	Judges 11 v 29–40
131	150	May 11	Daniel 8 v 15–27	163	182	Jun 12	Judges 12 v 1–15
132	151	May 12	Daniel 9 v 1–19	164	183	Jun 13	Judges 13 v 1–5
133	152	May 13	Daniel 9 v 20–27	165	184	Jun 14	Judges 13 v 6–25
134	153	May 14	Daniel 10 v 1 – 11 v 1	166	185	Jun 15	Judges 14 v 1–20
135	154	May 15	Daniel 11 v 2–35	167	186	Jun 16	Judges 15 v 1–20
136	155	May 16	Daniel 11 v 36–45	168	187	Jun 17	Judges 16 v 1–3
137	156	May 17	Daniel 12 v 1–4	169	188	Jun 18	Judges 16 v 4–22
138	157	May 18	Daniel 12 v 5–13	170	189	Jun 19	Judges 16 v 23–31
139	158	May 19	**ROMANS** 13 v 1–7	171	190	Jun 20	Judges 17 v 1–13
140	159	May 20	Romans 13 v 8–14	172	191	Jun 21	Judges 18 v 1–31
141	160	May 21	Romans 14 v 1–12	173	192	Jun 22	Judges 19 v 1–30
142	161	May 22	Romans 14 v 13–23	174	193	Jun 23	Judges 20 v 1–25

DAY	PAGE	DATE	BIBLE PASSAGE
175	194	Jun 24	Judges 20 v 26–48
176	195	Jun 25	Judges 21 v 1–25
177	196	Jun 26	**PSALM** 27
178	197	Jun 27	Psalm 28
179	198	Jun 28	Psalm 29
180	199–200	Jun 29	**1 TIMOTHY** 1 v 1–7
181	201	Jun 30	1 Timothy 1 v 8–11
182	202	Jul 1	1 Timothy 1 v 12–17
183	203	Jul 2	1 Timothy 1 v 18–20
184	204	Jul 3	1 Timothy 2 v 1–7
185	205	Jul 4	1 Timothy 2 v 8–15
186	206	Jul 5	1 Timothy 3 v 1–7
187	207	Jul 6	1 Timothy 3 v 8–16
188	208	Jul 7	1 Timothy 4 v 1–5
189	209–210	Jul 8	**MATTHEW** 15 v 1–20
190	211	Jul 9	Matthew 15 v 21–28
191	212	Jul 10	Matthew 15 v 29 – 16 v 4
192	213	Jul 11	Matthew 16 v 5–12
193	214	Jul 12	Matthew 16 v 13–20
194	215	Jul 13	Matthew 16 v 21–28
195	216	Jul 14	Matthew 17 v 1–13
196	217	Jul 15	Matthew 17 v 14–23
197	218	Jul 16	Matthew 17 v 24–27
198	219	Jul 17	Matthew 18 v 1–6
199	220	Jul 18	Matthew 18 v 7–14
200	221	Jul 19	Matthew 18 v 15–20
201	222	Jul 20	Matthew 18 v 21–35
202	223	Jul 21	Matthew 19 v 1–12
203	224	Jul 22	Matthew 19 v 13–22
204	225	Jul 23	Matthew 19 v 23–30
205	226	Jul 24	**1 TIMOTHY** 4 v 6–10
206	227	Jul 25	1 Timothy 4 v 11–16
207	228	Jul 26	1 Timothy 5 v 1–2
208	229	Jul 27	1 Timothy 5 v 3–8
209	230	Jul 28	1 Timothy 5 v 9–16
210	231	Jul 29	1 Timothy 5 v 17–25
211	232	Jul 30	1 Timothy 6 v 1–2
212	233	Jul 31	1 Timothy 6 v 3–10
213	234	Aug 1	1 Timothy 6 v 11–16
214	235	Aug 2	1 Timothy 6 v 17–19
215	236	Aug 3	1 Timothy 6 v 20–21
216	237–238	Aug 4	**RUTH** 1 v 1–13
217	239	Aug 5	Ruth 1 v 14–22
218	240	Aug 6	Ruth 2 v 1–16
219	241	Aug 7	Ruth 2 v 17–23
220	242	Aug 8	Ruth 3 v 1–18
221	243	Aug 9	Ruth 4 v 1–10
222	244	Aug 10	Ruth 4 v 11–15
223	245	Aug 11	Ruth 4 v 16–22
224	246	Aug 12	**MATTHEW** 20 v 1–16
225	247	Aug 13	Matthew 20 v 17–28
226	248	Aug 14	Matthew 20 v 29–34
227	249	Aug 15	Matthew 21 v 1–11
228	250	Aug 16	Matthew 21 v 12–17
229	251	Aug 17	Matthew 21 v 18–22
230	252	Aug 18	Matthew 21 v 23–32
231	253	Aug 19	Matthew 21 v 33–46
232	254	Aug 20	Matthew 22 v 1–14
233	255	Aug 21	Matthew 22 v 15–22
234	256	Aug 22	Matthew 22 v 23–33
235	257	Aug 23	Matthew 22 v 34–40
236	258	Aug 24	Matthew 22 v 41–46
237	259–260	Aug 25	**JOB** 1 v 1–22
238	261	Aug 26	Job 2 v 1–13

DAY	PAGE	DATE	BIBLE PASSAGE
239	262	Aug 27	Job 3 v 1–26
240	263	Aug 28	Job 4 v 1–21
241	264	Aug 29	Job 6 v 1–30
242	265	Aug 30	Job 8 v 1–22
243	266	Aug 31	Job 9 v 1–35
244	267	Sep 1	Job 11 v 1–20
245	268	Sep 2	Job 12 v 1 – 13 v 19
246	269	Sep 3	Job 15 v 1–35
247	270	Sep 4	Job 16 v 1–21
248	271	Sep 5	Job 18 – 19
249	272	Sep 6	Job 20 – 21
250	273–274	Sep 7	**2 TIMOTHY** 1 v 1–7
251	275	Sep 8	2 Timothy 1 v 8–12
252	276	Sep 9	2 Timothy 1 v 13–18
253	277	Sep 10	2 Timothy 2 v 1–7
254	278	Sep 11	2 Timothy 2 v 8–13
255	279	Sep 12	2 Timothy 2 v 14–19
256	280	Sep 13	2 Timothy 2 v 20–22
257	281	Sep 14	2 Timothy 2 v 23–26
258	282	Sep 15	2 Timothy 3 v 1–9
259	283	Sep 16	2 Timothy 3 v 10–17
260	284	Sep 17	2 Timothy 4 v 1–8
261	285	Sep 18	2 Timothy 4 v 9–15
262	286	Sep 19	2 Timothy 4 v 16–22
263	287–288	Sep 20	**NEHEMIAH** 1 v 1–11
264	289	Sep 21	Nehemiah 2 v 1–10
265	290	Sep 22	Nehemiah 2 v 11–20
266	291	Sep 23	Nehemiah 3 v 1–32
267	292	Sep 24	Nehemiah 4 v 1–9
268	293	Sep 25	Nehemiah 4 v 10–23
269	294	Sep 26	Nehemiah 5 v 1–19
270	295	Sep 27	Nehemiah 6 v 1–14

DAY	PAGE	DATE	BIBLE PASSAGE
271	296	Sep 28	Nehemiah 6 v 15 – 7 v 3
272	297	Sep 29	Nehemiah 7 v 4–73
273	298	Sep 30	**PSALM** 30
274	299–300	Oct 1	**MATTHEW** 23 v 1–12
275	301	Oct 2	Matthew 23 v 13–22
276	302	Oct 3	Matthew 23 v 23–28
277	303	Oct 4	Matthew 23 v 29–39
278	304	Oct 5	Matthew 24 v 1–14
279	305	Oct 6	Matthew 24 v 15–35
280	306	Oct 7	Matthew 24 v 36–51
281	307	Oct 8	Matthew 25 v 1–13
282	308	Oct 9	Matthew 25 v 14–30
283	309	Oct 10	Matthew 25 v 31–46
284	310	Oct 11	Matthew 26 v 1–16
285	311	Oct 12	Matthew 26 v 17–30
286	312	Oct 13	Matthew 26 v 30–35
287	313–314	Oct 14	**1 PETER** 1 v 1–2
288	315	Oct 15	1 Peter 1 v 3–12
289	316	Oct 16	1 Peter 1 v 13–16
290	317	Oct 17	1 Peter 1 v 17–25
291	318	Oct 18	1 Peter 2 v 1–3
292	319	Oct 19	1 Peter 2 v 4–12
293	320	Oct 20	1 Peter 2 v 13–17
294	321	Oct 21	1 Peter 2 v 18–25
295	322	Oct 22	**JOB** 22 v 1–30
296	323	Oct 23	Job 23 v 1–17
297	324	Oct 24	Job 25 – 27
298	325	Oct 25	Job 28 v 1–28
299	326	Oct 26	Job 29 – 31
300	327	Oct 27	Job 32 – 33
301	328	Oct 28	Job 34 – 37
302	329	Oct 29	Job 38 v 1–38

DAY	PAGE	DATE	BIBLE PASSAGE
303	330	Oct 30	Job 38 v 39 – 39 v 30
304	331	Oct 31	Job 40 v 1–24
305	332	Nov 1	Job 41 v 1 – 42 v 6
306	333	Nov 2	Job 42 v 7–17
307	334	Nov 3	**NEHEMIAH** 8 v 1–12
308	335	Nov 4	Nehemiah 8 v 13–18
309	336	Nov 5	Nehemiah 9 v 1–21
310	337	Nov 6	Nehemiah 9 v 22–37
311	338	Nov 7	Nehemiah 9 v 38 – 10 v 39
312	339	Nov 8	Nehemiah 11 v 1–36
313	340	Nov 9	Nehemiah 12 v 1–30
314	341	Nov 10	Nehemiah 12 v 31–43
315	342	Nov 11	Nehemiah 12 v 44 – 13 v 3
316	343	Nov 12	Nehemiah 13 v 4–14
317	344	Nov 13	Nehemiah 13 v 15–31
318	345	Nov 14	**1 PETER** 3 v 1–7
319	346	Nov 15	1 Peter 3 v 8–12
320	347	Nov 16	1 Peter 3 v 13–16
321	348	Nov 17	1 Peter 3 v 17–22
322	349	Nov 18	1 Peter 4 v 1–7
323	350	Nov 19	1 Peter 4 v 8–11
324	351	Nov 20	1 Peter 4 v 12–19
325	352	Nov 21	1 Peter 5 v 1–7
326	353	Nov 22	1 Peter 5 v 8–14
327	354	Nov 23	**MATTHEW** 26 v 36–44
328	355	Nov 24	Matthew 26 v 45–56
329	356	Nov 25	Matthew 26 v 57–68
330	357	Nov 26	Matthew 26 v 69–75
331	358	Nov 27	Matthew 27 v 1–10
332	359	Nov 28	Matthew 27 v 11–31
333	360	Nov 29	Matthew 27 v 32–44
334	361	Nov 30	Matthew 27 v 45–50

DAY	PAGE	DATE	BIBLE PASSAGE
335	362	Dec 1	Matthew 27 v 50–56
336	363	Dec 2	Matthew 27 v 57–66
337	364	Dec 3	Matthew 28 v 1–10
338	365	Dec 4	Matthew 28 v 11–15
339	366	Dec 5	Matthew 28 v 16–20
340	367–368	Dec 6	**JONAH** 1 v 1–3
341	369	Dec 7	Jonah 1 v 4–17
342	370	Dec 8	Jonah 2 v 1–10
343	371	Dec 9	Jonah 3 v 1–10
344	372	Dec 10	Jonah 4 v 1–4
345	373	Dec 11	Jonah 4 v 5–11
346	374	Dec 12	**PSALM** 31
347	375–376	Dec 13	**ESTHER** 1 v 1–22
348	377	Dec 14	Esther 2 v 1–20
349	378	Dec 15	Esther 2 v 21 – 3 v 15
350	379	Dec 16	Esther 4 v 1–17
351	380	Dec 17	Esther 5 v 1–14
352	381	Dec 18	Esther 6 v 1–14
353	382	Dec 19	Esther 7 v 1–10
354	383	Dec 20	Esther 8 v 1–17
355	384	Dec 21	Esther 9 v 1–17
356	385	Dec 22	Esther 9 v 18 – 10 v 3
357	386	Dec 23	**PSALM** 32
358	387–388	Dec 24	**2 PETER** 1 v 1–4
359	389	Dec 25	2 Peter 1 v 5–11
360	390	Dec 26	2 Peter 1 v 12–21
361	391	Dec 27	2 Peter 2 v 1–10
362	392	Dec 28	2 Peter 2 v 10–22
363	393	Dec 29	2 Peter 3 v 1–9
364	394	Dec 30	2 Peter 3 v 10–14
365	395	Dec 31	2 Peter 3 v 15–18

MATTHEW

The big picture

Ever read a biography? Maybe a sporting one or a celebrity memoir? You get to see how the big-name star in question started out. Perhaps with some embarrassing baby photos and the awkward teenage years with a bad haircut and goofy teeth, before they hit the big time and became impossibly glamorous.

Well, the book of Matthew is one of the four Gospels — biographies of Jesus — and seems to have been written for a largely Jewish audience. No amusing childhood pranks or Oscar wins here though. The opening verses of chapter 1 give us a big clue about what's important to Matthew as he writes. In verse 1 he points out that Jesus is descended from Abraham and David. In short, Jesus is heir to the promises of the Old Testament and heir to a throne.

Matthew wants to show how Jesus Christ came as the completion of Old Testament teaching and prophecy (words from God about the future). Matthew has 53 direct Old T quotes and loads more passing references. He's showing us how Jesus fits into the big picture of God's word.

MEET THE MESSIAH

Matthew uses the Old Testament to prove that Jesus is the long-awaited *Messiah* — the King God promised He would send to rescue His people — and the Saviour of the world. He'd come for all people, not just Jews. The news of this big rescue was now for everyone.

Matthew wants his readers (and that includes us) to realise just how significant Jesus' arrival on this planet was. The promised one, the perfect Son of God, the King of the universe was here. Will you bow the knee to Him now, or will you be forced to when He returns in glory? Will you take this biography to heart?

1 Family album

Does your heart sink when you see a long list of names in the Bible? Well this one is full of hidden treasures and surprises — it's also a neat summary of God's dealings with His people from the Old Testament 'til Jesus' birth.

👁 Read Matthew 1 v 1–17

ENGAGE YOUR BRAIN

▶ *What words or phrases are used in verse 1 to describe who Jesus is?*

The Messiah or Christ was the king promised in the Old Testament who would lead God's people. In fact, prophets such as Isaiah claimed this king would be God Himself! So why are David and Abraham mentioned? Take a look at the promises God made to both of them. This descendant, Jesus, was about to make God's promises come true!

▶ *What did God promise to Abraham in Genesis 12 v 1–3?*

▶ *And to David in 2 Samuel 7 v 12–16?*

A few names are worth mentioning — Abraham was a big hero, but his grandson Jacob was a bit of a mixed bag. Perez had a tough start in life. Rahab and Ruth weren't even Israelites; they were hated outsiders.

King Ahaz was evil, but Hezekiah had his heart in the right place.

▶ *What does this tell us about who God uses in His plans?*

▶ *What does this tell us about God?*

Matthew picks up on some major landmarks in Jewish history as he gives us a snapshot overview, not only of Jesus' human origins, but of God's dealings with His people over hundreds of years.

PRAY ABOUT IT

Thank God that He uses ordinary people to bring His plan of rescue to the world. Thank Him that He keeps His promises. Thank Him that He chose you despite your sin. Ask Him to help you learn more about Jesus — the Christ — as you read through Matthew.

2   What's in a name?

We've seen Jesus' family tree; now Matthew gives us a close-up as we zoom in to focus on Jesus' birth.

👁 Read Matthew 1 v 18–25

ENGAGE YOUR BRAIN

▶ *What was unusual about Jesus' conception? (v18, 25)*

▶ *Why is this so important?*

Jesus had a human mother and so was fully human but was also fully God — note the references to Him being conceived from the Holy Spirit. This makes Him uniquely qualified for His mission — we'll discover more about that later.

▶ *What would Joseph have assumed had happened?*

▶ *Why is Joseph described as righteous? What could he have done instead? (v19)*

▶ *How does God reassure him? (v20)*

▶ *What's the baby to be called?*

▶ *What other name will Jesus be known by, according to Isaiah's prophesy? (v23)*

What two crucial things do these names tell us about the reason why Jesus was born into our world?

A miraculous conception. God in human flesh entering our world — *Immanuel*, God is with us. And God with a mission — to save sinners.

PRAY ABOUT IT

God becoming human is one of the most incredible things to ever happen. The other is that He came to die for sinners like you and me. Take some time to really let that sink in and thank God for His incredible rescue plan.

THE BOTTOM LINE

Jesus is God with us.

3 We two kings?

Another well known part of the Christmas story today — or is it? No mention of camels and we aren't told how many Magi or wise men there were. But this *is* a story about kings: two to be precise.

👁 Read Matthew 2 v 1–12

ENGAGE YOUR BRAIN

▷ *Who are the two kings mentioned? (v1–2)*

▷ *What do we learn about Jesus?*
v2:
v6:
v11:

▷ *And Herod?*
v7–8:
v12:

▷ *Why do you think Herod was frightened by the thought of a new king?*

▷ *How did the wise men respond to the news of this king? (v10-11)*

Jesus still has this effect today. At one level Herod was right to see him as a threat. Jesus is THE King. But the Magi had a better reaction — they recognised Jesus' kingship and took great time and trouble to come and bow before Him.

GET ON WITH IT

Have you recognised Jesus' right to rule over your life? The Magi travelled a long way at great personal cost. Is that attitude part of your life? Do you spend time with Jesus even when you'd rather stay in bed? Do you make an effort to go to church or youth group even if other plans seem more tempting?

PRAY ABOUT IT

The Magi weren't Jews and yet they knew Jesus was their King. Thank God that Jesus came for the whole world; then pray for places where people still don't know Him.

THE BOTTOM LINE

There can only be one King in your life. Make sure it's Jesus.

4 Murder in mind

Herod was a puppet king, put in place by the Romans. Paranoid and dangerous, he had anyone he saw as competition murdered: even his own wife and sons. Now he's set his sights on Jesus. What's going to happen?

👁 Read Matthew 2 v 13–23

ENGAGE YOUR BRAIN

▷ *What are Herod's intentions? (v13)*

▷ *What does he do? (v16)*

▷ *How is Jesus protected? (v13–15)*

Even this horrific slaughter was foretold by the prophets (v18), as is Jesus' escape (v15) and even His childhood hometown (v23). There are no coincidences or mistakes here. God had a plan from the beginning of time.

▷ *What title was Jesus given back in verse 2?*

▷ *When is he called that again? (Hint: chapter 27 v 37)*

Jesus faced hostility, hatred and murderous violence almost from birth. His Father kept Him safe from Herod but only for a while — it was not yet time for Jesus to die.

His Father didn't save Jesus at Golgotha but turned His face away. Why? Remember why Jesus came? To save sinners.

PRAY ABOUT IT

Amazingly God turned people's sinful, hate-filled rejection of the King into the very means by which they could be rescued. Thank Him now.

SHARE IT

Your non-Christian friends and family probably don't come across like Herod. But rejecting Jesus is as serious and as ugly as what Herod did. Rejecting our King is treason and deserves the death penalty. Herod died (v19) and so will we. Only by accepting Jesus' death in our place can we live at peace under His rule in His kingdom for ever. Can you share that great news with someone today?

5 Make way for the King

Time has moved on. Jesus has grown up now and just as a king has a herald announcing his arrival, here we see John the Baptist doing exactly that.

👁 Read Matthew 3 v 1–12

ENGAGE YOUR BRAIN

▶ *What is John's message? (v2)*

Repenting means turning away from our sins and turning back to God.

The kingdom of heaven is near because the King is near!

▶ *Who does Isaiah say John is? (v3)*

▶ *So who is coming? (v3)*

Some people have called John the Baptist the last Old Testament prophet. He is pointing to the coming King, the Messiah. As Isaiah's prophecy makes clear, John's call means that the Lord, God Himself, is on His way. Cue Jesus!

▶ *What warning does John have for those who show no evidence of repentance? (v7–10)*

▶ *What does John tell us about the coming King? (v11–12)*

Jesus came to bring judgment (v12). We know that when He returns He will judge the earth, but that process began when He came the first time. People's reactions to Jesus — as we will see over the course of Matthew's Gospel — would either save them or condemn them.

GET ON WITH IT

The Pharisees and Sadducees thought they were OK because they were descended from Abraham, but they faced Jesus' judgment. Do you think you're OK because you go to church, or your parents are Christians, or you're a nice person? Repent! Turn to the King — He alone can save you.

THE BOTTOM LINE

The King is coming! Get ready!

6 Making a big splash

The King arrives. Jesus is now 30. The next big event confirms who He is. It's surprisingly soggy.

👁 Read Matthew 3 v 13–17

ENGAGE YOUR BRAIN

▷ Why has Jesus come to the Jordan? (v13)

▷ Why does John not want to baptise Jesus? (v14)

▷ Why does Jesus say John should baptise Him? (v15)

You can understand John's hesitation — here's the person he's just been talking about, someone massively above him, the King Himself, and He's asking to be baptised? John's baptism is for repentant sinners, not the perfect Messiah!

But what sort of a Messiah is Jesus? What sort of King is He? He's not up there with John telling sinners to repent, although He does preach that message later. No, He's down there in the water with the sinners; showing He's one of them even though He has no need of cleansing.

▷ What is God the Father's verdict on Jesus? (v16–17)

Bearing in mind Jesus' actions here and His Father's words, why is the cross such an extraordinary, amazing happening?

PRAY ABOUT IT

"God made him who had no sin to be sin for us, so that in him we might become the righteousness of God." (2 Corinthians 5 v 21)

Think about what this meant for Jesus, and what it means for you, and then talk to God about it.

THE BOTTOM LINE

Jesus came for sinners.

7 Temptation situation

The heavens opened and God spoke, confirming who Jesus was. Here, on earth, was His Son, the unique God-man. Would Jesus live up to that and complete His task? Or not trust God and disobey Him, like the rest of us?

👁 Read Matthew 4 v 1–11

Answer the following questions:

	Israel	Jesus
How long were they tested?	Numbers 32 v 13	Matthew 4 v 2
How do they respond to lack of food?	Exodus 16 v 1–3	Matthew 4 v 3–4
Do they put God to the test?	Exodus 17 v 1–2	Matthew 4 v 5–7
Do they worship God alone?	Exodus 32 v 1-6	Matthew 4 v 8–10

God's people failed to live His way again and again. They couldn't overcome their sin, but with Jesus' arrival we see a new Israel: a Jew who is totally obedient to God, someone who fulfils all the promises of the Old Testament. This is the start of something exciting.

PRAY ABOUT IT

Thank God that Jesus is the one perfect human being. Say sorry for the times when you fail to trust God, grumble and put other things before serving Him. Thank Him that Jesus was not only totally obedient to His Father but that His obedience led Him to die so that you could be forgiven.

8 Light and life

The preparation is over. Now this unique God-man can begin His public ministry. Again we see Jesus living up to prophecies made many hundreds of years before. God's plans are made reality.

👁 Read Matthew 4 v 12

ENGAGE YOUR BRAIN

▶ What has happened to John?

Read Matthew 14 v 1–12 for the distressing outcome.

👁 Read Matthew 4 v 13–17

▶ Are you prepared to face the consequences of living God's way, no matter how serious?

▶ What does Isaiah say about Jesus? (v16)

▶ What does Jesus say people need to do to enter His kingdom? (v17)

Repenting doesn't just mean feeling sorry for the things we've done wrong — most people feel like that at some point. No, it's an active decision to *turn away* from one way of living and to *turn back* to God.

Remember how John the Baptist preached the same message? But this time, the King is calling us to repent! It's His kingdom of light and life which is near. Get out of the darkness!

PRAY ABOUT IT

Have you done that? Pray for people you know who are living in darkness, that they would see Jesus' light and turn to Him.

THE BOTTOM LINE

Jesus is light and life.

9 | Something fishy

The kingdom is near and things are starting to gather momentum. Here we see Jesus calling the first disciples.

👁 Read Matthew 4 v 18–22

ENGAGE YOUR BRAIN

▶ *Who does Jesus see? (v18)*

▶ *What does He say to them? (v19)*

▶ *What do they do? (v20)*

▶ *How about verses 21-22?*

▶ *What is so surprising about their responses?*

Jesus is the King. When a king tells you to do something, you do it. Peter, Andrew, James and John don't fully realise who Jesus is yet, but they recognise something of His authority.

▶ *Are you following the King?*

▶ *What do you think Jesus means by "fish for people" / "fishers of men"?*

Being a fisherman wasn't a glamorous job. Antisocial hours, hard work, often with little success, and smelling fishy. Nice. We might not have to deal with the personal hygiene part but fishing for people will often be similar — hard work, often with limited "success"— but remember verse 16. We have a wonderful and life-saving message to share.

👁 Read verses 23–25

… and remind yourself what a powerful and compassionate King Jesus is.

PRAY ABOUT IT

Ask for God's help to fish for people.

GET ON WITH IT

As you head out into whatever you face this week — school, college, work, home — leave a mental "gone fishing" sign on your bedroom door.

10 Blessed is best

Here are the beatitudes: Jesus' teaching on what it means to be "blessed", on what sort of a life is worth having. What sort of life do you want? Think for a minute...

👁 Read Matthew 5 v 1–5

ENGAGE YOUR BRAIN

▶ *What sort of person do you think God would want in heaven?*

▶ *Do verses 3–12 sound like that?*

▶ *How would you define "blessed"?*

▶ *What might it mean to be "poor in spirit" (v3)?*

▶ *Why is this necessary to enter the kingdom of heaven?*

"Poor in spirit" could be rephrased as "spiritually bankrupt" — our state when we realise we have nothing to offer God. Ironically, the entrance requirement for God's kingdom is not hundreds of good works, but recognising you have nothing to offer. You can't receive a gift until your hands are empty.

▶ *How does the second beatitude follow on from the first? (v4)*

▶ *How do you think those who mourn will be comforted?*

▶ *What is meekness and how does it follow on from the previous two attitudes?*

Why do we have nothing to offer God? It's not just that we're not good enough. We're really bad. We are sinners who reject our loving Creator. We should mourn that. Once we have the right view about ourselves, we will be meek not arrogant, and, amazingly, that is when we are blessed and God approves of us, because of Jesus.

PRAY ABOUT IT

Think about verses 3–5. Have you realised you have nothing to offer God, mourned your sin, humbled yourself before Him? Spend some time praying through those verses.

THE BOTTOM LINE

Blessed are the poor in spirit.

11 Count your blessings

This list of "blessed are the..." is known as the beatitudes, sometimes called *beautiful attitudes*. As we saw from verses 3–5, they build up a picture of what it looks like to be part of the kingdom of heaven.

👁 Read Matthew 5 v 6–12

ENGAGE YOUR BRAIN

▶ *Try to define each of these six beatitudes in your own words.*

v6:

v7:

v8:

v9:

v10:

v11–12:

THINK IT OVER

Do you really hunger and thirst for righteousness? Do you long for the day when Jesus will return and your sin will vanish for ever?

GET ON WITH IT

Do you ever think about that part of the Lord's Prayer that says *"forgive us our sins as we forgive those who sin against us"* and feel a bit guilty? Jesus tells us that His followers should be merciful to others for they have received and will receive God's mercy. Are you holding a grudge? Need to forgive someone even if they haven't said sorry? Do it.

▶ *Why might being a peacemaker (v9) show a family resemblance to God?*

▶ *What does Jesus warn us about in verses 10–11?*

▶ *How does he encourage us?*

PRAY ABOUT IT

Thank God that when Jesus died on the cross, He washed our sinful hearts clean so that one day we will see Him face to face.

THE BOTTOM LINE

Blessed are the pure in heart for they will see God.

ROMANS

Basic Christianity

Are you sitting comfortably?

Well, you won't be for long because we're about to throw ourselves into one of the most in-your-face and challenging books in the Bible.

LIFE-CHANGING LETTER

Romans is actually a letter written by Paul around AD 60 to Christians in Rome (centre of the world back then). To ordinary people like you and me. Paul didn't start the church there, but he would soon visit it.

Paul was the one chosen by Jesus to take the good news of the gospel to Gentiles (anyone who's not a Jew).

Paul wanted this Gentile church (though there were Jewish believers in it too) to grab hold of its responsibilities towards other members of God's people. In this case, to step outward to Jews — across a big, fat cultural divide.

POWERFUL STUFF

Many people think Romans is the most important book they've ever read. Some have come to trust in Jesus for the first time after reading it. Some are stunned by its amazing truths about God and about people. Some find their faith shaken into life like never before.

Romans may be a hard read at times, but it very clearly lays out the gospel — the basic truths of Christianity. All the stuff we need to get our heads around. And it slaps down the implications of believing it and living as a Christian.

Be careful, this book could change your life...

12 Dear Romans...

When people write letters, they usually begin: "Dear Bob..." and don't sign their name until the end. But Paul's style is different. In fact, he gets completely distracted by something else during his introduction.

👁 Read Romans 1 v 1–7

ENGAGE YOUR BRAIN

▶ *How does Paul introduce himself? (v1)*

▶ *What and who does Paul go off on a tangent about? (v2–4)*

▶ *What facts are we told about Jesus? (v3–4)*

Paul was God's specially chosen apostle, sent out by God to tell people the truth about Jesus. He was "set apart" to spread the gospel — the good news about Jesus — which is what he gets so excited about.

Paul wants everyone to hear the gospel that was promised by Old Testament prophets. It was fulfilled in Jesus — God's Son, who became human, to die and be raised back to life through the power of the Holy Spirit. But how does all that affect us?

👁 Read verses 5–7 again

▶ *How does Paul describe his job? (v5)*

▶ *What does faith in Jesus lead to? (end of v5)*

▶ *How does he describe the Christians in Rome? (v6–7)*

Paul was sent to call ordinary Christians (some Jewish, but mostly Gentiles) to believe in Jesus Christ. His readers belonged to Jesus. And so do you, if you're a Christian: in fact, you are "loved by God" and can be called "holy" or a "saint"! (v7)

PRAY ABOUT IT

Ask God to show you the whole truth of the gospel in Romans and to use it to build up your faith and make you more obedient to Him.

THE BOTTOM LINE

The gospel makes saints — people set apart to be holy and live for God.

13 | The power of God

Do you ever pray for Christians overseas who you've never met? Paul was doing the same, and encouraging them too. And he also had some more challenging words about the gospel.

⊚ Read Romans 1 v 8–13

ENGAGE YOUR BRAIN

▶ What was Paul thankful to God for? (v8)

▶ Even though he'd yet to meet them, what did Paul do? (v9–10)

▶ Why did Paul want to visit Rome? (v11–13)

The faith of these Christians in Rome had become big news (v8). So much so that Paul regularly prayed for them and longed to visit them and help strengthen them in their faith (v12). So that even more people in Rome would become Christ-followers.

PRAY ABOUT IT

Which faraway Christians can you pray for? Go on then — do it!

Have you ever thought of visiting them or writing/emailing to encourage them?

⊚ Read verses 14–17

▶ How does Paul describe his commitment to spreading the gospel? (v14–15)

▶ Why shouldn't we be ashamed of the gospel? (v16)

Paul is passionate about sharing Jesus with people, whatever their background (v14). We shouldn't be ashamed of the gospel — it is the power of God to save people! And Christians have a duty to share what God has entrusted to them.

SHARE IT

▶ How do these verses make you think differently about sharing the gospel?

▶ Who can you talk to about Jesus, who you wouldn't normally consider?

14 No excuses

Paul says that the truth about Jesus — the gospel — is the power of God to *save* those who believe. Save them from what?

👁 Read Romans 1 v 18–20

ENGAGE YOUR BRAIN

▶ *Why is God angry with human beings? (v18–19)*

▶ *What's one way we know that God exists? (v20)*

▶ *Why should we know better than to walk out on God? (v20)*

People need saving from God's wrath — His anger and punishment for rejecting Him. Paul says that no one has an excuse for not believing in God or living for Him. Nature screams at us that God exists and shows us how powerful and perfect He is (v20). But people still live as if God isn't there.

👁 Read verses 21–23

▶ *What is God particularly angry about? (v21)*

▶ *Does anyone have an excuse for disobeying God?*

This is serious stuff. Sadly, many people refuse to admit that God exists, even though they know it deep down. Or they admit His existence but refuse to let Him rule their lives or give Him the glory and thanks He deserves as their powerful Creator. In fact, people will worship anything rather than God (v23).

PRAY ABOUT IT

▶ *Who do you know who refuses to trust in God?*

▶ *What about yourself?*

Spend a longer time than usual bringing these people before God in prayer. Plead with Him to change them and forgive them.

THE BOTTOM LINE

There's no excuse for rejecting God.

15 Trampling truth

More tough stuff today. Yesterday we discovered that no one has an excuse for rejecting God. Today, Paul tells us that God is already punishing people who go their own way, shunning Him.

👁 Read Romans 1 v 24–27

ENGAGE YOUR BRAIN

▶ *What has God "given us over" to for rejecting Him? (v24)*

▶ *Why is it so dumb to worship anything other than God? (v25)*

▶ *What does Paul say about same-sex sexuality? (v26–27)*

God is already revealing His anger at those who reject Him — by allowing them to sin. People want to ignore Him and do whatever they want. So God lets them. But people are living a lie if they think it's better than serving God (v25). Paul says that rejecting God leads to abuse of sex, same-sex sexuality* and social breakdown.

👁 Read verses 28-32

▶ *What do people know about God? (v32)*

▶ *But what is their response? (v32)*

Deep down, people know that God exists and will punish sin, but they bury these facts and ignore them. They reject Him. So God is right to be angry with them and punish them.

None of us has lived up to what we know about God — we've deliberately kicked Him out of our lives. We can't plead ignorance or make excuses either. God's not an idle spectator, overlooking His world, happily letting evil continue. He's expressing His anger for all to see, and one day He'll carry out a final judgment. See why we need Jesus?

PRAY ABOUT IT

Talk openly with God about how today's bit of Romans has made you feel. Thank Him for sending Jesus to rescue us from sin.

Finding this hard to get your head around? Read "Is God anti-gay?" by Sam Allberry (The Good Book Company) for brain-stretching help.

16 Passing judgment

"Did you hear what Sasha did? Unbelievable — none of us would have done it." Almost without realising it, we can point an accusing finger at people. But God's finger is more accurate than ours.

👁 Read Romans 2 v 1–4

ENGAGE YOUR BRAIN

▶ What's the problem with judging others? (v3)

▶ What do people fail to realise about God? (v4)

We all think we're on the "good" side and look down our noses at others and their sin. But none of us are sinless — we're just as bad. None of us have the right to criticise others. Only God judges fairly, seeing all the facts (v2).

👁 Read verses 5–11

▶ How would you describe God's anger and punishment in v5–6?

▶ How do verses 8–9 make you feel?

▶ And how about verse 7 and verse 10?

If we fail to admit we've sinned against God, then we're storing up God's wrath (v5). We can't hide behind claims of being good. God is completely fair and will judge everyone as they deserve (v6). That includes rewarding everyone who *always* does good and pleases God. But who lives like that? No one!

THINK IT OVER

▶ Who do you criticise harshly?

▶ What will you do about that?

▶ Know anyone who thinks their Christian upbringing or good behaviour means they're all right with God?

PRAY ABOUT IT

Talk honestly with God about your answers to these questions.

THE BOTTOM LINE

Only God judges fairly.

17 Justice for all

It must be tricky being a judge, wondering if the sentence you've dished out is fair or not. Paul says even though we get things wrong sometimes, God doesn't. He's the perfect, totally fair judge who doesn't show favouritism.

👁 Read Romans 2 v 12–16

Slowly. It's difficult stuff.

ENGAGE YOUR BRAIN

These Jews had grown up being taught God's law and knew it well.

▷ *Why wasn't knowing God's law enough? (v13)*

God's judgment will be absolutely fair. Paul says whether you're a Jew or a Gentile, *everyone* has sinned against God and we'll all face His judgment.

We're a lot like the Jewish people Paul mentions, because we have God's law in the Bible. That is a great privilege — in some parts of the world, hardly anyone has a Bible. But, because the Bible tells us clearly what's right and wrong, we have *no excuse* when we disobey God.

People who don't have the Bible are like the Gentiles Paul talks about.

But God's law is written on their hearts (v15). Their conscience tells them what's right or wrong. They too have no excuse. *Everyone* has broken God's law and deserves to be punished.

▷ *Who will judge everyone? (v16)*

Whether or not God punishes us depends on our reaction to Jesus. If we accept Him, He'll rescue us as our Saviour. If we reject Him, He'll condemn us as our Judge.

Tough but fair.

PRAY ABOUT IT

Talk honestly with God about where you're at and your response to Jesus. And pray for friends who think they're good enough, yet refuse to accept Jesus.

THE BOTTOM LINE

God will judge everyone fairly.

18 Practise what you preach

"Josh is always talking behind people's backs; only yesterday I heard him say..." Does hypocrisy get on your nerves? God hates double standards too.

👁 Read Romans 2 v 17–24

ENGAGE YOUR BRAIN

▶ *What's Paul's criticism of these over-confident Jews? (v21)*

▶ *What's the terrible result of their actions? (v24)*

It's dangerous to focus on other people's faults — we end up missing our own. These Jews were so confident that they were right with God and were top dogs that they looked down on others. They were blind to their own double standards.

👁 Read verses 25–29

Circumcision was a sign of being one of God's people. Jewish men were proud of being circumcised: of being God's chosen people.

▶ *Would it protect them from God's anger? (v25)*

▶ *What does God look for in a person? (v29)*

Being Jewish or being circumcised (or having Christian parents) is not enough to put you right with God. These Jews had nothing to be smug about. God isn't interested in what a person is like on the outside. It's all about your heart being devoted to Him; living your life God's way.

THINK IT OVER

▶ *Do you think you deserve preferential treatment from God?*

▶ *Do you ever congratulate yourself for being "good"?*

▶ *Are you practising what you preach?*

PRAY ABOUT IT

Ask God to help you practise what you preach, so that you don't just look like a Christian on Sundays, but devote your whole life to Him.

19 What's the point?

It seems as if Paul's been saying there was no advantage in being one of God's chosen people — the Jews. But he wasn't saying that at all. Check out Paul arguing with himself!

👁 Read Romans 3 v 1–4

ENGAGE YOUR BRAIN

▶ Is there any advantage in being Jewish? (v2)

▶ Does God's ability to keep His promises rely on His people having faith in Him? (v4)

A great privilege of being Jewish was that they'd been given God's own words (the Old Testament). But a privilege can do nothing for you if you abuse it. It's the same for people brought up in a Christian home — they get taught about Jesus from a young age. But if they refuse to follow Jesus, they only have themselves to blame.

Paul says: Don't think that because some Jews have no faith in Jesus, God has broken His promises. God's faithfulness is never in doubt, even if that makes everyone else a liar. God always keeps His promises.

👁 Read verses 5–8

▶ Our sin shows how holy and forgiving God is. Isn't God being unfair to punish us for it? (v6)

▶ Isn't our sinfulness doing God a favour? Can't we just carry on sinning? (end of v8)

Paul barely answers these questions. It's so ridiculous to suggest that God is unfair or that it's OK for us to keep sinning against Him that Paul dismisses these arguments. God is perfect, holy and totally fair. People who reject God deserve His punishment. End of story.

PRAY ABOUT IT

Ask God to help you be more like Paul — to know your Bible well so that you can answer people's arguments against God and His word.

20 No one's perfect

I expect you've had no problem following all of Paul's ideas and arguments in Romans so far. In fact, I bet you could sum it all up in one sentence. No? Me neither. We'd best let Paul sum it all up...

👁 Read Romans 3 v 9–18

ENGAGE YOUR BRAIN

▷ *What big point is Paul making with all these Old Testament quotes? (v10–18)*

▷ *What are humans naturally like, according to these verses?*

▷ *Any exceptions?*

Have you got the message? NO ONE is sinless. NO ONE is good enough for God. We've all turned away from Him and sin can be found in every part of our lives.

👁 Read verses 19–20

▷ *Can we say anything to God to defend ourselves? (v19)*

▷ *Who is good enough for God? (v20)*

I may think I live a good life or am a better person than other people I know, but that counts for nothing. NO ONE meets God's perfect standards. None of us can say anything to excuse us from the punishment we deserve. Which is exactly the point God's law was designed to get us to.

Don't worry, that's not the end — there's good news tomorrow.

SHARE IT

▷ *When you talk about Christianity, do you miss out the bits about sin and punishment?*

▷ *How vital is it to understand that we're all guilty before God?*

▷ *So how will you talk about these things with friends?*

PRAY ABOUT IT

Talk to God about these issues and ask Him to help you be honest but sensitive with your friends.

21 | God's free gift

We've all sinned and deserve God's punishment. No one is good enough for God. That's devastating news but it's not the end of the story. Now read what some people say is the most important paragraph ever written...

👁 Read Romans 3 v 21–26

ENGAGE YOUR BRAIN

Now read it again verse by verse and we'll unpack Paul's incredible words.

v21 None of us can keep God's perfect law. So He's made a way for us to be put right with Him.

v22 It's not based on how good we are. We can only be made right with God by relying on Jesus and what He's done for us.

v23 There's no difference between Jew or Gentile or anyone. We've all rejected God and all deserve His punishment.

v24 So we don't deserve God's forgiveness, but He offers it to us anyway. It's a free gift. That's *grace*. Because of Jesus, we can be *justified* — forgiven; just as if I'd never sinned. Christians have been *redeemed* — bought back by Jesus.

v25 God sent His Son to die to take away God's anger against us. But we've got to trust in Jesus.

v26 Through Jesus, we see God's perfect justice and incredible patience with sinners like us.

THINK IT OVER

▶ *Summarise the good news from these verses in your own words.*

▶ *What does Jesus' death tell us about God?*

SHARE IT

How can you use the ideas in this mind-blowing passage to tell your mates about what God has done for sinful people like us? Take time to work out how you can clearly explain this great news. Write it down. Practise it. And then do it.

22 Faith the facts

Paul sounds a bit strange, having this conversation with himself. But he's answering some really important questions and concerns that Jews had about the gospel message.

👁 Read Romans 3 v 27–28

ENGAGE YOUR BRAIN

▶ *Could Jews boast about being God's special people? (v27)*

▶ *Can we boast about being God's people, Christians?*

▶ *Why not?*

No one can boast about being chosen by God — we haven't earned it by living good lives. It's a free gift, achieved by Jesus dying on the cross for us. We've got nothing to be proud about — Jesus did all the hard work! We just have to trust in Him.

👁 Read verses 29–30

▶ *Who is the gospel for?*

The great news is that God offers forgiveness to EVERYONE, whatever their background. There is only one God, and there's only one way to be put right with God: faith in Jesus.

And that's true for everyone.

👁 Read verse 31

If faith in Jesus is the only way to God, was God's law pointless? Absolutely not! By trusting in Jesus, we become what God's law wants us to be but can't make us.

The law shows it's impossible for us to please God, and so urges us to trust in Jesus. But because of what Jesus has done, God will accept us as perfect law-keepers! Amazing. And it's all down to Jesus.

PRAY ABOUT IT

Ask God to help you...

• not be proud about your faith or look down on others

• share the gospel with other people; it's good news for everyone

• live God's way, not your own.

23 | Faith works

Paul says that we're "justified" (put right with God) by faith in Jesus, not by doing good works. He backs up his claims with two great Jewish heroes — Abraham and David.

👁 Read Romans 4 v 1–5

ENGAGE YOUR BRAIN

- ▶ *Was Abraham accepted by God because he worked hard and earned it?*

- ▶ *Does God only forgive "good" people? (v5)*

Many people believe that if they live good lives they'll be accepted by God. But we're ALL sinful and are not good enough for God — even Abraham, the Jews' hero. God accepted Abraham (in fact, treated him as righteous), not because he lived a good life, but because he believed God. Trusted in Him.

Incredibly, God justifies (forgives) wicked people if they trust in Him to save them (v5). How awesome is that?

👁 Read verses 6–8

- ▶ *How do you think King David felt when he wrote this?*

- ▶ *What's the great news for believers? (v7–8)*

King David was so excited! God accepted him even though he messed up many times. David trusted in God, so the Lord forgave his sins and would never hold them against him. The same goes for anyone who trusts Jesus' death in their place to wipe out their sins.

PRAY ABOUT IT

If you truly mean it, admit to God that you're not good enough to be with Him.

Now thank God that if you trust in Jesus your sins are forgiven and God won't count them against you! Plenty to praise God for!

THE BOTTOM LINE

We're justified by faith, not works.

24 ¦ Showing promise

Is it just me, or do you find Paul's letter to Christians in Rome tricky to understand? It's brain-achingly hard at times, but it's vital truth about Christianity. So stick with it — it's worth it.

👁 Read Romans 4 v 9–12

ENGAGE YOUR BRAIN

▶ *When was Abraham counted righteous (right with God)? (v10)*

▶ *So, who is Abraham the "father" of? (v11–12)*

This was really controversial at the time. Most Jews couldn't cope with the idea that they weren't the only ones special and acceptable to God. Paul says that being circumcised and being Jewish doesn't make you right with God. Abe was circumcised as a sign to *show* that he belonged to God — it didn't make him right with God.

👁 Read verses 13–17

▶ *Did God make great promises to Abraham because of his law-keeping or his faith? (v13)*

▶ *So who is God's promise to — only Jews or all believers? (v16)*

God's promises to Abraham can be found in Genesis 12 v 1–3. God didn't make these promises because Abraham obeyed His law. It was because of Abe's faith in God.

God's promise to Abraham is for *all believers*. He promised that Abraham would be the father of many nations. That promise means that anyone can be part of God's people, not just the Jews. We don't deserve to be God's people — it's an undeserved gift. *Grace.*

PRAY ABOUT IT

Thank God that we don't have to earn His love and forgiveness. Thank Him that it's a gift to anyone who accepts it. Pray for people you know who haven't accepted God's gift.

25 Credit note

"We'll win this match!" promises your coach. But you're losing badly, half your team is injured and the opposition is HUGE! Would you believe his promise? Abraham had an even harder promise to believe.

👁 Read Romans 4 v 18–22

ENGAGE YOUR BRAIN

▷ *Why did God's promise that Abraham would have many children seem so unlikely? (v19)*

▷ *How would you describe Abraham's faith in God? (v20-21)*

God promised Abraham millions of offspring. But Abe was 100 years old and his wife was unable to have kids. Yet Abraham believed God's promise against all the odds. So he was counted "righteous" — right with God.

True faith in God realises that nothing is impossible for God. He keeps His promises. Even when all hope is lost. Faith rests entirely on what God has promised, not on what we do.

👁 Read verses 23–25

▷ *What's God's promise for those who trust in Jesus? (v24–25)*

We deserve to be condemned to eternal death for rejecting God. Instead, God sent Jesus to die in our place and then raised Him from death, providing a rescue for everyone who has faith in Him. Those of us who believe will be counted as right with God.

GET ON WITH IT

Learn verse 25 by heart. This is an incredible truth for all Christians to hold on to. The resurrection is proof that Jesus has paid for our sins.

PRAY ABOUT IT

Thank God for keeping His promises. Thank Him for His promise to make us right with Him.

THE BOTTOM LINE

Have faith in God who keeps His promises.

26 Peace and joy

Paul says we're "justified by faith" — we're declared right with God as we trust in Jesus' death on the cross. We won't be condemned by God as we deserve to be. Now Paul tells us that more goodies are coming our way.

 Read Romans 5 v 1–2

ENGAGE YOUR BRAIN

▶ What do people who trust in Jesus now have? (v1)

The problem
God is rightly angry with our sin against Him. We deserve to be punished.

The solution
"We have been justified through faith" — Jesus took God's anger and punishment on Himself for everyone who has faith in His death for sinners.

The result
"We have peace with God through our Lord Jesus Christ." God's anger has been dealt with by Jesus, so Christians have peace with God.

What a sensational result! Even their sin can't alter that, since Jesus has already taken God's punishment for it.

 Read verses 1–2 again

▶ What else have believers gained? (v2)

▶ What should be their response?

Having faith in Jesus is like a door that lets you into the great room full of God's blessing ("grace"). Sin was the barrier stopping us getting in, but now we have full access to it. And that should fill us with great joy.

PRAY ABOUT IT

Think about God's grace — all He's done for you and given you. Praise Him for specific things. Thank Him. Tell Him how it makes you feel.

THE BOTTOM LINE

Faith in Jesus gives us peace with God.

27 | No pain, no gain

We've been reading about Jesus' death in our place and how it puts believers right with God. But we're not just passive observers of Jesus' suffering — Christians can expect to share in it too.

👁 Read Romans 5 v 3–5

ENGAGE YOUR BRAIN

▶ *What surprising thing can Christians get excited about? (v3)*

▶ *Why should we be happy to suffer? (v3–5)*

Jesus suffered and died to save us. Suffering for being a Christian comes with the territory. We're promised that people will persecute us. But why be happy about it?

Paul tells us that we should see the difficulties of life as opportunities to grow spiritually. God has a great plan for our lives but it doesn't guarantee an easy, relaxing life.

Instead, God allows us to face times of suffering which make us trust in Him more, and help us grow in spiritual character. *"Suffering produces perseverance; perseverance, character; and character, hope."* God allows us to experience hard times so that we develop spiritual muscles, and are made more fit to serve Him.

And that really is something to celebrate, especially as we have the certain hope of sharing God's glory. And the Holy Spirit in us reminds us of God's overwhelming love for us (v5). The Christian life really is a matter of "no pain, no gain". Let's look at our troubles as opportunities to learn and grow spiritually.

TALK IT THROUGH

Think about hard times you've faced. Can you see God at work in those situations, making you stronger?

PRAY ABOUT IT

Ask God to help you through any tough situations you face. Ask Him to help you not give up. Thank Him that He's with you, building you up along the way. Thank Him for the certain hope of eternal life.

28   Unbeatable love

Does God love you?
Do you genuinely feel that He does?
Is there any evidence that God loves you?

👁 Read Romans 5 v 6–8

ENGAGE YOUR BRAIN

▶ *How does God show His love for us? (v8)*

▶ *How would you describe God's timing? (v6)*

Simple. We know God loves us because His own Son Jesus died for us. While we were still God's enemies. And God has given His Spirit to all who trust Him.

You may have read stories of people giving their own lives to save loved ones. But God's love shown on the cross beats all human love hands down. We were God's enemies, sinning against Him when He gave His Son to die in our place.

👁 Read verses 9–11

Verse 9 talks of the final day when God will judge His world.

▶ *What's true for those who trust in Jesus? (v9)*

▶ *Why can we be sure of this? (v10)*

If God's done the difficult thing (v10a), of course we can be sure He'll complete the job and hold on to us when His judgment comes (v10b). And there's even more to get excited about (v11).

PRAY ABOUT IT

Will you praise and thank God for what He's done? Spend time thanking Him for sending His Son Jesus to die for sinners like yourself.

THE BOTTOM LINE

While we were still sinners, Christ died for us.

JOSHUA

Invade and conquer

After years of slavery in Egypt and 40 years in the desert, the Israelites were finally going to enter the promised land of Canaan. The problem was that Canaan wasn't empty. It was full of people who were enemies of God and His people. They wouldn't give up their land without a fight.

ATTACK!

At the end of the book of Deuteronomy, the Israelites were camped on the east side of the River Jordan. God wanted His people to conquer the land on the west of the river, and He appointed Joshua to lead them into battle. Would God keep His promise to give His people this land flowing with milk and honey?

DEJA VU

If this all sounds a little familiar, it's because the Israelites had reached this point before. But they hadn't trusted God to give them victory and success in Canaan. So He punished them by making them wait a further 40 years in the desert until that disobedient generation had all died out. All except faithful Joshua and Caleb.

SECOND CHANCE

Now God's people were back with a second opportunity. Would they trust God this time and go in to claim the land?

For Christians, this book teaches us loads about God and His relationship with His people. He has made great promises in the Bible — will we trust and obey Him?

Let battle commence...

29 | Promising start

Ready for a history lesson? What do you mean "No"? Give us a chance! Joshua is the sixth book in the Bible and continues the history of God's people, the Israelites. Time for a recap.

👁 Read Genesis 12 v 1–3

ENGAGE YOUR BRAIN

▶ *What promises did God make to Abram?*

👁 Read Genesis 50 v 20–25

▶ *Which of the promises had come true by the end of Genesis?*

▶ *What was Joseph confident about? (v24)*

God promised Abram *people, land* and *blessing*. His family would become a great nation, with their own country to live in, and they would be a blessing to everyone. By the end of **Genesis**, only the first promise had come true.

In **Exodus**, God rescued His people from terrible slavery in Egypt by opening up the Red Sea as a national escape route. God then met their leader Moses on Mount Sinai and gave them His law (the Ten Commandments in **Deuteronomy**

and other stuff in **Leviticus**) so they knew how to live as God's people in the land He would give them.

Disastrously, the people rebelled and chose not to go into Canaan. That's in **Numbers**. They were punished by God. 40 years on, after Moses had died, what had happened to the promises?

👁 Read Joshua 1 v 1–5

▶ *How did God encourage Joshua?*

▶ *How should it encourage us too?*

God gave Joshua a tough task — leading His people into battle. But the Lord promised to be with them, giving them victory and a new home.

PRAY ABOUT IT

Thank God for keeping His promises made years ago. Ask Him to speak to you through the book of Joshua.

30 Following orders

**"Pull yourself together!" "Don't be sad; cheer up."
Now and then concerned friends tell us what to do.
Sometimes they're worth listening to; sometimes they're
not. But God's orders must always be taken seriously.**

👁 Read Joshua 1 v 6–9

ENGAGE YOUR BRAIN

▶ *What does God tell Joshua to do? (v6, 7, 9) Why was this important? (v6)*

▶ *What was the key to success? (v7–8)*

The Israelites had a huge task ahead of them — conquering Canaan. They had to be brave and strong. God gave them Joshua and a book to guide them. Success relied on obeying God's word. They could be courageous in a terrifying situation because God would be with them (v9). He promised to make them successful (v8).

These verses are important to believers now. God calls us to be brave as we share our faith. He's always with us, and we have the whole Bible to teach us. One day we'll have success and prosperity — eternal life with God!

👁 Read verses 10–18

Two and a half of the twelve Israelite tribes would live on the other side of the river Jordan from Canaan.

▶ *But what did Joshua expect of them? (v14–15)*

▶ *How did they respond? (v16)*

GET ON WITH IT

▶ *Through the Holy Spirit, God is always with His people — do you remember that?*

▶ *God's word, the Bible, should be our guide — are you reading it enough?*

▶ *It's full of His promises — are you relying on them? What about obeying his commands?*

THE BOTTOM LINE

Be strong and courageous.

God is always with His people.

31 | Faith in strange places

I spy with my little eye something beginning with J. And R. In this section of his book, Joshua sends spies to check out the land over the river. Their risky expedition would have extraordinary twists to it...

👁 Read Joshua 2 v 1–11

ENGAGE YOUR BRAIN

▷ *Who surprisingly helped God's spies? (v1)*

▷ *What had she heard about the Lord? (v9–10)*

Jericho was the first place the Israelites would have to defeat on their way into the promised land.

God often uses the least likely people to serve Him. This time it was Rahab the prostitute. She'd heard all about God and how He'd rescued the Israelites and destroyed their enemies. She feared the Lord and pleaded for her life to be spared...

👁 Read verses 12–24

▷ *What deal was struck? (v14)*

▷ *What was Rahab told to do?*

▷ *What did the spies report? (v24)*

God had chosen the Israelites to be His people. They were to respond with faith — trusting His promises. But God's plan was for the whole world. Incredibly, here was an outsider (a non–Israelite) who turned to God for rescue.

The New Testament shows how Jesus came to rescue sinful people whatever their background or history. Brilliant news. And Jesus wants us to trust Him completely.

PRAY ABOUT IT

Are you a Christian? Thank God for making you one of His people. And think (then pray about) what it will mean to trust Him... in all your decision making; in difficult situations; in the face of doubt or abuse; with everything.

THE BOTTOM LINE

God's rescue is available to everyone.

32 Water proof

Joshua's spies reported that people in Jericho were shaking in their boots about the Israelites' God. Time to invade! Oh, hold on, there's a huge, rushing river in the way.

👁 Read Joshua 3 v 1–6

ENGAGE YOUR BRAIN

▶ *What three instructions did Joshua give? (v3–5)*

The *ark of the covenant* was a portable throne/chest which held the Ten Commandments. It was a symbol of God's presence — the Lord was leading the way. And it reminded the Israelites of the covenant promises God had made. They were God's rescued people, who must depend on His promises. They had to consecrate themselves (v5) — special ceremonial washing to make them clean for God's presence.

👁 Read verses 7–17

▶ *What did Joshua remind them about God? (v10, 13) What would He do for them? (v10)*

▶ *What proof of God's greatness did they witness? (v15–17)*

In the Old Testament, the Israelites regularly forgot how powerful their God was. Here was another miraculous reminder. Just as He had brought the previous generation through the Red Sea, God showed them here that He'd really be with them. He would give them victory.

GET ON WITH IT

Through the Holy Spirit, God is always with His people today, too. They can still rely on His promises, knowing He's the living God (v10) and the Lord of all the earth (v13).

▶ *Find Deuteronomy 10 v 14. Make a poster of it or memorise it.*

PRAY ABOUT IT

Our God is the God of the whole earth. Praise and thank Him. And bring your requests to Him, knowing that nothing is impossible for God.

33 Set in stone

Yesterday we zoomed through the story of God holding back the river Jordan so the Israelites could cross into the promised land. Today we get a slo-mo replay and a big reminder.

Read Joshua 4 v 1–18

ENGAGE YOUR BRAIN

▶ Who had to do what? Why? (v6-7)

▶ What did God do for Joshua? (v14) Then what happened? (v18)

Read verses 19–24

▶ What great rescue were they reminded of? (v23)

▶ How would other nations react to news of this miracle? (v24) How should God's people react? (v24b)

God's people had been bullied slaves in Egypt and He'd rescued them by parting the Red Sea. They then rejected His rule so He sent them into the desert. Yet He went with them and gave them food out of nowhere. Now, at the Jordan, He'd done the miraculous again. The Israelites were now in the land God had promised to give them.

God would continue to lead them, care for and fight for them. His people were expected to trust Him and tell others about all He'd done. They were also to fear Him (v24) — respect, trust and obey Him fully.

The Israelites looked at these stones to remind them of God's greatness. We look back to the cross of Jesus to see God's greatest rescue — the supreme reminder of God's greatness, love and care, showing us He's always with us.

PRAY ABOUT IT

If you're thankful for God's great acts, especially the cross, tell Him. Ask Him to help your lifestyle match your words.

THE BOTTOM LINE

Remember God's great rescue. Fear the Lord.

34 Snip snip hooray!

God's people were now in the land He'd promised them. Their punishment was over at last. Time to start again with God.

👁 Read Joshua 5 v 1–3

ENGAGE YOUR BRAIN

▶ *What was great news for God's people? (v1)*

▶ *What was eye-watering news for them? (v2)*

Once they had arrived in the promised land, God ordered Joshua to have all the males circumcised (cutting the foreskin off the penis).

▶ *Why did Joshua need to do that???*

👁 Read verses 4–8

Centuries before, in Abraham's time, God wanted the Israelites to be circumcised. Why? As a sign of being God's people. Like wearing a badge which said: *"I'm living under God's care with His people!"* It was actually a big privilege. But it wasn't a ticket to heaven. Circumcised or not, you still had to trust God.

▶ *Why hadn't there been circumcision for 40 years? (v6)*

No trust in God, no circumcision. Now the punishment was over, God's people could start again. By being circumcised, they were promising to trust God.

God's people were to be different. These days, Christians don't need circumcision to mark them as belonging to God. The Bible talks about *"circumcision of the heart"* (Jeremiah 4 v 4). Our attitude to God is what really counts. Living God's way marks us out as different.

THINK IT THROUGH

▶ *Are you any different from non-Christians you know? What marks you out as loyal to God?*

▶ *How does your attitude to God need to change?*

Talk your answers over with the Lord honestly.

35 Surround sound

Ever been surprised by someone's sudden appearance? An unwanted teacher or boss silently appearing at your shoulder. Bumping into a friend in the unlikeliest place. Well, Joshua is about to have the shock of his life...

👁 Read Joshua 5 v 13 – 6 v 5

ENGAGE YOUR BRAIN

▶ What was Joshua's right response to his visitor? (5 v 14–15)

▶ What did God promise Joshua? (6 v 2) How? (v3–5)

What an incredible encouragement to know that God's army was on his side! The instructions were weird but that wasn't the point. What mattered was that Joshua obeyed God, giving Him the respect He deserved (5 v 14–15).

👁 Read Joshua 6 v 6–14

▶ Remember what the ark was a symbol of? (See day 32)

▶ So what did marching with the ark show?

How could this possibly defeat a fortified city? We'll find out tomorrow.

Back in Joshua 1 v 9, God said: "Be strong and courageous. Do not be afraid ... for the LORD your God will be with you wherever you go."

GET ON WITH IT

▶ How can you show more respect to the Lord?

▶ In what ways do you need to be more obedient to God?

▶ What do you need to be courageous about?

▶ How will it help to remember that God is with you?

PRAY ABOUT IT

Spend 5 minutes talking over your answers with the Lord. Thank Him that He's fighting on the side of His people and is always with them.

THE BOTTOM LINE

God is fighting for His people.

36 Wall fall down

God commanded the Israelites to march around Jericho with His ark, blowing their trumpets. They did this once a day for six straight days. On day seven there was a noisy and devastating change of routine.

👁 Read Joshua 6 v 15–21

ENGAGE YOUR BRAIN

▶ *What special instructions were the attackers given? (v18)*

▶ *What was the outcome of this bizarre battle plan? (v20)*

The city was devoted to the Lord — it was up to God what He did with it. Some bits were to be kept (v19), while the rest of Jericho was to be wiped out (v21).

👁 Read verses 22–27

▶ *Remember Rahab? What happened to her and her family?*

▶ *What happened to everyone and everything else? (v21, 24)*

▶ *What happened to Joshua? (v27)*

God was in control. He rightly punished the people of Jericho who had refused to live His way. But He rescued Rahab, who had turned to Him.

God expected total allegiance and trust from His people. And He wanted them to be pure. That's why the ungodly people of Jericho had to be wiped out — so God's people would not be tempted by them to follow other gods.

We live after Jesus came. The situation has changed but God hasn't. On the cross, Jesus defeated our worst and most fearsome enemy: death. The Bible warns us that people will ridicule Jesus and the cross. They'll think it's weird. Impossible.

But God says it's His way of rescue, so we're to trust Him, obey His commands and kick out the wrong things in our lives.

PRAY ABOUT IT

Pray for people you know who reject God and are headed for destruction. Plead with God to rescue them, as He did Rahab.

37 Achan pain

Israelites 1 Jericho 0. Well, God 1 Jericho 0. Would His people now trust Him? Or would they take matters into their own hands rather than let God rule in His way? If they did, the consequences would be fierce.

👁 Read Joshua 7 v 1–9

ENGAGE YOUR BRAIN

▶ What had Achan done wrong? (See Joshua 6 v 18–19)

▶ How did God punish His disobedient people? (v3–5)

▶ Who did Joshua blame? (v7)

Joshua couldn't work out what had gone wrong so quickly after the magnificent victory at Jericho. Why would God allow the Israelites to be beaten up by a small town? Joshua would soon find out...

👁 Read verses 10–15

▶ Why were they defeated? (v11)

▶ What would happen if they didn't take urgent action? (v12)

The Israelites had broken their covenant agreement with God. Unless the culprit was found and put to death, God would leave His people.

👁 Read verses 16–26

▶ How do you feel about this tragic story?

▶ Was the punishment deserved?

God couldn't just forgive and forget as if nothing had happened. He hates sin. One day He will judge finally. And it's only the death of Jesus that can satisfy God's anger and rescue us from God's punishment.

PRAY ABOUT IT

▶ What do you need to confess?

▶ What do you need to ask God?

▶ What will you thank Him for?

THE BOTTOM LINE

God hates sin and will punish it.

38 ┆ Ai II – The Revenge

Question: What's the name for people from Ai?
Aiites? Aiish? Ailiens?
Less stupid question: After the lesson God taught His people in ch 7, would they start trusting Him again?

👁 **Read Joshua 8 v 1–29**

ENGAGE YOUR BRAIN

▶ *How did God reassure Joshua? (v1)*

▶ *How was God generous to His people? (v2)*

▶ *Who would win this victory? (v7)*

The Israelites followed God's plan closely and He gave them success. God's people knew the Lord was on their side again. He also showed them great generosity. When they'd defeated Jericho they'd had to stay away from its treasures. This time they could keep the plunder (v2).

👁 **Read verses 24–29**

▶ *How would you describe the destruction of Ai?*

▶ *What happened to its king? (v29)*

Gruesome. The king of Ai was hanged on a tree/pole after his death to act as a warning against

going against God. It was also a sign of God's anger at sin. God's people needed to realise how seriously God treats sin. It's so easy to treat sin lightly. But it matters to God. So sin must matter to us and we should fight it in our lives.

1400 years after the Ai incident, God gave us another picture of sin — the King of the Jews was hung on a tree/pole. Jesus was nailed to a cross as the punishment for our sins. Can you still treat sin as though it doesn't matter?

PRAY ABOUT IT

Only you know exactly what you need to say to God today. Don't hold back.

THE BOTTOM LINE

God punishes sin, yet shows great generosity to His faithful people.

39 Mountain tension

What's the biggest crowd you've ever been in? Imagine being part of the huge Israelite horde, gathered together in front of two mountains, to pledge their allegiance to God. A sea of thousands of faces, all committed to God.

👁 Read Joshua 8 v 30–31

ENGAGE YOUR BRAIN

▶ *What did Joshua do first?*

Sacrificing fellowship offerings meant burning meat on the altar as an offering to God. It was a sign that God was at peace with the Israelites, had forgiven them, and that the Israelites were devoted to Him. But there was another sign of their devotion…

👁 Read verses 32–35

▶ *What did Joshua do? (v34)*

▶ *How much of it did he read? (v35)*

▶ *Who was there while it happened? (v33, 35)*

Yesterday we read how God gave His people victory in battle at Ai. But it wasn't to be a one-sided relationship — the Israelites were expected to show their devotion to God by obeying His word. And it wasn't just for the elders and priests, it was for everyone — including women, children and foreigners (*"aliens"*) like Rahab, who now lived with God's people.

On the cross, Jesus won the victory over sin and death. He brought forgiveness to believers. Our response must be to keep turning back to Him and to go on living by His word, the Bible. It's so simple, yet it can seem the hardest thing to do.

THINK IT THROUGH

▶ *What practical things can you do to make sure you read the Bible and obey God more?*

▶ *What specific things do you need to work on?*

THE BOTTOM LINE

Get back to God's word.

40 Trick or treaty

God was giving success to Joshua and the Israelites as they invaded Canaan. News of their victories soon got around. Some of the local nations banded together to fight the Israelites. Others had more cunning plans.

👁 Read Joshua 9 v 1–15

ENGAGE YOUR BRAIN

▷ How did the Gibeonites/Hivites deceive Joshua?

▷ Why did the Israelites fall for this deception? (v14)

▷ What was the outcome? (v15)

👁 Read verses 16–27

▷ What did the Israelites discover? (v16)

▷ Why was this a big problem?

▷ What happened to these crafty neighbours? (v20–21)

The first eight chapters of Joshua have showed us that God wanted a pure people who served Him and were not tempted away to follow false gods. That's why God commanded His people to have nothing to do with their enemies in Canaan. The Israelites failed to ask God for help (v14), were deceived and so compromised. Big mistake. It would come back to haunt them later.

THINK IT THROUGH

Christians shouldn't compromise their faith. We're called to obey God in this world, but not to be tempted by its sinful ways.

▷ In what ways are Christians tempted to compromise?

▷ Which affect you particularly?

PRAY ABOUT IT

Incredibly, the deceitful Gibeonites were not destroyed. Even their punishment was a privilege (v27). They were brought into God's people. God is mind-bogglingly gracious. Thank Him now and ask Him to bring "deceitful" or unlikely friends of yours into His family.

41 | Romans: Sin disease

We're turning back to Paul's letter to Christians in Rome. So far, he's pointed out that no one is good enough to meet God's perfect standards — but while we were still sinners, Christ died for us.

👁 Read Romans 5 v 12–14

ENGAGE YOUR BRAIN

▶ *Who have sinned and deserve to be punished with death? (v12)*

▶ *Who sinned first?*

▶ *So why is it that we all deserve to be punished?*

Adam disobeyed God, bringing sin into the world. God's punishment was death — Adam died. And death has also been the end for every human since. Sin is like a disease. Adam brought it into the world and spread it. Sin entered the world through Adam and Eve, but we've all caught the sin disease by disobeying God. We're all just as bad.

When Adam fell into sin, we all fell with him. But there's no point blaming him and thinking we could have done any better. Every one of us has chosen to sin. Chosen to live for ourselves instead of living for God.

Adam, the first man, sinned for all of us. But we've all sinned too. Adam brought death into the world. But we all deserve death because we're all sinners. Tomorrow, Paul will tell us all about the cure, which he hints at in verse 14.

PRAY ABOUT IT

We're all naturally sinful. Ask God to help you fight specific sins that hound you. And pray for friends who don't yet realise they need a cure for their sin disease.

THE BOTTOM LINE

By one man's sin, everyone was plunged into sin, guilt and death.

42 Full of life

Yesterday Paul told us the tragic truth — one man (Adam) plunged us all into sin and death. Today he gives us the good news — one Man (Jesus) can rescue us from sin and death.

👁 Read Romans 5 v 15–17

ENGAGE YOUR BRAIN

▶ *How much more did Jesus do than Adam? (v15–16)*

▶ *What's the result for those who receive God's great gift? (v17)*

Jesus did far more than reverse the death sentence brought by Adam's sin. Out of His overflowing grace pour the riches of eternal life! Freedom from sin and the gift of eternal life are on offer for all who receive them, by trusting in Jesus. Earth–shattering stuff.

👁 Read verses 18–21

▶ *What was the result of Adam's action? (v18)*

▶ *And what about Jesus' action? (v18–19)*

▶ *What's Paul's point in verses 20–21?*

Adam may have brought sin and God's punishment into the world, but Jesus Christ has made it possible for us to be made right with God and experience eternal life, through *"one act of righteousness"* — His death on the cross.

Verses 20–21 are slightly tricky. They say that God's law in the Old Testament shows up our sin — it shows us that we fail to obey God. Once we realise how sinful we are, we're more likely to ask for God's forgiveness. That's God's grace at work, bringing people to eternal life through Jesus.

PRAY ABOUT IT

If you're a Christian and you're not bursting with excitement and thanks to God right now, there's something seriously wrong.

43 Evil twin

A pair of twins look the same, sound the same, but aren't the same age. They were born years apart. The first one died at exactly the time the second was born. How can this be? Well, they're both you if you're a Christian.

👁 Read Romans 6 v 1–4

ENGAGE YOUR BRAIN

▶ *If Christians' sins are forgiven, can they carry on sinning? (v1–2)*

Jesus died on the cross to take the punishment we deserve. He died for our sin. So when you become a Christian you have all your wrongs forgiven by Jesus. It is as though your sinful life has died with Jesus. You no longer want to disobey God — you want to please Him. That's the plan, anyway.

Back in Jesus' time, everyone who chose to follow Him was baptised — it symbolised the death of their old, sinful life. Twin one was dead; twin two was now alive, living for Jesus. People who trust in Jesus have *shared* in Jesus' death and *shared* in Jesus' resurrection. Stop and take that in for a moment.

👁 Read verses 5–7

▶ *What has happened to our old, sinful twin? (v6)*

▶ *So what's true of our new life as a Christian? (v7)*

Our old self dies when we trust in Jesus and His death in our place. We're born again, freed from the grip sin had on our lives. Free to serve God. Yes, we'll still mess up sometimes, but sin no longer rules us — God does.

PRAY ABOUT IT

Thank God that He frees His people from sin. Ask Him to help you with specific temptations you battle with.

THE BOTTOM LINE

A Christian's sinful self has died.

44 Alive and kicking

Christians are dead to sin — it no longer rules them. So why do we still struggle to say "no" to sin and temptation? How do we make sure our sin is put to death?

 Read Romans 6 v 8–11

ENGAGE YOUR BRAIN

▶ Who did Jesus live for? (v10)

▶ So who do Christians (Christ-followers) live for?

Christians share in Jesus' death and also in His risen life. They are dead to sin — it no longer rules them. It's as if they have become fully alive to God for the first time. Verse 10 calls this "living to God" instead of living to sin.

THINK IT OVER

In your attitude, have you drawn a line under sin or have you left the door open to it coming back?

▶ Yes, we still fail — but what can you do to kick sin from your life?

▶ How can you be more committed to living for God?

Read verses 12–14

▶ What does Paul tell Christians not to do? (v12–13)

▶ So what should Christians do?

▶ Think of specific things you need to stop doing, and start doing.

It's going to be hard, so don't miss the great promise in verse 14. If you're a Christian, you're dead to sin and alive in Christ. So live like it — get pleasing God and kick out the wrong stuff in your life. Don't think about going back to sinful living. How could you when you've shared in Jesus' death and resurrection?

PRAY ABOUT IT

Read through verse 13 and pray about the issues it raises.

THE BOTTOM LINE

Christians are dead to sin and alive to God.

45 Slaving away

How do you feel about being a slave? It's not a positive thought, is it? Paul says we're all slaves, but that's only a bad thing if you're a servant to the wrong master.

◉ Read Romans 6 v 15–18

ENGAGE YOUR BRAIN

▶ *What's the choice of masters on offer? (v16)*

▶ *What change of ownership has happened to Christians? (v17–18)*

Everyone's a slave. When you trust in Jesus, you're set free from one master (sin) to become a slave (a willing servant) to another — God. Verse 18 says we've been set free — to become slaves…

◉ Read verses 19–23

▶ *How should Christians be different from their old sinful selves? (v19)*

▶ *Did you have more freedom before you became a Christian? (v21)*

▶ *So what are the benefits of being God's slaves? (v22–23)*

Freedom isn't doing as we please: it's doing as God pleases. As our master, sin pays us *wages* (what we deserve) — death. But God as our master gives us a *gift* (what we don't deserve) — eternal life. Christians should live in a way that honours God, not turn back to their old boss, sin.

THINK IT OVER

Grab another Christian and chew over these questions: How should being a slave to God affect…

• what films you watch?

• how you spend your money?

• choices you make in life?

• who you spend time with?

PRAY ABOUT IT

Talk to God about who you're a slave to, and how you're getting on at the moment.

46 Wedding bells

They make adults cry. They keep dressmakers in business. They swallow your whole Saturday. Paul's talking about weddings.

👁 Read Romans 7 v 1–3

ENGAGE YOUR BRAIN

▶ What does Paul say about God's Old Testament law? (v1)

▶ How does the story (v2–3) back this up?

A husband and wife promise to be married to each other as long they're both alive. But once of them dies, the marriage is over and they are released from their promise. But Paul's not really talking about weddings — he's making a point about sin and God's law.

👁 Read verses 4–6

▶ Who do Christians now belong to? (v4)

▶ What effect should that have on us? (end of v4)

▶ What changes when a person trusts in Jesus? (v5–6)

A Christian's situation is similar to the widow who remarries. Our old sinful selves have "died", so we're released from our marriage to the law — trying to meet God's perfect standards. We can't do it. But we don't have to, because Jesus has freed us from sin and death and our old way of life.

Christians are married to Christ. They want to serve Him and bear fruit for God (v4). The law has no hold on them any more. They want to keep God's law and live His way, but they're now free to serve God far more effectively — with the Holy Spirit's help (v6).

PRAY ABOUT IT

Talk to God about how fruitful you are for Him.

THE BOTTOM LINE

Christians are married to Christ.

47 The law on trial

Paul's been talking a lot about God's law. It's been a bit confusing at times. Some people thought Paul was claiming that law-keeping was sinning or caused people to do wrong. Check out his response.

👁 Read Romans 7 v 7–8

ENGAGE YOUR BRAIN

▶ *What does God's law show us? (v7)*

Paul never said that God's law was bad. It came from God, so it can't be wrong. But Paul does say that it isn't enough to save us from sin. If it was, Jesus wouldn't have had to die on the cross.

Ever seen a KEEP OFF THE GRASS sign? Doesn't it make you want to run all over the grass? Even though you didn't want to before you saw the sign? That's the way sin makes us react to God's law. It tempts us to disobey God's commands.

👁 Read verses 9–13

▶ *How does Paul describe God's law? (v12)*

▶ *So what's the real problem? (v11)*

God's law is *"holy, righteous and good"*. It's perfect — it comes from God. It's our failure to keep God's law that is the problem. God's law shows up our sin. It points out how useless we are at obeying God. That sounds bad, but we need to realise how sinful we are so that we can turn to Jesus to be rescued.

PRAY ABOUT IT

What sin has God's word shown up in your life?

Talk to God about it — confessing, repenting and asking for help.

THE BOTTOM LINE

God's law shows up our sin.

48 | Sin inside

Sin can take over people's lives. As much as they want to do what's right, they can't seem to stop themselves from sinning. There's only one answer to the sin problem — Jesus Christ.

👁 Read Romans 7 v 14–17

ENGAGE YOUR BRAIN

▶ *What can rule people's lives? (v17)*

Paul's words can be hard to get your brain around. Here he's saying:

"God's law is perfect and holy. But it couldn't make me holy. Even though I knew God's law, sin was in charge of my life."

👁 Read verses 18–25

▶ *What did Paul long for? (v24)*

▶ *What did he need? What's the only way to be free from sin? (v25)*

People's real problem isn't God's law: it's the sin in us. The law can't save us because we can't possibly keep it. The sin inside us stops us from doing so.

Only Jesus and His Spirit living in us can help us please God. There's loads more about that in chapter 8.

PRAY ABOUT IT

Talk to God about anything you don't understand from this chapter of Romans.

Re-read it, asking God to make it clear and to teach you through it.

Thank Him that Jesus' death on the cross defeated sin.

49 That's the spirit

As we begin one of the most mind-blowing chapters of the Bible, Paul sums up what he's told us so far. His first sentence is a cracker.

👁 Read Romans 8 v 1–4

ENGAGE YOUR BRAIN

▶ *What must every Christian remember? (v1)*

▶ *What makes this possible? (v2)*

The gospel (*"the law of the Spirit who gives life"*) has done what the Old Testament law could never do (v3a) — bring us rescue. And it's all through Jesus taking God's punishment instead of us (v3b). Christians are not condemned — they won't be punished by God, because Jesus has set them free!

👁 Read verses 5–8

▶ *How does Paul describe people who are ruled by sin?*
v5:

v6:

v7:

v8:

▶ *What about people with God's Spirit in their lives?*
v5:

v6:

If you're a Christian, it should be obvious in the way you live. Your mind is no longer set on doing sinful stuff and it's no longer set against God. Your mind should be set on pleasing God, with the Holy Spirit helping you to live God's way. You're heading for everlasting life and peace with God (v6)!

THINK IT OVER

Is your life the same as everyone else's? How are you different? How can you please God more?

PRAY ABOUT IT

Thank God that there is no condemnation for Christians. Talk through the *Think it over* questions with Him.

50 Dead bodies

"Death doesn't really worry me ... I just don't want to be there when it happens." (Woody Allen)
Thoughts about death can fill our minds sometimes. Let's read what Paul said on the subject.

👁 Read Romans 8 v 9–11

ENGAGE YOUR BRAIN

▶ *Who's in control of Christians? (v9)*

▶ *What will happen to their bodies? (v10–11)*

All Christians have the Holy Spirit in them, helping them live God's way. Christians' bodies will die, just like everyone else. But God's Spirit raised Jesus from death and He will also give new life to Christians. Their bodies will die but they will go on to live with God for ever.

👁 Read verses 12–17

▶ *What does Paul call Christians? (v16)*

▶ *So how should we live? (v12–13)*

▶ *What do Christians share in with Jesus? (v17)*

Christians are God's children. That means they have to stop being ruled by sin (v12). They're no longer slaves to fear — they can cry out to God their Father (*"Abba"* means *"Daddy"*) with their needs (v15). God loves His children.

Christians are also God's heirs, along with His Son, Jesus. The inheritance has an up side and a down side. Christians will share in Christ's sufferings — they will be persecuted for serving God. But they will also share in God's glory — they will one day live with Him and see what He's really like. Phenomenal.

PRAY ABOUT IT

Thank God for the work of His Spirit in us, His children. Tell Him the things you need the Spirit's help to change.

THE BOTTOM LINE

Christians are God's children. Death is not the end for them.

51 Waiting for God

Last time, Paul talked about Christians sharing God's glory. And also sharing Christ's sufferings too. For Christians, the two things go hand in hand. So how do we cope with the tough stuff before eternal glory?

👁 Read Romans 8 v 18–22

ENGAGE YOUR BRAIN

▶ *What does Paul say about our suffering? (v18)*

Life isn't a breeze for Christians. But Christians can always look with certainty to an amazing future. One day God will finish making us more like Him. Christians won't just see God's glory — they'll be part of it!

When sin entered the world through Adam and Eve, God cursed the world (v22). But one day, He will make everything perfect again (v20–21)

👁 Read verses 23–27

▶ *Who else is groaning? (v23)*

▶ *What are Christians waiting for? (v23)*

▶ *Who helps them? How? (v26)*

Believe it or not, Christians aren't happy all the time. We're still waiting for God's rescue plan to be completed. We're waiting to claim our inheritance in eternity with God. We cling on to this certain hope.

As we groan our way through the suffering of this life, we struggle in prayer, barely knowing what to say to God sometimes. The Holy Spirit groans along with us. He understands, and helps us to pray.

PRAY ABOUT IT

Read through today's verses and talk to God about them. Don't know what to say? Then ask God's help.

THE BOTTOM LINE

Current suffering is nothing compared to a future with God.

52 It's all good

"Why does God allow such suffering?"
"I can't believe God let that happen to a Christian."
Ever thought or heard things like that? Well, Paul has something surprising to say on this topic.

👁 Read Romans 8 v 28

ENGAGE YOUR BRAIN

▶ *What's the surprising truth?*

▶ *How does Paul describe Christians in this verse?*

Christians are people who love God — they've been called by Him as part of His perfect plans. God's at work. In all things. For the good of those who love Him. *Astonishing.* Our brief time of pain on this planet fits into God's eternal plans. We may not see it at the time, but God uses the hard things in life to do us good.

👁 Read verses 29–30

▶ *How does this help us understand how God works everything for the good of His people?*

God FOREKNEW His people

He knew them intimately and loved them, even before they were born.

He PREDESTINED them

All Christians have been chosen by God to be His children for ever.

He CALLED them

Christians are called to turn away from their sinful lives to Jesus.

They're JUSTIFIED too

Put right with God — their sins cancelled by Jesus' death.

And GLORIFIED

Believers will share in God's glory in eternity with Him.

God will stop at nothing to make His people like His perfect Son, and bring them into glory with Him. Any suffering will be worth it.

PRAY ABOUT IT

Thank God that however hard life seems, we can trust Him. His plans are perfect and will work out.

53 Winning team

Ever wonder what's the point of being a Christian? Ever worry you might not actually make it to eternal life with God? Can we really be sure? Check out one of the most encouraging Bible passages there is to spur you on.

👁 Read Romans 8 v 31–34

ENGAGE YOUR BRAIN

▷ Why shouldn't Christians worry about opposition? (v31–33)

▷ Where is Jesus now and what is He doing? (v34)

Whoever is against us, God is greater, and He won't abandon us or let us go. He gave up His own Son to rescue us, so of course He will protect us and give us everything we could possibly need. No one else can condemn us — God is the ultimate Judge and He has already justified us. Jesus is with God in heaven right now, speaking for us.

Read through those incredible verses again right now, praising God.

👁 Read verses 35–39

▷ What should Christians expect in this life? (v36)

▷ But who can separate them from God? (v35)

▷ What can take eternal life away from them? (v38–39)

Christians will experience suffering and persecution in this life. We must be prepared to face death for Jesus, if necessary (v36). But whatever the danger or difficulties that tempt us to give up, nothing will separate us from Jesus' love, or from sharing His victory (v37). Jesus isn't just a friend for life, He's a friend for eternal life.

PRAY ABOUT IT

▷ What are you most afraid of?

Add those things to Paul's list in verses 38–39. And thank God that not even those things can stop His plans or His love for you.

THE BOTTOM LINE

Nothing can separate Christians from God's love.

54   Matthew: the big picture

Back to Jesus teaching on the hillside. Have you ever been called "salt of the earth"? Unlikely. But salt of the earth is what Jesus calls members of His kingdom, regardless of their age or background.

👁 Read Matthew 5 v 13–16

ENGAGE YOUR BRAIN

▶ *How do you think living out the beatitudes (v3-12) makes Christians salt and light in our world?*

▶ *What function does salt have? (It must be good for something — see v13.)*

Various ideas have been suggested for what Jesus means in verse 13. Salt is a preservative — it stops food from rotting — so Christians must be there to slow the decay of society's morals. Salt is antiseptic — it stops germs — same idea again. Salt adds flavour. Salt was very valuable in ancient times. Whatever Jesus means by using this metaphor, it's clear that Christians should be having a positive effect on the world around us.

▶ *What purpose does a light serve? (v15)*

▶ *How are we to be lights? (v16)*

▶ *How have these verses challenged you personally?*

PRAY ABOUT IT

Ask God to help you to have a positive impact on the world around you and that as people see your good deeds they would give glory to our Father in heaven.

GET ON WITH IT

Is there an issue in the news, or locally or at school/college/work where you could make a positive contribution as a Christian? How can you glorify God in the way you get involved?

THE BOTTOM LINE

Jesus says: "YOU are the salt of the earth".

55 Law-full

A bit of a mind-bender today; Jesus tells us He didn't come to abolish the Law but to fulfil it. What's that mean? Surely Christians today don't have to keep the Old Testament Law?

👁 Read Matthew 5 v 17–18

The Law and the Prophets means the Old Testament. One of the best ways to understand "fulfil" is that Jesus "filled it full" — He made it 3D. All the pictures and prophecies were pointing to Him. He completed the Old Testament; He gave it its full meaning.

👁 Read verses 19–20

ENGAGE YOUR BRAIN

▶ *What's your first reaction to these verses?*

▶ *How can we meet the standards Jesus sets in verse 20?*

Verse 20 would have sounded impossible — the Pharisees and teachers of the law were seen as super-holy — so how can anyone be more righteous than that? But the Pharisees actually reduced the law to a set of rules to keep. Over the next few days, Jesus will show us that true righteousness goes much deeper than that. And no one can keep the law perfectly… except Jesus. The only way we can be "righteous" is to be "in Christ" — to be saved by Him so that God treats us like His Son.

Jesus is the answer to the Old Testament, the final piece in the jigsaw. It points to Him. It's completed in Him. He's the one with ultimate, universal authority. And He says that entering God's kingdom isn't about keeping laws, but looking to Jesus.

PRAY ABOUT IT

Thank God that if you are a Christian you are "in Christ" and His righteousness is your own.

THE BOTTOM LINE

Jesus came to fulfil the Law.

56 Killer instinct

Jesus starts to explain what He means by fulfilling the Law now as He shows us the principles that the Law was designed to reflect. The first one is a real killer.

⊙ Read Matthew 5 v 21–22

ENGAGE YOUR BRAIN

▷ *What rule did the Pharisees and teachers of the law teach? (v21)*

▷ *How is Jesus' command more demanding? (v22)*

▷ *Have you ever been guilty of breaking the Pharisees' rule?*

▷ *What about Jesus' command?*

Murdered anyone recently? No? How about being really angry with someone? Ah… Jesus isn't interested in merely keeping the rules; He wants our hearts to be right. His kingdom is about far more than looking OK and being religious.

PRAY ABOUT IT

Say sorry to God now for the times when you have murdered someone in your heart.

⊙ Read verses 23–26

Offering a gift to God at the altar was serious stuff. What does Jesus say is more important?

So, when you remember (maybe when you're in a Christian meeting) that a friend is upset with you, what's the only appropriate action? OK, it might interrupt the meeting, but get the point? It's got to be immediate.

GET ON WITH IT

Anyone you need to make peace with? Do it. RIGHT NOW!!!

THE BOTTOM LINE

God's as serious about anger in His disciples as He is about murder. So mend broken friendships. Now.

57 Serious sex stuff

Adultery sounds old-fashioned these days, unless we call it cheating. And divorce is just part of life now, isn't it? What have such topics got to do with you? A lot more than you think, says Jesus.

👁 Read Matthew 5 v 27–32

ENGAGE YOUR BRAIN

▶ What rule did the Pharisees and teachers of the law teach? (v27)

▶ How is Jesus' command more demanding? (v28)

▶ Have you ever been guilty of breaking the Pharisees' rule?

▶ What about Jesus' command?

When God gave the Ten Commandments to Moses, He wasn't just saying: "Don't commit adultery". He was reminding His people that marriage is special, and that He is a loving, promise-keeping, faithful God and His people should be like Him. The Pharisees are reducing this heart attitude to a series of rules they can claim to keep or bend (v31). Jesus is having none of it.

▶ How seriously does Jesus take our sin? (v29–30)

▶ Where is our sin really located? Hand? Eye? (Hint: v28)

PRAY ABOUT IT

• Pray for the married couples you know, that God would bless them and help the husbands and wives to keep their marriage promises.

• Pray for people you know who have gone through the pain of divorce, that they would know the comfort of God, who always keeps His promises.

• Pray for yourself, that God would enable you to be pure in heart in your relationships.

THE BOTTOM LINE

Take your sin seriously.

58 Yes = yes? Eye = eye?

Some slightly more unusual rules now — we don't spend much time swearing oaths these days unless we're in court. Although we all make promises. And what about grudges and taking vengeance?

👁 Read Matthew 5 v 33–37

ENGAGE YOUR BRAIN

▶ *What rule did the Pharisees and teachers of the law teach? (v33)*

▶ *How is Jesus' command more demanding? (v37)*

▶ *Have you ever been guilty of breaking the Pharisees' rule?*

▶ *What about Jesus' command?*

▶ *Are you a man/woman of your word? Do you keep your promises? Can people trust you when you say you'll do something?*

👁 Read verses 38–42

▶ *What's the Old Testament rule in verse 38?*

▶ *How is Jesus' command even harder? (v39–42)*

▶ *How did Jesus live out the principles of verse 39?*

It's one thing to react proportionally to someone who wrongs you — she broke my pen, so I'll take hers. That seems fair to us. But Jesus takes things to a whole different level. Christians will be wronged and persecuted and we must take it (v39). We should share our stuff generously (v42) and go out of our way for others (v41). After all, Jesus gave His life for us, so we should show His attitude to people around us.

TALK IT OVER

Get hold of another Christian and talk about whether verse 39 applies when we see people doing evil to others. Why? Why not? How would you back up your argument from the Bible?

THE BOTTOM LINE

Let your yes be yes and your no be no.

59 | Love your enemies

By now the message is sinking in. God doesn't want us to be good, He wants us to be perfect! And we're not. Problem?

👁 Read Matthew 5 v 43–48

ENGAGE YOUR BRAIN

▷ What rule did the Pharisees and teachers of the law teach? (v43)

▷ Is that easy to do?

▷ How is Jesus' command more demanding? (v44)

▷ Is that easy?

One of the distinctive things about Christians is their ability to love their enemies. Just as Jesus prayed on the cross for those crucifying Him: "Father forgive them", Christians who were in concentration camps or who have had their families murdered have been able to forgive, pray for and love their enemies.

▷ What is your reaction to Jesus' command in verse 48?

▷ How can we meet the standards which Jesus sets in verse 20 and verse 48?

We can't. That's the simple answer. We're not perfect. But that's the whole point! Remember Matthew 5 v 3: *"Blessed are the poor in spirit, for theirs is the kingdom of heaven."* We have nothing to offer God; we can only accept what His Son has done. Jesus is perfect; He fulfils the Law and His heart is pure. Everything we have been reading about in chapter 5 that we can't do — He can!

PRAY ABOUT IT

Thank Jesus for all that He's done on your behalf. Pray for specific people you find hard to love. Thank God that He loves them and ask for His help to be truly loving towards them.

THE BOTTOM LINE

Be perfect as your heavenly Father is perfect. In Christ, you are!

60 Godly giving

Being part of God's kingdom is about being pure in heart and not merely obeying rules. Jesus now tackles our sinful human desire to look as if we're holy on the outside when our motives are all wrong on the inside.

Read Matthew 6 v 1–4

ENGAGE YOUR BRAIN

- *What is the headline warning for this next section, according to Jesus? (v1)*

- *What is the first example He gives of how we might do this? (v2)*

- *What is the danger we might fall into when giving money away?*

Jesus is warning us of the dangers of hypocrisy. A hypocrite is someone who says one thing and does another, or whose life doesn't match up with what they claim about it. The word originally meant "actor", and it's very easy to play the part of a Christian without being different on the inside.

GET ON WITH IT

- *Do you give to charities/people in need?*

- *What will you start doing?*

- *How might you be tempted to be hypocritical when giving money or time to good works?*

- *Where do we look for approval?*

- *Where should we want our reward to come from? (v4)*

PRAY ABOUT IT

Ask for God's help to have pure motives when giving money or time to help others. Use Psalm 139 v 23–24 and 2 Corinthians 8 v 7–9 to help you pray.

THE BOTTOM LINE

Beware of publicising your good deeds in front of others.

61 How to pray

Jesus is warning us not to be hypocrites or to boast about good stuff we do. What other "religious" activities might we be tempted to show off about? How about prayer?

Read Matthew 6 v 5–15

ENGAGE YOUR BRAIN

▶ *What marked out a hypocrite's prayer in Jesus' day? (v5)*

▶ *How might a hypocrite pray today?*

▶ *How should our praying be different, according to Jesus?*

▶ *Look at verses 5–6. How are these two rewards different?*

▶ *Why don't we need to repeat certain "magic" words, phrases or mantras when we pray? (v7–8)*

It's hard for us today to understand just how revolutionary it was for Jesus to say that God is our Father, who hears us and cares about our needs. The example of how to pray that He gives us in verses 9–13 is so familiar but is a brilliant way to help us pray.

PRAY ABOUT IT

Use the Lord's Prayer now to help you pray. After each line add in your own prayers on that topic:

Our Father in heaven, hallowed be your name,

Your kingdom come,

Your will be done, on earth as it is in heaven.

Give us today our daily bread.

And forgive us our debts, as we also have forgiven our debtors.

And lead us not into temptation, but deliver us from the evil one.

62 Banking on God

We've seen how easily we can be tempted to do things for the approval of others, rather than God. And now we see a fresh temptation — to put our trust and energies into something other than God.

👁 Read Matthew 6 v 16–18

ENGAGE YOUR BRAIN

Although not many of us do it, fasting is something Jesus assumes Christians will do.

▶ *What should fasting be about?*

When you miss a meal to spend extra time with God or to help others, don't let anyone know. Just do life as normal (v17) and God will reward you with a closer relationship with Him.

GET ON WITH IT

Is fasting something you've ever thought about doing? It might not just be food. Maybe you could fast from social networking, or the internet or TV or gaming for a while so you can focus on prayer instead?

👁 Read Matthew 6 v 19–24

List some of the ways we might "store up treasures on earth":

•

•

•

•

What is the heart attitude behind storing up earthly treasures?

▶ *How can we store up treasure in heaven?*

▶ *What is the problem Jesus highlights in verse 24?*

We can't put all our trust in money and God at the same time — it's like having one foot in a boat and the other on the shore: sooner or later you'll end up falling into the water!

THE BOTTOM LINE

You can't serve both God and money.

63 Why worry?

Trusting God is the foundation of our faith. We've seen how money and possessions can erode our trust in God, and now Jesus highlights another easy way that we can stop trusting Him.

👁 Read Matthew 6 v 25–34

ENGAGE YOUR BRAIN

▶ If trusting in wealth is one way we can fail to trust God, what's another way we can show our lack of trust? (v25–34)

▶ What's the problem with worrying? (v27)

▶ How does Jesus reassure His followers? (v26–32)

▶ What should our priority be? (v33)

TALK ABOUT IT

Ever wonder why, if God promises to feed and clothe his children, there are so many Christians in need? Get hold of an older Christian and see if you can work out why that is. (Remember Matthew 5 v 10–12 and look up Matthew 25 v 41–45 for another suggestion.)

▶ How do you fail to trust God?

▶ Do you hedge your bets by trusting in exam results, getting a good job, relationships etc? And are you always worrying?

Jesus is not saying that life will always be easy — we've already seen that Christians will face hostility and persecution. But He is telling us not to worry. Worry shows a lack of trust in our loving heavenly Father, who cares for us and is in control, no matter what happens to us.

PRAY ABOUT IT

Jesus says there are only two sorts of ambition. Either you can be self-centred or God-centred. Tell God which one yours is. Ask for God's help to trust Him and not to worry.

THE BOTTOM LINE

Seek first God's kingdom and His righteousness.

64 Plank you very much

We pass judgment (in our heads, if not aloud) on others' hair, clothes, taste in music and, if they're Christians, on their lifestyle and Christian "performance". But this isn't what life in God's kingdom should look like.

👁 Read Matthew 7 v 1–6

ENGAGE YOUR BRAIN

▶ *What are the dangers of judging others? (v1–2)*

▶ *How can 5 v 7 and 6 v 14–15 help us avoid being judgmental?*

▶ *Why is it stupid to judge our brothers and sisters (other Christians)? (7 v 3–4)*

Ever noticed that the things that annoy you about others are often things that you do yourself? It's much easier to moan about how unreliable X is than to make an effort to keep our promises or arrive on time. But more than that, when we start judging others, we forget that we deserve God's judgment and are only saved by His mercy.

▶ *Does Matthew 7 v 5 suggest we should ignore the speck in our brother's eye (the sin in their life)?*

▶ *So, how should we deal with helping each other to overcome sin in our lives (v5)?*

▶ *What and who do you think verse 6 is talking about?*

While being judgmental is something to avoid, there will be times when we need to be discerning — to judge whether something should be avoided. The most precious thing we have is the gospel. Verse 6 is saying that there will be exceptional circumstances when taking Jesus' good news (the pearl) to unbelievers provokes such crazed rejection that we'll have to back off and leave those people in God's hands.

PRAY ABOUT IT

Take a look at Luke 18 v 9–14 and ask God to keep you from being judgmental and self-righteous.

THE BOTTOM LINE

Don't judge or you too will be judged.

65 | Knock-on effect

Why do we find it so hard to believe that God is there and that He rewards those who seek Him? Read on for some very famous words.

👁 Read Matthew 7 v 7–11

ENGAGE YOUR BRAIN

- ▶ What should our attitude be when approaching God? (v7–11)

- ▶ Why is verse 8 so reassuring?

- ▶ But what do we have to do?

- ▶ What does Jesus remind us about God's character in verse 11?

Whether it's a request, a worried insistence or long-term searching, such prayers are answered by God. That's the promise. But they'll be answered in God's way, and sometimes that means a loud "No" or "Not yet". Think how rubbish it would be if God answered all your prayers the way you wanted. It would make us so selfish.

PRAY ABOUT IT

Do you find it difficult to pray? Do you think that God is too busy, too disappointed by you sinning yet again, or that your needs are so insignificant that He won't listen to you? Read verses 7–11 again and trust your loving, heavenly Father with your needs and worries.

👁 Read verse 12

- ▶ How does God want us to treat each other? (v12)

- ▶ How can you put that into practice today?
  At home:
  At school/college/work:
  Chatting to friends:

THE BOTTOM LINE

Ask and it will be given to you; seek and you will find; knock and the door will be opened to you.

66 | Hit the road

**Two gates, two roads, two destinations.
This really is the bottom line.**

👁 Read Matthew 7 v 13–14

ENGAGE YOUR BRAIN

▷ *Why do you think the gate is wide and the road is easy that leads to destruction?*

▷ *Why do you think Jesus describes "the road that leads to life" (v14) in the way He does?*

▷ *Is it hard or easy living as a Christian?*

Have you ever caught yourself thinking: "Life would be so much easier if I wasn't a Christian"?

Or: "If I wasn't a Christian, I could go to that party / see that film / say what I really think to…"? Yes, the road is easy through the wide gate, but it leads to destruction.

In 1 Corinthians 15 v 19, the apostle Paul says: "If only for this life we have hope in Christ, we are of all people most to be pitied." BUT he goes on to remind us we have an eternal hope — Jesus was raised from the dead as a guarantee of our future too. The road might be hard now, BUT it leads to life! Perfect life with Jesus.

PRAY ABOUT IT

Ask God to help you live with an eternal perspective, remembering where you are headed when life is tough and remembering that Christ has walked the path first and His Spirit goes with us now.

SHARE IT

Sadly, there are many who take the road to destruction. Can you point out the way to eternal life to a friend or family member today? Jesus is the gate, the way in to eternal life.

THE BOTTOM LINE

Two gates, two roads, two destinations.

67 Bad taste

Ever picked a juicy-looking piece of fruit, taken a nice big bite out of it and... YEUCH!!! It tastes disgusting. So bitter. Today Jesus tells us about people who leave a bad taste in the mouth.

👁 Read Matthew 7 v 15–20

ENGAGE YOUR BRAIN

▶ *According to these verses, how can we tell if someone is a true follower of Jesus?*

▶ *What is Jesus talking about when He mentions fruit?*

▶ *Why are our actions such a good indication of our hearts?*

▶ *Can you think of a practical example of bad fruit?*

The sort of people Jesus is talking about here — false prophets — are the type of people who have power and influence in the church. Imagine you heard a church leader or youth leader completely denying something in the Bible, or you see them stealing money, or you find out they're always nasty and sarcastic behind people's backs. Their *fruit* — their actions — shows the reality of their hearts. Now that's not to say our leaders are always

going to be perfect, but if the fruit is overwhelmingly bad, so is the tree.

▶ *What is the final outcome for these false prophets? (v19)*

▶ *Bearing in mind the first part of chapter 7, how can we be watchful (v15) without becoming judgmental?*

PRAY ABOUT IT

Ask God to help you to have a pure heart so that your fruit is good.

Ask Him for His help to be watchful and not deceived by false teachers and leaders.

68 | Lord! Lord!

So you talk the talk but do you walk the walk? Are you going to put your money where your mouth is? As James puts it elsewhere in the New Testament, faith without actions is dead.

⊙ Read Matthew 7 v 21–23

ENGAGE YOUR BRAIN

▶ What test does Jesus apply to people who claim to follow Him?

▶ What is the evidence these people present to Jesus? (v22)

▶ How do they look as if they are true Christians?

Many people use the right language (the people in verse 22 call Jesus "Lord") and say the right things. They might look impressive and have high-profile roles in the church (v22) but if they're not doing what God wants, then they're not true disciples.

▶ When does this test take place? (v22)

▶ What is so terrifying about verse 23?

▶ What does God want us to do? (v21) Clue: John 6 v 29.

On the Day of Judgment, all our impressive deeds will count for nothing. We can't earn our way into heaven. All we can do is trust in the mercy of God shown in Christ. If Jesus knows us, we are safe.

GET ON WITH IT

Have you done that? Make sure you're not trusting in anything except Jesus.

PRAY ABOUT IT

Pray for anyone you know who's not currently trusting in Jesus. Pray that God would open their eyes and ears to see who Jesus is and to listen to and obey Him.

THE BOTTOM LINE

It's not what you do, it's who you know.

69 | Firm foundations

As we reach the end of the Sermon on the Mount (well done!), Jesus gives us a stark warning. It's a million miles away from jolly little Sunday-school songs about building your house on the rock too!

👁 Read Matthew 7 v 24–29

▶ *What does Jesus want us to do after listening to His teaching (and when we read the Bible generally)? (v24)*

▶ *How can we make sure we do this?*

▶ *Re-read verses 24–27. What sort of builder are you?*

▶ *What do you think the storm and floods signify?*

You could interpret the storm and floods that the wise and foolish men face as life's trials and difficulties, and it's certainly true that listening to and obeying Jesus is our anchor through tough times. But look back at the previous verses — what was Jesus talking about in verse 22? The ultimate test will come when we all stand before Jesus on the Day of Judgment. Again, Jesus points out that it is *obeying* Him — doing what He has told us to do — that will enable us to stand.

▶ *Why is it so important to listen to and obey Jesus? (v29)*

▶ *Do you just talk about being a Christian or do you live it?*

Don't be downhearted when you fail to be perfect. Remember the beatitudes — what sort of person pleases God? (Matthew 5 v 1–12)

PRAY ABOUT IT

The most important thing God has told us to do is to listen to His Son (Matthew 17 v 5). Pray now that you would listen to Jesus and obey Him.

THE BOTTOM LINE

Hear Jesus' words and act on them.

70 Joshua: Invade and conquer

The story so far: The Israelites have invaded Canaan, the land God promised them. So far, God has brought them great victories in Jericho and Ai. But the Israelites have been disobedient several times — a worrying trend.

👁 Read Joshua 10 v 1–8

ENGAGE YOUR BRAIN

▷ *Why was the king of Jerusalem nervous? (v1–2)*

▷ *So what did he do? (v3–5)*

▷ *What was the good news for the people of Gibeon? (v7–8)*

👁 Read verses 9–15

▷ *What amazing things happened? (v10, 11, 12–14)*

▷ *Who was behind this spectacular victory? (v8, 10, 11, 12, 14)*

Joshua and the Israelites won a remarkable victory over these five kings and their armies. But God was the real hero. He fought for His people, throwing the enemy into confusion, raining huge hailstones on them and even stopping the sun in the sky. God is the mighty Warrior who fights for His people. Take courage from being on God's side!

Joshua's prayer was unbelievable. He asked the Lord to make the sun and moon stand still until the Israelites had defeated their enemies. And God did it! But the most amazing thing wasn't the sun and moon stopping. It was almighty God listening to a man (v14).

THINK IT THROUGH

God listens to us! How can we possibly be flippant or bored or repetitive when we pray? We're talking to the God who created the whole universe and can stop the sun and moon at will. He listens to us!

PRAY ABOUT IT

Prayer is a great privilege. Take extra time to talk to God today. Thank Him for fighting on our side. Praise Him for His incredible power. Thank Him that He listens to you. And then tell Him exactly what's on your mind now.

71 | Rock and roll

God gave the Israelites a great victory over five enemy kings and their combined forces. But the five kings ran away, so it's time for Operation Rock and (heads) Roll.

👁 Read Joshua 10 v 16–21

ENGAGE YOUR BRAIN

▶ *What happened to God's enemies? (v20)*

▶ *What effect did this have on the surrounding nations? (v21)*

The enemy kings were tracked to a cave in Makkedah and were trapped there to be dealt with later. Meanwhile, the Israelite army completed its rout of the enemy. The victory was so thorough that no one dared even whisper a word against God and His people. It's a very dangerous thing to oppose God. He will destroy His enemies.

👁 Read verses 22–27

▶ *What bizarre order did Joshua give to his commanders? (v24)*

▶ *What point was he making? (v25)*

This was not a macho show of strength. Joshua was showing the people that God was fighting for them against their enemies. With God on their side, they could be brave, knowing He would defeat anyone who stood in their way. God had placed enemy armies beneath their feet and would continue to do so.

THINK IT THROUGH

▶ *When you have "victories" in life, do you give God the glory?*

▶ *What can you do to make sure you remember that God is fighting on your side?*

PRAY ABOUT IT

Read through verse 25, thanking God for each great truth in it.

THE BOTTOM LINE

The Lord fights for His people.

72 It's grim up north

Jabin, the most powerful northern king, heard about the Israelites' great success in battle. So he gathered all the other kings and armies in northern Canaan to crush Joshua and the Israelites with their might.

👁 Read Joshua 11 v 1–15

ENGAGE YOUR BRAIN

▷ *How huge was the enemy army? (v4)*

▷ *What did God say when faced with this immense army? (v6)*

▷ *So what happened? (v8)*

The Lord told Joshua how to win this seemingly hopeless battle. Not only was the enemy's army massive, they had horses and chariots too. So the Israelites attacked their camp before they could get their chariots into battle. Brilliant. Joshua did exactly what the Lord commanded (v15) and God's people won a famous victory.

👁 Read verses 16–23

▷ *Was it a quick and easy victory for Israel? (v18)*

▷ *What did God do to His enemies? (v20)*

▷ *What did God do with the land He conquered? (v23)*

It doesn't take us long to read about these victories, but the Israelites were fighting for a long time (v18) — several years. The conquest of Canaan was a long, gruelling series of battles. God always keeps His promises, but we often have to wait and work hard for Him.

Verse 20 seems harsh but these people turned against God, taking part in disgusting religious practices. God rightly hardened their hearts so they couldn't turn to Him. They chose to go their own way, so God let them.

PRAY ABOUT IT

Thank God that He is in complete control; He keeps His promises; He's on the side of His people; He punishes those who reject Him; and He gives His people a great inheritance they don't deserve.

73 | True inheritance

God promised to give His people their own land. He gave them many great victories over their enemies, and now it's time to dish out the land they'd conquered. This is what they'd been waiting for years for.

👁 Read Joshua 13 v 1–14

ENGAGE YOUR BRAIN

▶ *What did God promise Joshua? (v6)*

▶ *What mistake did the Israelites make? (v13)*

Joshua was now in his 90s and there was still loads of Canaan to be conquered. God promised to drive out their enemies — then all the Israelites had to do was divide up the land and live in it. However, God's people were already taking their job lightly. God had commanded them to completely drive out their enemies, but they weren't always doing this (v13). That would come back to haunt them later.

👁 Quickly read verses 15–33

▶ *Why didn't the tribe of Levi inherit any land? (v33)*

This may seem like a long list of rivers, hills and towns but this was exciting for the Israelites! God was giving them this land He'd promised them many years before. He had given them great victories over kings and nations (v12, 21–22, 30) and continued to look after His people.

But the real inheritance wasn't this land, it was God Himself (v33). This is true for Christians today. Through Jesus we have a real and eternal relationship with God. That's the greatest prize, one we must treasure.

PRAY ABOUT IT

Thank God for all He's given you. Thank Him that you can have a real relationship with Him. Ask Him to help you treasure it and grow closer to Him.

THE BOTTOM LINE

God's people inherit a relationship with Him.

74 Caleb's comeback

Remember how the Lord punished a whole generation of Israelites for disobeying Him, making them wander in the desert for 40 years? Well, there were two exceptions, two survivors — Joshua and Caleb.

👁 Read Joshua 14 v 6–9

ENGAGE YOUR BRAIN

▶ *How did Caleb (and Joshua) differ from the other spies? (v7–8)*

▶ *What did God promise Caleb? (v9)*

45 years earlier, Moses had sent twelve spies to report on what they saw in Canaan. Ten of them were terrified and gave negative reports. Only Caleb and Joshua trusted God to give His people victory against their enemies. But the Israelites listened to the ten and so refused to enter Canaan at that time. They didn't trust God, so He punished them. Now Caleb had come to collect his reward.

👁 Read verses 10–15

▶ *What did 85-year-old Caleb claim? (v11)*

▶ *How would he be able to drive out his enemies? (v12)*

▶ *Why was he given this land? (v14)*

▶ *What was the great news for God's people? (v15)*

Faith in God gave Caleb energy, courage and enthusiasm. He was so thankful for what God had done for him. And he knew that God would help him drive out his enemies, even though he was 85! Caleb followed God wholeheartedly (v14) and God blessed him.

GET ON WITH IT

▶ *What do you need to trust God more with?*

▶ *What can you boldly do for Him?*

▶ *How can you serve God (and others) enthusiastically?*

Pray about your answers.

THE BOTTOM LINE

Be bold for the Lord.

75 God's goodness

Job done. All the land had been dished out to the twelve Israelite tribes. Now for some stuff about safe cities, Levite towns and a brilliant summary of the whole book.

Read Joshua 20 v 1–9

ENGAGE YOUR BRAIN

▶ *What were these cities of refuge for? (v3)*

Life is important to God, so He protects it. He is just — demanding that everyone receives a fair trial, whatever they're accused of.

Skim-read Joshua 21 v 1–42

▶ *Remember what the Levites didn't get? (Joshua 13 v 33)*

▶ *So where did they live? (21 v 3)*

God kept His promise to the Levites. They didn't inherit any land because God Himself was their inheritance. So God's people provided them with everything they needed. Christians today still have a responsibility to make sure that people who work for God are provided for.

Read verses 43–45

▶ *How many of God's promises came true?*

▶ *What did God's people have at last? (v44)*

These three verses sum up Joshua. Verse 43: land distribution of chapters 13–21; verse 44: God's great victories in chapters 1–12; and verse 45: the whole book — God kept His promises. Joshua shows how great God is to His people.

Verse 44 is a promise for us too. God will wipe out all His enemies and give rest to His people. One day Jesus will return — He will punish everyone who has rejected Him. And He will gather His people and bring them to eternal rest and safety.

PRAY ABOUT IT

Thank God that He keeps His promises, defeats His enemies and gives His people rest.

76 Tribal trouble

Joshua told the two and a half tribes who'd helped in the fighting to hike back to the other side of the Jordan and settle in the land there. But, no sooner had they gone, than trouble started brewing.

👁 Read Joshua 22 v 1–8

ENGAGE YOUR BRAIN

▷ *How had these tribes behaved? (v2)*

▷ *What did Joshua say they must do? (v5)*

👁 Read verses 9–20

▷ *What did they do as they reached the border of Canaan? (v10)*

▷ *What did the other Israelites think? (v11–12)*

▷ *What was the accusation? (v16)*

▷ *Why were they afraid? (v18, 20)*

The Israelites thought these tribes were rebelling against God. They knew that the sin of one part of God's people would mean punishment for all of them. No wonder they were ready to wage war.

👁 Read verses 21–34

▷ *Why had they built the altar? (v24–27)*

▷ *What did the other Israelites think of this? (v31) What did they do? (v32–34)*

No need for a panic. The altar hadn't been built as competition — it was actually a monument showing that they were committed to God.

GET ON WITH IT

Read verse 5 again. What could you do to… Love God more? Walk in all His ways? Serve Him with all your heart and soul?

PRAY ABOUT IT

Talk these things over with God.

THE BOTTOM LINE

Worship God and nothing else. Walk in His ways.

77 Remember remember

As Joshua was reaching the end of his long and eventful life, he gathered the leaders of Israel to tell them what was on His wise mind. Let's listen in.

👁 Read Joshua 23 v 1–5

ENGAGE YOUR BRAIN

▶ *What had God done for them in the past? (v3–4)*

▶ *What would He do for them in the future? (v5)*

Joshua wanted to remind the people of all that God had done for them. Because they could look back on His faithfulness, they could be sure He would continue to be with them and fight for them. Whenever you doubt that God is with you or on your side, look back on all He's done for you.

👁 Read verses 7–11

▶ *What advice does Joshua repeat?*

v6:

v7:

v8:

v11:

Remembering what God has done should spur us on to serve Him. He has done incredible things for us, so we should obey His word, have no idols and love Him completely.

👁 Read verses 12–16

▶ *What dangers were they to avoid? (v12–13, v16) Why?*

Joshua spelled it out: God's been faithful; now will you obey Him or turn from Him? If they turned away, they'd show they weren't truly His people. God would punish them — they'd lose their land and their lives.

Christians today must go on trusting God, doing what He says. Or we risk finding out that we were never one of His people. Christians, hang on!

THINK IT THROUGH

What are the traps you face? What will you remember about God to spur you to live His way?

78 God did it

Joshua gathered all of Israel together to speak to them one last time before he died. They got together in Shechem: the place Abraham received his great promise from God, and the place where Jacob turned to God.

👁 Read Joshua 24 v 1-13

ENGAGE YOUR BRAIN

▶ What did all these great episodes in Israel's history have in common? (v3-11)

▶ What should they remember about their victories? (v12)

▶ And where they lived? (v13)

A brilliantly brief summary of Israelite history. And no less than 18 times God says, "I did that". God was behind all these great moments in their history. God is incredibly gracious to His people.

THINK IT THROUGH

Think over your personal history — it's an exciting exercise to list all that God has done for you. And don't forget that He chose you before you were born and has an unbelievable eternal future lined up for you. Anything you want to thank Him for right now?

👁 Read verses 14-15

▶ What should be the response to all that God's done? (v14)

▶ What's the alternative? (v15)

How else can we respond to God's amazing grace? It would be ludicrous to turn around and say: "Thanks, but no thanks, God." That's what we're doing if we turn away from God. We have the same choice the Israelites had — serve God or live our own way, rejecting the Lord.

PRAY ABOUT IT

What choice have you made? Have you actually made it yet? Talk over your thoughts with God.

If you truly mean it, tell God you're committing your life to Him.

THE BOTTOM LINE

Choose life with God — He's done so much for you.

79 Stones and bones

It's the end of Joshua's book and the end of Joshua's life. But he won't stop reminding the Israelites how vital it is to be committed to God and live His way.

👁 Read Joshua 24 v 16–24

ENGAGE YOUR BRAIN

▶ *Why did they want to serve God? (v17–18)*

▶ *What's Joshua's warning? (v20)*

▶ *What must the people do? (v23)*

Joshua wasn't convinced by their enthusiasm — he'd heard it all before and then seen the Israelites turn away. Commitment to God is a lifelong thing, not a casual fling. And it means throwing out anything that might take God's place in our lives.

👁 Read verses 25–33

▶ *What did the Israelites have to remind them of the covenant agreement with God? (v25–27)*

▶ *What else had God given His people to remind them of His greatness? (v28)*

Does the end of Joshua seem like an anti-climax? It's not. Check out verse 28 again. Everyone was sent off to their *own inheritance*. God had given His people remarkable victories. He had kept His promise and given the Israelites their own land. Their inheritance. That's why Joseph, Joshua and Eleazar all wanted their bones buried in the promised land. God had been faithful to His people. They were now living in God's place, under His rule, enjoying His special care and His rest.

PRAY ABOUT IT

Thank God for promising Christians an incredible inheritance — eternal rest with Him. Ask Him to help you be truly committed to Him and to living His way.

THE BOTTOM LINE

God keeps His promises to His people, so get on with living His way.

DANIEL

Dare to be different

Do you ever feel pressure to fit in? Stupid question, we all do! Whether it's something as harmless as your choice of footwear or what music to listen to — or more serious such as deciding whether to join in with underage drinking or drugs or sex before marriage — we face peer pressure all the time.

Now picture yourself in this situation: you're forcibly removed from your home, taken to a different country, given a new name, taught to speak a different language, sent to a foreign university and even given new gods to worship. Imagine the pressure to fit in!

That's exactly what happened to Daniel and his friends. Despite many warnings over hundreds of years, God's people (Israel) kept rejecting Him, so (as He'd warned them) they were sent away from the promised land. Enemy nations conquered Israel (the northern kingdom) and then Judah (the southern kingdom) and took God's people into exile.

Daniel was from Judah and was carried off to Babylon (present-day Baghdad), where all of the above things happened to him. But despite being almost brainwashed by his new masters, Daniel was helped by God to stay faithful.

OVER TO YOU

Your situation isn't very different from Daniel's. Your citizenship is in heaven (Philippians 3 v 20), but you're living in a hostile world that would love to brainwash you with its values and ideas. Let's immerse ourselves in this life-changing book and see what we can learn from the way God helped Daniel to be different.

Controlling interest

The beginning of the book of Daniel is a national tragedy for God's people. Although God's people are taken away from God's promised land, God doesn't desert them. He's with them even in a hostile, foreign land...

Read Daniel 1 v 1–7

ENGAGE YOUR BRAIN

▶ *What happens to Jerusalem?*

▶ *Who is behind this attack? (v2)*

▶ *What is King Nebuchadnezzar's tactic for making his enemies part of his empire? (v3–5)*

▶ *Who did he pick? (v3–4)*

Imagine having everything going for you and then being deported, taught a new language, given new food, a new boss, even new names.

▶ *How likely is it that these Jewish exiles would stay true to God?*

▶ *Yet who is in control? (v2)*

TALK IT OVER

Be honest. Do you ever catch yourself thinking: "Life would be so much easier if I wasn't a Christian"? Have you ever thought of yourself as an exile like Daniel and his friends?

You're surrounded by people with different values and beliefs. How can you keep trusting God and depending on Him? Talk it over with a Christian friend, and share some ideas.

PRAY ABOUT IT

God was in charge. It wasn't just that He knew what was happening — He was actively encouraging it (v2). Even when we can't understand why things happen, we can hold on to the fact that God is in control.

Thank God that He's in control even when events look dire. Thank Him that He's able to keep you going as a Christian — ask Him to do that today.

THE BOTTOM LINE

God is in control.

81 Food for thought

"Start as you mean to go on." Often your first actions have an impact on what follows. What will Daniel do? Will he stand up for God in enemy territory or will he worship their gods and enjoy the good life?

👁 Read Daniel 1 v 8–21

ENGAGE YOUR BRAIN

- ▶ *What were the king's arrangements for Daniel and his friends? (Look back to v5.)*

- ▶ *What is Daniel's concern? (v8)*

The food that came from the king's table probably included food that God had told His people not to eat as it was unclean (pork, shellfish etc) and it may also have been dedicated to the Babylonian gods — a double no-no.

- ▶ *What does Daniel propose as an alternative? (v12)*

- ▶ *What happened? (v14–16)*

- ▶ *Why? (v9)*

There would have been consequences for the chief guard if Daniel's proposal didn't go well (v10), but God was in control.

- ▶ *How does God bless Daniel and his friends? (v15, 17)*

- ▶ *Where do they end up? (v19)*

It's not always easy to do things God's way. But when we trust Him in the little things, He builds our Christian character so we can trust Him in the big things.

GET ON WITH IT

Is there something in your life that you know God wants you to do or stop doing?

PRAY ABOUT IT

Ask for God's help to be like Jesus, who was obedient even to death (Philippians 2 v 8). Thank Him that, because Jesus was obedient, we can be forgiven when we aren't.

THE BOTTOM LINE

Trust God in the little things; He won't let you down.

82 Nightmare situation

Dreams about flying mean you're gaining a new perspective... er... apparently. Let's face it, most dream interpretation is made up by the so-called interpreters. King Nebuchadnezzar was well aware of that.

👁 Read Daniel 2 v 1–9

ENGAGE YOUR BRAIN

🔹 *Who does the king turn to? (v2)*

🔹 *What does he promise them if they can/can't interpret his dream?*

🔹 *What's the catch? (v9)*

That's clever. Any fool can make up a plausible interpretation for a dream they've heard about. But you'd have to have supernatural knowledge to know what the dream was without being told, in which case you must also know its true meaning.

👁 Read verses 10–23

🔹 *Are the wise men of Babylon able to help the king? (v11)*

🔹 *Who do they say is able to do what he asks? (v11)*

🔹 *What is the king's response? (v12)*

🔹 *How does Daniel react? (v14–18)*

Daniel is wise in how he handles the executioner, polite in his request to the king, and humble in seeking God's mercy and help. He's not just concerned for his and his friends' safety but also the rest of Babylon's wise men.

🔹 *How does God respond? (v19)*

🔹 *Why is God the only one who can answer this request? (v20–23)*

PRAY ABOUT IT

Why not uses verses 20–23 to praise God now for who He is?

83 | The interpreter

So the king's dream and its meaning were a mystery. But not to God. And now, not to Daniel. Imagine the suspense as, at the eleventh hour, before all the wise men face the chop, in comes Daniel with the interpretation.

👁 **Read Daniel 2 v 24–49**

ENGAGE YOUR BRAIN

▶ Who does Daniel say is responsible for interpreting the dream? (v27–28)

▶ Why is this so important?

▶ What was the dream about? (v37–45)

▶ How does God remind Neb who is the most powerful King of all?

  v37:

  v44:

  v45:

Bible historians have matched up all these different kingdoms to the Mede and Persian, Greek, and Roman empires, etc., but the main point is that God is in control of history. He gave Nebuchadnezzar his power and He is in charge of the future too.

▶ How does Nebuchadnezzar respond to all this? (v46–48)

▶ What is the position of Daniel and his friends at the end of this chapter?

▶ Who is in control of their lives?

PRAY ABOUT IT

In Matthew 28 v 18, Jesus says: "All authority in heaven and on earth has been given to me". Thank God now that Jesus is in control of our world and our destiny.

THE BOTTOM LINE

The LORD is the greatest King of all.

84 Feel the heat

More testing times for God's people in Babylon. This time it was Daniel's friends in the firing line. The heat is on.

👁 Read Daniel 3 v 1–15

ENGAGE YOUR BRAIN

▶ *Just how big is Nebuchadnezzar's ego?! (v1–7)*

▶ *Does it look as if he's learned anything about who the ultimate Ruler is? (2 v 47)*

▶ *How do Shadrach, Meshach and Abednego respond? (3v12)*

▶ *What is the king's reaction?*

Nebuchadnezzar seems to have a little bit of an anger-management problem. This is the second time we're told he flies into a rage, and if you remember chapter 1 v 10, it seems that his staff were constantly under the threat of execution!

👁 Read verses 16–30

▶ *What is Shadrach and co's brilliant answer? (3v16–18)*

▶ *How does Neb take it? (v19–23)*

▶ *Why is it astonishing that these guys survive this furnace? (v22)*

▶ *Who is with them? (v25)*

God is with Shadrach, Meshach and Abednego. Right there, in the fire with them. It's a little foretaste of "Emmanuel" — one of Jesus' names — when God came to be with us and rescue us in person.

▶ *What does Nebuchadnezzar realise? (v26, 28–29)*

▶ *How does the chapter end? (v29–30)*

▶ *Any similarities to chapter 2?*

GET ON WITH IT

Do you need to stand up for what you believe in today? Is everyone around you worshipping other gods — money, popularity, appearance, relationships?

God is with you. Ask Him to help you to worship Him only.

85 | God rules

King Nebuchadnezzar is incredibly powerful and he has an ego to match. Remember the huge gold statue and the orders to worship him? With all that in mind, this letter from King Neb comes as quite a shock!

👁 Read Daniel 4 v 1–25

ENGAGE YOUR BRAIN

▷ What has Nebuchadnezzar come to realise? (v1–3) Surprising?

▷ What prompted all this? (v5)

▷ Who did he turn to? (v8)

▷ What was his dream about? (v10–17)

▷ What did it mean? (v22, 24–25)

Nebuchadnezzar had everything going for him, but none of it was his own doing. In his pride he forgot that God is the true King.

👁 Read verses 26–37

▷ What is Daniel's advice to the king? (v26–27)

▷ Does he take it? (v29–30)

▷ How is Nebuchadnezzar restored to his position? (v34)

▷ What does he realise? (v34–37)

PRAY ABOUT IT

Are you tempted to pat yourself on the back for your achievements, good looks or popularity? How about your prayer life or Bible knowledge? Repent and remember that all things come from God (see Psalm 24 v 1 and Philippians 2 v 13).

SHARE IT

Were you surprised that someone like Nebuchadnezzar came to acknowledge God as his King?

Is there anyone you know who you doubt could ever become a Christian? Why not talk to them about Jesus? God is the one who can change them!

THE BOTTOM LINE

God is the King, not you.

86 God's graffiti

Have you heard the phrase "The writing's on the wall"? Well, this is where it comes from! We've moved on from the reign of Nebuchadnezzar to his son (or possibly grandson, the term "father" could mean ancestor), Belshazzar.

👁 Read Daniel 5 v 1–17

ENGAGE YOUR BRAIN

▶ What is Belshazzar's big mistake? (v2–3) How does he make it worse? (v4)

▶ What attitude does this show towards God?

▶ What is God's response? (v5)

▶ Who does the king look to for answers first? (v7) What does that show us?

▶ Who does the queen suggest? (v10–12)

▶ What is Daniel's attitude toward Belshazzar? (v17)

When you compare the way he spoke to Nebuchadnezzar, Daniel seems rude to Belshazzar – "You can keep your rewards!" Maybe Daniel could see that Nebuchadnezzar would genuinely turn towards God whereas his descendant had no real desire to know the LORD.

👁 Read verses 18–31

▶ What does Daniel remind Belshazzar about Nebuchadnezzar? (v18–21) And his own behaviour? (v22–23)

▶ What is God's verdict? (v26–28, 30–31)

▶ Who does Belshazzar honour? (v29) Who should he have honoured?

Belshazzar said "No" to God and, tragically for him, God said "No" to him. God's word is final.

PRAY ABOUT IT

God graciously gives us time and opportunity to repent. Have you done this? Your friends and family? Spend some time now praying for God's mercy.

THE BOTTOM LINE

Are you listening to God?

87 Lion and cheating

Daniel in the lions' den is a great kids' story. But it's not just for kids and it's not really about lions. Just like yesterday's graffiti story, it's the tale of a human king meeting the heavenly King.

👁 Read Daniel 6 v 1–11

ENGAGE YOUR BRAIN

- ▶ *What position did Daniel hold in Darius' kingdom? (2–3)*

- ▶ *What was exceptional about him? (v4)*

- ▶ *What did his enemies do? (v5–9)*

- ▶ *Who were they really setting themselves up against?*

- ▶ *How did Daniel respond? (v10-11)*

Daniel might have been a big shot in Babylon, but his home was still Jerusalem and he still depended on God to help him in everything.

👁 Read verses 12–28

- ▶ *How is the king tricked? (v12–16)*

- ▶ *What does the king recognise about Daniel? (v20)*

- ▶ *And about God? (v20)*

- ▶ *How about after Daniel's miraculous rescue? (v26–27)*

Notice that the lions aren't cuddled up with Daniel like in the pictures in a children's Bible. These beasts were starving — God's angel had to shut their mouths! See what they do to Daniel's (and God's) enemies in verse 24!

PRAY ABOUT IT

What have these three kings (and you) learned about God in the last three chapters? Thank Him that He reigns eternally, that He is utterly in control, that He is powerful and that He cares for those who trust Him.

THE BOTTOM LIFE

God is the King who rescues.

88 | Psalms: Psongs from the heart

King David (you can read his story in 1 and 2 Samuel), wrote many of the Psalms. Here, he pours out his heart to God, praising, thanking and mourning in times of trouble and triumph. We'll be looking at these Psalms and what they show us about David's relationship with God.

👁 Read Psalm 24 v 1–10

ENGAGE YOUR BRAIN

Psalm 24 introduces God as the planet's founder and landlord.

▶ *What kind of person is fit for a close encounter with Him? (v3–4)*

Verses 7–10 could be describing the excitement when the ark of the covenant was brought to Jerusalem. The ark (not the boat; more like a treasure chest) was a symbol of God's presence and blessing. If God was moving in, no wonder they wanted to get the doors wide open!

👁 Read verses 7–10 again

▶ *List the words that accompany "King" and "Lord" to describe God.*

▶ *What can stand in the way of someone like that?*

THINK IT OVER

In the New Testament, God's people, are called "the temple" (2 Corinthians 6 v 16–18). If God's at home in us, He's calling us to live clean lives, devoted to purity.

PRAY ABOUT IT

Yourself

How do your heart (attitudes) and hands (actions) need a good scrub?

Your church

How might it need styling less like the world and more like God?

Thank God that, though we're a work in progress, He longs to bless and forgive those seeking Him (v5–6).

89 Shameless

Life is sometimes lonely and difficult. We can feel out of control or lost. David knows how it feels.

👁 **Read Psalm 25**

ENGAGE YOUR BRAIN

▷ *When does David come to God? (v5 and 15)*

▷ *What does he share with God? (v1 and 16-21)*

▷ *Which verses show that David was a sinner?*

Think you have to be perfect to pray for God's help? David was far from perfect, yet he still had the confidence to ask God for some big things. David's demands and needs are big, but God is bigger.

In verse 19 David mentions his enemies. Our greatest enemy is Satan — he hates us (v19) and tries to trap us in sin and guilt (ensnares us – v15). He relishes the fact that we've all done things to be ashamed of.

On spare paper, or the right side of this page, write down stuff you've done which you know is wrong —

'fessing up is the first part of your strategy to thrash Satan. Then, get the fattest pen you can find. Write verse 20 across your confessions in large letters!

▷ *What does David ask God to remember? (v6-7)*

▷ *And to forget?*

▷ *According to this psalm, what is God like?*

Interestingly, David doesn't ask God to remember what a good guy he's been (he knows he hasn't). He asks God to remember what a merciful, loving God He is. Awesome news! God's rescue plan is trustworthy because it depends on His perfection, not ours.

PRAY ABOUT IT

Read verses 1–7 out loud to God as a prayer (unless you're on the bus, in which case, read it in your head), praying it to God.

Clear-cut Christian

You meet another Christian at a party. Can they tell from your behaviour that you're a Christian too? Maybe it's not always obvious — but don't give up! God's great at taking our tarnished lives and creating clear-cut Christians.

👁 Read Psalm 26

ENGAGE YOUR BRAIN

▶ *What does David want God to do? (v1–3) Why?*

David knew he was sinful, but he also knew he needed to live God's way. David is saying: "Prove I'm right to live your way, Lord." Can you relate to that prayer? Been dissed for not getting drunk, or respecting God's laws on sex and relationships?

Obeying God is totally worth it. Living blamelessly ultimately leads to eternal life. But isn't David an ordinary sinner? Why's he now harping on about his "blameless life"?

▶ *What's a blameless life? Write a summary of each verse with your own words (eg: v1 Always trust in God):*
v2:

v3:

v4–6:

v7:

v8:

Are verses 4-5 saying: "Non-Christian friends are not allowed"? Nope. We should share God's greatness with them (v7). But we shouldn't share their lifestyle. David avoids "evildoers" to avoid temptation, knowing he's not good enough to survive in their company.

TALK IT OVER

Do any of your friends drag you away from God? Chat to an older Christian about it.

PRAY ABOUT IT

If you love Jesus, God sees you as blameless. You've been forgiven. Look back at the hallmarks of a blameless life. Pick one you need to work at. Ask for God's help.

ROMANS

Passionate Christianity

This is one sequel that really won't make sense unless you've read the first part! Have you read Romans 1–8 yet?

ROAMING ROMANS

Paul is writing to a bunch of Christians in Rome — one of the first churches. Initially this church would have been mostly Jewish converts but, as time went on, the Roman emperor started persecuting Jews (see Acts 18 v 2) and they got kicked out of Rome. So it was down to the Gentile (non-Jewish) believers to run the show.

DIFFERENCES

By the time Paul writes this letter, the Jews are coming back to Rome, and the church is a real mixture of Jew and Gentile. Obviously this causes a few issues, and sorting that out is one of the reasons why Paul is writing.

WISH I WAS THERE

It's also a *"see you soon"* kind of letter, as Paul is planning to visit Rome shortly. As we've already seen in chapters 1–8, it's also a *"Wow, isn't the gospel about Jesus amazing!"* letter. In fact it's that same gospel which will sort out all the Jew/Gentile issues in Rome and is the reason for Paul's pit stop there too.

So, if chapters 1–8 are all about what God has done in Christ, then chapters 9–16 are about what He is doing in His people — *Christians*, whether Jew or Gentile. And that means us too! It's exciting and vital stuff — so read on…

91 | God's choice

Romans chapters 1–8 have shown us how amazing God's rescue plan truly is. But hang on a minute — why haven't the Jews responded to their long awaited Saviour? Paul is absolutely devastated that they are missing out.

👁 Read Romans 9 v 1–5

ENGAGE YOUR BRAIN

▶ *What is upsetting Paul so much (v1–5)?*

▶ *Why does he feel so passionately about it?*

Paul says the Jews received so many privileges from God, so how could they possibly have rejected Jesus? Paul so badly wishes his fellow Jews would accept Jesus' rescue.

👁 Read verses 6–13

▶ *What might people think when they see God's people, the Jews, missing out? (v6)*

▶ *How does Paul answer this misconception? (v6-13)*

"Not all who are descended from Israel are Israel" (v6). Huh? Just because you were genetically Jewish didn't mean you were spiritually one of God's people.

Remember, no one has a right to God's forgiveness. Jews may be Abraham's descendants, but that doesn't make them His children — the true people of God. God's true people are the ones God chose (like Jacob). More about this tomorrow…

What makes Paul so sad is that the Jewish people were especially privileged — they'd seen so much of God's mercy and had special insight into His plan for the world. It was terrible that so many of them missed the point and missed seeing Jesus for who He is.

PRAY ABOUT IT

Think about God's grace — all He's done for you and given you. Praise Him for specific things. Thank Him. Tell Him how it makes you feel.

THE BOTTOM LINE

God is free to act as He pleases.

92 | Oh mercy!

The idea that God chooses some people and not others can make people very angry. It just doesn't seem fair. Let's see what Paul says about it.

👁 Read Romans 9 v 14–23

ENGAGE YOUR BRAIN

▶ *What is the accusation against God in verse 14?*

▶ *What do you think of Paul's statement in verse 15?*

Paul then uses the example of Pharaoh and the Exodus. Pharaoh simultaneously hardened his own heart against God and was also hardened by God.

▶ *Why does the Bible say this happened? (v17)*

▶ *How is verse 18 similar to verse 15?*

▶ *How do you feel about that?*

OK, so God decides who He will have mercy on — surely that means you can't blame human beings for rejecting Him? They have no choice.

▶ *What is Paul's surprising reply in verses 20–23?*

PRAY ABOUT IT

Be honest with God about how this makes you react. Ask Him to help you see Him for who He really is and to trust Him.

👁 Read verses 24–33

▶ *How are we made right(eous) with God?*

▶ *Does anyone deserve His mercy?*

The definition of mercy is God *not* giving us the punishment we deserve. The earlier chapters of Romans have made it clear that no one deserves to be saved. How then should we respond to the amazing mercy God shows to us?

PRAY ABOUT IT

Chances are that you're not from a Jewish background. If so, how do verses 25–26 make you feel? Spend some time thanking God for His great mercy.

93 One-way street

Righteousness — being seen as perfect and holy in God's eyes; being able to have a relationship with Him, no longer facing His deserved anger and punishment. Time for a quick course in Righteousness 101...

Read Romans 10 v 1–13

ENGAGE YOUR BRAIN

- How are people made right with God? (v4)

- What mistake did many Jews make? (v2–3)

- What is the only real way we can be right with God? (v9–10)

- What wonderful assurance do we have if we trust in Jesus rather than in our own efforts to be good? (v11–13)

When it comes to getting right with God, the law can't help — because none of us can keep it. We can't save ourselves. Only trusting in the death of Jesus can put us right with God.

Notice who this is true for (v12) — Jew and Gentile. *Everyone* is saved in the same way. God is the God of everyone.

- So what is Paul's prayer for his Jewish relatives? (v1)

PRAY ABOUT IT

Is this your heart's desire and prayer? List your top ten people to pray for and spend some time asking God to save them.

THE BOTTOM LINE

Jesus is the only way to be put right with God.

94 Stubborn and disobedient

So did Israel miss out because God only chose a "remnant"? Or was their rejection of God their own fault? And why does it matter to us, anyway?

Read Romans 10 v 14–15

ENGAGE YOUR BRAIN

▷ What are the stages that need to happen in order for someone to be saved? (You might need to work backwards.)

GET ON WITH IT

Have you taken verses 14–15 to heart? Can you be part of the answer to your own prayers for friends and family who don't know Jesus yet?

Read verses 16–21

▷ Did Israel hear the message? (v18)

▷ Did they understand it? (v19)

▷ So why haven't they accepted the word of Christ, according to Paul? (v21)

Sadly, very few of God's chosen people followed Him faithfully. In fact, right the way through the Old Testament, you can see how few actually trusted Him (see 1 Kings 19 v 10–18 for one example). The Israelites were especially privileged but — like the rest of us — they would rather go their own way than God's way.

▷ How has God dealt with non-Israelites? (v20)

▷ How has He dealt with Israel? (v21)

▷ What does this teach us about God?

PRAY ABOUT IT

Thank God that even though we are frequently just as stubborn and disobedient as the Israelites, God is patient and merciful with us.

THE BOTTOM LINE

Faith comes through hearing the word of Christ (v17).

95 The end for Israel?

Surely God must be fed up with Israel by now? They rejected God and threw His love back in His face. Surely it's time for God to wash His hands of the Israelites...

Read Romans 11 v 1–5

ENGAGE YOUR BRAIN

▷ *How does Paul answer the suggestion in verse 1?*

Don't forget, Paul was an Israelite. In Philippians 3 v 4–6 he boasts about his Jewish credentials. So, obviously, God hadn't given up on Jews — the first disciples were Jewish!

▷ *What do verses 2–5 tell us about those who were really God's people in the Old Testament?*

Just because you were genetically related to Abraham, didn't mean you were automatically one of God's people — Jesus makes the same point in John 8 v 31–47. We are not entitled to God's favour; it is a gift.

GET ON WITH IT

▷ *Do you think that because you go to church and/or were baptised that makes you automatically right with God?*

Read Romans 3 v 9–26

▷ *Have you understood that?*

▷ *Accepted it personally?*

Read Romans 11 v 5–10

▷ *What does Paul remind us about the way God operates? (v5-6)*

▷ *So even within the people of Israel there were two groups. How are they described? (v7)*

Since Israel rejected God, He let them become what they chose to be: spiritually blind and deaf (v8). But He'll never let go of those He has chosen by grace (v5–6) — people who rely on Jesus' death.

PRAY ABOUT IT

Be honest. What do you find hard about verses 8–10? Use earlier verses in Romans to help you: 3 v 10–18; 9 v 20–24.

96 Roots and branches

How much of advertising is based on envy? "Ooooh that looks nice, I want one!". Paul uses pretty similar tactics in his efforts to win over fellow Jews.

👁 Read Romans 11 v 11–14

ENGAGE YOUR BRAIN

▶ Is Jewish opposition to Christ beyond saving? (v11)

▶ What does Paul hope will be the side-effect of his sharing the gospel with non-Jews? (v13–14)

Let's not forget this was the man who fiercely persecuted the early church and gave orders for many to be executed (see Acts 7 v 54 – 8 v 3). This was a man who pretty much embodied Romans 11 v 8 but God changed him spectacularly.

▶ What does Paul want the Jews to be envious of? (v12)

The riches of a relationship with God that we have as Gentile (non-Jewish) believers are precisely those which the anti-Jesus Jews had lost. But Paul certainly didn't want Gentile Christians to be smug…

👁 Read verses 15–24

The first Jews (Abraham, Isaac etc) trusted God. They're the *roots*. The *branches* are those Jews who've believed the gospel and trust Jesus. The *wild olive shoot* means Gentile Christians, like us. Paul says: *"Of course God hasn't rejected His true people."* Great stuff.

▶ So what should our attitude be towards those branches that have been broken off? (v18a, 20b)

▶ What about our attitude towards God? (v18b, 20b–22)

PRAY ABOUT IT

What have you learned about God? And about yourself? Talk to Him about that right now.

THE BOTTOM LINE

Thank God for the riches of knowing Him.

97 Jews for Jesus

Paul is still helping the Roman Christians to get their thinking straight about non-believing Israelites. It's a little tricky to get our heads around, but Paul's also teaching us loads about our awesome God.

👁 Read Romans 11 v 25–36

ENGAGE YOUR BRAIN

- ▶ *Use the space on the left to summarise Paul's argument so far.*

- ▶ *What does Paul remind us of in verses 25–32?*

Step one: partial hardening; some Israelites accept Christ, some don't.

Step two: the full quota of chosen Gentile believers come into God's kingdom.

Step three: the full quota of chosen Israelites are also saved.

As we've already seen, this pattern happened in the life of Paul himself and continues to happen all over the world today as Jewish people respond to Jesus.

👁 Read verses 26 & 32 again

- ▶ *Is Paul saying that every single Jewish person will eventually be saved? (v14 and v23).*

- ▶ *Why is it especially amazing when an Israelite turns to Jesus?*

GET ON WITH IT

The promises and the great figures of the Old Testament belong first to the Jewish people — it's a huge tragedy when they fail to see how Christ is the perfect fulfilment of them all. What can you do to share Jesus with Jewish people? Take a look at www.jewsforjesus.org.uk for inspiration.

PRAY ABOUT IT

If you find this whole topic is making your brain hurt a bit, take courage from verses 33–36 and join Paul in praising our wise, holy and in-control God.

THE BOTTOM LINE

God is in control and He is merciful.

98 | Conform or transform?

Sometimes it's really hard going against the flow, sticking your neck out, being the odd one out. But that's what being a Christian is all about — we are not to conform but to transform. How? Why? Read on...

👁 Read Romans 12 v 1–8

ENGAGE YOUR BRAIN

▷ *What is the "therefore" in verse 1 there for?*

It's always a good idea when you come across a word like *"therefore"* or *"so"* in the Bible to look back at what has gone before. In this case, Paul is referring back to God's mercy — the whole wonderful gospel message he's been explaining so far in Romans. Everything from this point on in Romans is *therefore* a response to God's mercy.

▷ *What does Paul want the Roman Christians to do? (v1)*

▷ *What is a sacrifice normally like? So what does Paul mean?*

▷ *How are we transformed? (v2)*

▷ *What will the end result be? (v2)*

▷ *What does this mean in practice with other Christians? (v3–8)*

Paul says Christians should give their whole lives over to God. That means pleasing God in everything we do, say and think about. And the place to start showing our thanks to God is among His people — using our God-given abilities to serve Him and other Christians.

GET ON WITH IT

What has jumped out at you particularly from verses 3–8? How can you act on that today?

PRAY ABOUT IT

As you read God's word here in Romans, ask Him to renew your mind and transform your behaviour so that it's in line with what He wants.

THE BOTTOM LINE

We do everything as a response to God's mercy.

99 Transformers

More practical tips on what it means to be transformed — to live God's way in response to His mercy. Ready?

👁 Read Romans 12 v 9–21

ENGAGE YOUR BRAIN

▶ *What do verses 9 and 21 have in common?*

▶ *From those verses, can you summarise what this section is all about?*

▶ *Read verses 10-13. Does this reflect the reality in your church/ CU/youth group?*

GET ON WITH IT

▶ *How exactly can you love your brothers and sisters in Christ like this?*

▶ *How do verses 14–20 help us to interact with the world around us?*

▶ *What difficulties are you likely to face as a Christian?*

▶ *How are you to deal with them?*

Obviously we want to get along with everyone and, as far as it depends on us, Paul wants us to do that. But he also recognises that we will face hostility and persecution from non-believers. In which case we're not to get angry and seek revenge, but to put our trust in God. Think about Jesus' example.

PRAY ABOUT IT

Read verses 18–20. Is there anyone you are finding it hard to get on with at the moment? Perhaps someone who has hurt or annoyed you. Pray for them and ask for God's help to love them rather than seeking revenge.

THE BOTTOM LINE

Good always overcomes evil. God is in charge.

MATTHEW

Follow the leader

According to legend, the great British polar explorer Ernest Shackleton placed an advert in a newspaper before his expedition. "Men wanted for a hazardous journey. Small wages, bitter cold. Long months of complete darkness. Constant danger, safe return doubtful. Honour and recognition in case of success." He received more than 5,000 applications.

If you were to write an advert for joining Jesus' team, then chapters 8 to 14 of Matthew's Gospel would be a good place to start. However, they would give you an equally mixed idea of what to expect!

The hazards are personal cost, opposition, people trying to mislead you and persecution, even to death.

But the benefits include forgiveness, close relationship with the God who created you, His Spirit in you, eternal life and God's care for you every day.

The big question is: will you trust your leader? It's a hazardous journey, but travelling with Jesus guarantees our safe arrival and our eternal reward.

THE ONE TO FOLLOW

The disciples are slowly learning what it means to have faith in Jesus, to find rest in Him, to focus on Him and not the things they fear. We'll see that He is the centre of history — the one promised all through the Old Testament. The only one who can open our eyes to see God.

And sadly, we'll see a lot of people on the outside: people rejecting Jesus and facing the bitter cold and complete darkness of being without their true leader and King.

Are you ready to follow your leader?

100 Healing power

Three healing episodes follow the famous Sermon on the Mount, but what are they revealing about Jesus?

◉ Read Matthew 8 v 1–4

ENGAGE YOUR BRAIN

▶ *What is the man's problem in v2?*

▶ *How does Jesus respond? (v3)*

Jesus' command (v4) showed His respect for the Old Testament. It would also restore the man back to society, and the priests would hear of Jesus' power over illness.

◉ Read verses 5–13

▶ *What is the centurion's problem? (v6)*

▶ *This man is an enemy Roman, yet how does Jesus respond to his request? (v7)*

▶ *What's so amazing about the centurion's faith? What does he recognise about Jesus? (v8–9)*

▶ *What's the outcome? (v13)*

Jesus reminds His listeners here that the kingdom of heaven is the same kingdom promised to Abraham, Isaac and Jacob — a kingdom you enter by faith (v10–12).

◉ Read verses 14–17

▶ *What's the illness Jesus deals with in verse 14?*

▶ *What's the woman's response to Jesus? (v15)*

Matthew points us to Isaiah, one of the greatest Old Testament prophets, to explain what Jesus is doing (v17).

PRAY ABOUT IT

Thank Jesus that He is willing and able to heal. Thank Him for His death, making us clean. Ask Him to give you eyes to see your sinfulness and faith to enter His kingdom.

THE BOTTOM LINE

Jesus is the living, loving, powerful fulfilment of the Old Testament.

101 No compromise

Have you ever volunteered for something only to realise when the time comes to actually do it that... it's raining, no one you know will be there, or it's going to be too much like hard work?

👁 Read Matthew 8 v 18–22

ENGAGE YOUR BRAIN

▶ *What do these two guys have in common? (v19 & 21)*

▶ *What is Jesus' answer to the first man? (v20)*

▶ *What about the second man?*

▶ *What are the two men putting ahead of their desire to follow Jesus?*

▶ *What about you? What gets in the way of following Jesus wholeheartedly?*

For some of us it might be physical comfort, or material possessions, like the first guy. Jesus won't necessarily ask us to sleep rough as He did, but would you be prepared to? Or maybe, like the second disciple, it's your family relationships, or your friends holding you back. Maybe a boyfriend or girlfriend? (Just to say, Jesus isn't being really cold here as if the guy's father has only just died. The sense of the man's request is that he wants to wait until his parents have grown old and died before he's free to leave and follow Jesus.)

PRAY ABOUT IT

Be really honest with yourself and with Jesus (He already knows anyway!). What's stopping you following Him properly today?

Ask Him to help you to follow Him.

GET ON WITH IT

And what are you going to do as a result? It might be painful; in fact it probably will be. But take a look ahead to Matthew 16 v 24–27.

THE BOTTOM LINE

Following Jesus is costly; but the reward is priceless.

102 | Storming stuff

Have you ever been really frightened? Actually feared for your life? If so, you'll know just how the disciples felt here.

👁 Read Matthew 8 v 23–27

ENGAGE YOUR BRAIN

▶ *How bad was this storm?*

▶ *What's right about the disciples' reaction? (v25)*

▶ *What's wrong? (v26)*

Let's not forget that at least four of the disciples were fishermen. They'd seen bad storms before, and this one was obviously pretty serious. And at least they turn to the one person who can help, but Jesus is disappointed by their lack of faith.

Think of it this way — they are in the safest place in the world, with the one who not only commands the wind and waves but created them.

▶ *Why are the disciples so amazed? (v26–27)*

Even after a storm is over, it takes a while for the waves to die down. Jesus simply speaks and everything is instantly calm. In the account of this episode in Mark's Gospel, the word Jesus uses to calm the storm is the sort of thing you would say to a family dog – "Sit"!

▶ *Read Psalm 107 v 23–32 and see if you can answer the question the disciples ask in Matthew 8 v 27.*

PRAY ABOUT IT

Have you recognised who Jesus really is? Talk to Him now about the things that scare you.

THE BOTTOM LINE

Who is this man?

103 Pigging out

The kingdom of heaven will be free from sin, sickness and chaos. It will also, importantly, be free from evil. Check out this piggy situation to see the King in action!

👁 Read Matthew 8 v 28–32

ENGAGE YOUR BRAIN

▶ *Who does Jesus encounter in verse 28? What are they like?*

▶ *What do they recognise about Jesus?*

▶ *What do the evil spirits know will happen to them? (v29)*

▶ *What happens to them in verse 32?*

Jesus has a zero-tolerance approach to evil. However threatening or scary these things can seem, Jesus is more than able to deal with evil.

PRAY ABOUT IT

Christians should remind each other that the devil is defeated but not yet destroyed. (Check out Ephesians 6 v 10–20 and also Ephesians 1 v 18–23.) Remember that, although we are living with spiritual opposition, our King Jesus has triumphed and reigns over everything.

👁 Read Matthew 8 v 33–34

▶ *Is the town's reaction to these events surprising?*

▶ *Why do you think they react this way?*

▶ *How might you have expected them to respond?*

TALK IT OVER

Chat to an older Christian about the idea of evil and demons if it confuses or unsettles you. Perhaps it all seems a bit unbelievable — but the New Testament is quite clear, both that evil forces exist, and also that Jesus is far more powerful. Romans 8 v 38–39 is a brilliant passage to learn by heart!

THE BOTTOM LINE

Jesus has defeated the devil.

104 Power point

If you've broken your leg, you need an ambulance, not a bunch of flowers, right? In this next episode, it looks as if Jesus has lost his marbles to begin with...

👁 Read Matthew 9 v 1–2

ENGAGE YOUR BRAIN

▶ *What is the man's problem? What is Jesus' response? (v2)*

▶ *How would you describe the way Jesus speaks to the man? What does this show us about Him?*

▶ *What does Jesus see as the man's biggest need?*

▶ *Does the paralysed man do anything?*

Obviously the man can't do anything, he's paralysed! Plus it was his friends that brought him — Jesus responds to their faith, not the man's. But this man isn't just physically helpless: he is spiritually helpless too. He needs God's forgiveness and Jesus gives it to him.

👁 Read verses 3–8

▶ *Why do the teachers of the law react the way they do? (v3)*

▶ *Who can forgive all our sins? What is Jesus claiming about Himself?*

▶ *Which do you think is easier to say and why? (v5)*

▶ *How does Jesus prove His authority? (v6–7)*

▶ *What is the crowd's reaction? Have they got the big picture about Jesus yet?*

Of course it's easier to say your sins are forgiven, but Jesus shows His power and authority by doing the visible miracle too. But which is easier to do? Healing someone was easy compared to going to the cross so that our sins could be forgiven.

PRAY ABOUT IT

Thank Jesus that He went to the cross so that we could be forgiven; that He did the hard thing that we could never do.

105 | Doctor and bridegroom

Ever wondered who this guy Matthew was, who wrote this Gospel? Well, it's more than likely he's the same man we meet now in verse 9.

👁 Read Matthew 9 v 9–13

▶ What was Matthew's job? (v9)

▶ What does Jesus say to him?

▶ And his reaction?

Tax collectors were usually corrupt money-grabbers who, worst of all, colluded with the enemy Romans. Nice followers you pick, eh Jesus? And having dinner with him and his shady mates too? At least, that's what the Pharisees were saying.

▶ How does Jesus explain His behaviour? (v12)

▶ What do the Pharisees need to work out? (v13)

Bit of an insult there for the Pharisees, who thought they were super holy. They hadn't understood the Old Testament at all. Jesus looks at people's hearts, not their outward behaviour, and we all need open heart surgery.

👁 Read verses 14–17

▶ What issue do John's disciples have with Jesus' followers? (v14)

▶ Why was fasting not appropriate for Jesus' disciples? (v15)

▶ What do you think Jesus is getting at in verses 16–17?

Jesus is saying that you can't apply old rules to something new. Yes, Jesus is the fulfilment of the Old Testament, but the movie trailer is not the film. A whole new way of doing things is inevitable now that Jesus is here.

PRAY ABOUT IT

Have you ever honestly admitted to Jesus that you're spiritually sick and need Him to be your doctor? Thank Him that He came for sinners.

THE BOTTOM LINE

Jesus came to call sinners.

106 Healing words

How do people react to Jesus? Are they respectful? Patronising? Indifferent? Hostile? What about your friends and family? What about you?

👁 Read Matthew 9 v 18–34

ENGAGE YOUR BRAIN

▶ *What is Jesus asked to do? (v18)*

▶ *How much does this ruler trust Jesus?*

▶ *Is he justified in doing so? (v25)*

That is serious faith. But it's not over the top if Jesus is the Son of God.

▶ *Who else is seeking a miracle from Jesus? (v20–21)*

▶ *Is she as upfront as the ruler?*

▶ *How does Jesus treat her? (v22)*

That gentle, encouraging word again (see v2). "Take heart, daughter, your faith has healed you." Jesus wants us to trust Him. However timidly we try, He accepts us with love and encouragement.

▶ *Do the blind men show faith in Jesus? (v27–30)*

▶ *Is the mute demon-possessed man able to contribute anything to his cure?*

▶ *How does the crowd respond to all these miracles? (v33)*

▶ *And the Pharisees? (v34)*

▶ *Why is their response so terrible?*

It's almost unbelievable that the Pharisees could get it so wrong. If you reject the rescuer, you cannot be rescued…

PRAY ABOUT IT

Powerful, death-defying, yet gentle and loving. Thank God that we have such a great King!

SHARE IT

Ask someone today what their response to Jesus is. If they say they don't know, challenge them to read a Gospel (keep some yourself to give away) and then get back to you.

107 Mission possible

A new phase in Matthew's Gospel starts here. Jesus, the one with unique authority in teaching (chapters 5–7) and miracles (chapters 8–9), hands authority on to His disciples. They're sent out to continue His mission.

👁 Read Matthew 9 v 35–38

ENGAGE YOUR BRAIN

▸ *How does verse 35 sum up Jesus' mission?*

▸ *What is Jesus' attitude towards the crowds? (v36)*

▸ *Why is it so bad for sheep to be without a shepherd?*

▸ *Who is ultimately responsible for the success of God's growing kingdom? (v38)*

PRAY ABOUT IT

Do you see non-Christians ("the lost") in this way — like sheep without a shepherd? Ask Jesus to help you have His compassion for the lost, and pray verse 38!

👁 Read Matthew 10 v 1–15

▸ *Who sends out the twelve? (v1)*

▸ *How does Jesus describe the people the disciples would be preaching to? (v6)*

▸ *What are the disciples to do? (v7–8)*

▸ *Do you think it will all be straightforward for them? (v14)*

We know that Jesus' mission is for the whole world and He certainly hasn't shown any bias against non-Jews (look back at chapter 8 v 10–11), but He wants His disciples to start with Israel. God's plan in the Old Testament was to bless the world through His chosen people (see Genesis 12 v 3).

THE BOTTOM LINE

People without Jesus are like sheep without a shepherd.

108 Christians in conflict

Jesus sent His disciples to continue His mission. Now He spells out exactly what that work involves. And that spelling reads C-O-N-F-L-I-C-T. Christians should expect exactly the same.

👁 Read Matthew 10 v 16–31

ENGAGE YOUR BRAIN

▷ What should characterise the disciples as they set out on their good-news-sharing mission? (v16)

▷ What will they encounter? (v17–23)

▷ What is Jesus' warning in verse 17?

▷ Why shouldn't they be surprised by all this opposition? (v24–25)

▷ What is Jesus' next piece of advice? (v26)

▷ Why can the disciples react this way? (v26–31) List the reasons.

•

•

•

•

Following in Jesus' footsteps will mean persecution. But we, like the first disciples, are to expect that. Don't forget to spot the promises too (v20, 30). God, our heavenly Father, is with us by His Spirit.

PRAY ABOUT IT

Who or what are you fearing today? Man or God (v28)? Are you more concerned about being teased or rejected than about standing firm for Jesus? Ask for the Holy Spirit's help to have a healthy fear of God today wherever you find yourself.

TALK IT THROUGH

Do you really expect to suffer as a follower of Jesus? Why? Why not? Get together with a Christian friend and think about how you can encourage each other to stand firm without being afraid.

109 Faith flight

Do you ever hear people saying that Jesus was a peacemaker? Well that's partly true, but this next section shows that He could also be the opposite!

👁 Read Matthew 10 v 32–33

ENGAGE YOUR BRAIN

▶ *Are verses 32–33 fair?*

▶ *How do they make you feel?*

Hands up if you're feeling guilty/panicked? Don't get things out of perspective — look ahead to chapter 12 v 20; Jesus will not break a bruised reed: He knows that we are weak. Peter, a key disciple, denied knowing Jesus but was restored and forgiven after the resurrection. This verse (this whole section!) is about loyalties.

👁 Read Matthew 10 v 34–39

▶ *What does Jesus say about His mission? (v34)*

▶ *Does this surprise you?*

▶ *Would it surprise your non-Christian friends?*

▶ *What is your reaction to verses 35–39?*

The amazing thing about verse 37 is that none of us is worthy of Christ. And because of that, He lost His life so that we could find ours. But if we are to follow Him, we need to give up everything that might come between us and Jesus. We need to hold onto Jesus with both hands.

👁 Read verses 40–42

▶ *What is the result of holding onto Jesus?*

▶ *What do you think this reward is? (Clue v32, 39)*

PRAY ABOUT IT

Is your first loyalty to Christ? Look back at what He did for you at the cross and ask for His help to live full-on for Him today.

THE BOTTOM LINE

Jesus comes first.

110 Identity parade

How would you identify someone famous? There might be little clues like bodyguards or a car with flags on. Here, John the Baptist's disciples are trying to identify Jesus, and Jesus in turn tells people how to identify John.

👁 Read Matthew 11 v 1–6

ENGAGE YOUR BRAIN

▶ What do John's followers want to know about Jesus? (v3)

▶ What clues does Jesus give to His identity? (v4–5)

If you were familiar with your Old Testament, the things Jesus was doing were signs screaming out "THIS IS THE MESSIAH"! Check out Isaiah 61 v 1–3. Jesus is the one who was promised; we shouldn't expect anyone else (v3). That's why all these so-called modern prophets or cult leaders are clearly frauds.

PRAY ABOUT IT

Even John the Baptist was a little unsure and wanted reassurance about who Jesus is. Thank God for the evidence He gives us, and pray for yourself or anyone you know who suffers doubts about their faith from time to time.

👁 Read Matthew 11 v 7–19

▶ What does Jesus ask the crowd about John? (v7–9)

▶ Who does Jesus say John is?
v9:
v10:
v14:

▶ What criticism does Jesus have of the generation who saw both John and Jesus? (v16)

Like kids in an argumentative mood, Jesus' audience was never satisfied. John the Baptist was too severe for them; Jesus was too free and easy. But notice verse 19. John's actions show who he was just as Jesus' do.

SHARE IT

All the evidence stacks up to show that Jesus is God's King. Ask God to help you share Jesus' identity with someone this week.

JUDGES

Heroes and zeros

It's a book about judges. No surprises there. But not the kind who hang out in court all day — these were action-packed rescuers, picked by God and helped by His Spirit to rescue God's people, the Israelites.

Judges continues the Old Testament story of God and His people. So what happened before Judges? Well, the people God created in the beginning lived in the Garden of Eden, under His command and care. It was perfect — God's people in God's place living under His rule. But Adam and Eve rejected God's rule and turned against Him, earning His anger and punishment. Booted out of Eden, they lost that perfect face-to-face relationship with God.

But it wasn't all over. God's plan, formed before creation, was to reveal the depths of His love. He launched a rescue mission. In time, God's people would worship Him not just because He created them but because He'd won them back. God promised to reverse the effects of His people's rebellion against Him. He said He'd do that by choosing a people (starting with Abraham) who'd belong to Him and benefit from Him. He promised to bless the world through His people.

God rescued them from slavery in Egypt and made sure they got to the land He'd promised them — Canaan — despite huge obstacles on the way, which would make them rely on Him. Under Joshua, they conquered the land and kicked out its occupants, and life began to look good for the Israelites.

Would it continue that way, or would they hit a depressing downward spiral? And how does all this point us to the ultimate Rescuer, Jesus? There's only one way to find out. Get ready for loads of action in one of the wildest books in the Bible...

111 So far, so good

Moses and the Israelites had disobeyed God and failed to conquer Canaan. So they were punished, wandering the desert for 40 years until the whole generation had died out. But life was more successful with Joshua in charge...

👁 Read Joshua 21 v 43–45

ENGAGE YOUR BRAIN

▶ *What did God give to His people?*

▶ *How had God failed them? (v45)*

Life was awesome. God kept all His promises and gave His people great victories as they conquered the promised land. They were God's people, living in His land, under His rule. Then Joshua died...

👁 Read Judges 1 v 1–10

▶ *Which Israelite tribes fought these great battles? (v3)*

▶ *Who really won the battles? (v4)*

▶ *Why didn't Adoni-Bezek complain about his horrific torture? (v6–7)*

👁 Read verses 11–15

▶ *Who took up Caleb's challenge?*

▶ *What was his reward?*

(Remember the name Othniel — he'll be big news in chapter 3.) So far, so good for the Israelites. They're obeying God and He's given them great victories, including conquering Jerusalem, which would become the main city for God and His people.

In the Old Testament, God seems to punish people loads. But notice that when His people loyally obey Him, He keeps His amazing promises and gives them great rewards. Tomorrow, we'll see what happens when people are casual with God's commands.

PRAY ABOUT IT

Think of some of God's great promises to His people. Thank Him that He always keeps His word and gives His people great things.

THE BOTTOM LINE

God always keeps His promises.

112 Total wipeout

Yesterday we saw the Israelites get off to a good start in Canaan — God giving them victory over their enemies as they conquered loads of territory. They were obeying their great God. But how long would it last?

Read Judges 1 v 16–21

ENGAGE YOUR BRAIN

▶ *Who was behind these successes?*

▶ *What went wrong? (v19, 21)*

This may not seem so bad. But God had commanded His people to drive out all His enemies from the land He was giving them (Numbers 33 v 52). If they failed to do this, they'd be turned against God by these people (Exodus 23 v 33). This was serious — there was no room for failure.

Read Judges 1 v 22–36

▶ *Which of the twelve Israelite tribes failed to complete the job?*
v19:
v21:
v27–28:
v29:
v30:
v31–32:
v33:
v34:
v35:

There were some great victories, but most of the Israelite tribes didn't fully carry out God's commands. They seemed happy to live alongside their enemies. Sometimes we think we've made good progress in the Christian life and can afford to leave some areas only partly dealt with. Sliding away always starts gently...

THINK IT THROUGH

Which sins do you leave in your life? What do you need to do about it?

PRAY ABOUT IT

We're not alone — God wants to help us fight our sin. Ask Him to help you. Mention the specific sin you can't seem to beat.

113 Round and round

The people of Israel conquered Canaan, but didn't make a thorough job of it. They didn't clear all the locals out. And they soon found that where there was a Canaanite, there was a Canaanite god as well. Disaster loomed.

👁 Read Judges 2 v 1–5

ENGAGE YOUR BRAIN

▷ *Where did they go wrong? (v2)*

▷ *Why shouldn't they have done this? (v1)*

▷ *What would be the result? (v3)*

👁 Read verses 6–15

▷ *What were the Israelites like when Joshua was around? (v7)*

▷ *What about the next generation? (v10–12)*

▷ *What happened to them? (v14–15)*

👁 Read verses 16–23

▷ *What great thing did God do for His disobedient people? (v16)*

▷ *How did they respond? (v17)*

▷ *What did God do next and why? (v20–22)*

There's a big pattern running through the book of Judges:

PRAY ABOUT IT

• Confess your current sins to God.

• Thank Him that He's totally fair and punishes sin.

• Cry out to Him to rescue you and help you fight the sin in your life.

• Thank Him for sending His Son to rescue you once and for all.

114 | Judge number one

"We're in the book of Judges, but we haven't met a judge yet!" I hear you (almost) cry. Well, today we'll briefly get acquainted with Israel's first judge sent by God to rescue them. Actually we've met him before...

👁 **Read Judges 1 v 11–13**

👁 **Then read Judges 3 v 7–11**

Yesterday we read chapter 2, which outlined the whole of Judges. This pattern occurs again and again:

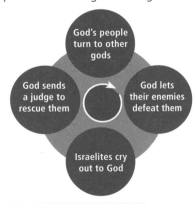

God's people turn to other gods

God lets their enemies defeat them

Israelites cry out to God

God sends a judge to rescue them

ENGAGE YOUR BRAIN

Check how Othniel's story fits the pattern:

▶ *What did God's people do wrong? (3v7)*

▶ *How did God punish them? (v8)*

▶ *So what did the Israelites do? (v9)*

▶ *So what did God do? (v9)*

▶ *How was Othniel able to rescue God's people? (v10)*

▶ *So what did God bring to His undeserving people? (v11)*

When His people cried out to Him, God rescued them. Even though they deserved to be wiped out for the way they'd treated Him. And God will rescue anyone who cries out to Him to rescue them from their sin.

It was God who gave Othniel the power to save the Israelites. Life may seem impossible sometimes, but God is in control. Only He has the power to defeat sin and win the victory for His people.

PRAY ABOUT IT

Think about what this short story tells us about God and His people. Let this influence your prayers.

115 Eglon the king...

As judges go, Othniel was quite normal. Today we read about a much stranger character. Get ready for one of the weirdest, most exciting and disgusting stories in the Bible.

👁 Read Judges 3 v 12–23

ENGAGE YOUR BRAIN

▶ How is the circular pattern of Judges shown again in verses 12–15?

▶ What opportunity did Ehud use to get to King Eglon?

The Israelites were invaded by enemies again after turning away from God. After 18 years, they cried to God for help and He gave them lefty Ehud to deliver (rescue) them. And what a way to do it. Look at the pointed message he gave to Eglon from God (v20).

👁 Read verses 24–31

▶ What did Eglon's assassination lead to? (v27–29)

▶ What was the great result for God's people? (v30)

This weird tale is all about God using an unusual rescuer who uses strange ways to save people. As we'll see through the rest of Judges (and the whole Old Testament), God continued to use unusual rescuers to save His people in surprising ways.

THINK ABOUT IT

▶ Who was the most unusual rescuer of all time?

▶ And in what surprising way did He save people? (Check out Romans 5 v 8.)

PRAY ABOUT IT

Thank God that He can use unlikely people like us to serve Him in amazing ways. And thank Him for the perfect Rescuer He sent to save us — Jesus.

THE BOTTOM LINE

God uses surprising methods to rescue His people.

116 Here come the girls

After Ehud and 80 years of peace, the Israelites were back to their old, evil ways. Get ready for another surprising rescuer and more disgusting deaths.

👁 Read Judges 4 v 1–16

ENGAGE YOUR BRAIN

▶ In which verses do you see the same old Israelite pattern?

▶ What were God's people up against? (v2–3)

▶ What was surprising about God's next hero? (v4)

▶ What did God promise to do, using Barak? (v6–7)

▶ What was Barak's response? (v8)

▶ How was Deborah's response different? (v14)

▶ What happened and who was behind it? (v16)

👁 Read verses 17–24

▶ What happened to Sisera? (v21)

▶ What did God do for His people? (v23–24)

Another gruesome death. And yet again God used unusual methods to rescue His people. He used two women and a nervous wreck to conquer a mighty enemy with 900 iron chariots! God's rescue is always impressive and perfect, even if the methods seem weird at the time.

And He has patience with timid believers like Barak. Look at the huge difference between verses 8 and 14. Barack was transformed by God from cowardly to courageous.

PRAY ABOUT IT

Thank God for His patience in developing your feeble faith. Ask Him to give you the confidence and belief to serve Him courageously.

117 Deborah: The Musical

Yesterday we read the amazing story of Deborah the prophetess, nervous Barak, iron chariots and death by tent peg. Now imagine putting all that into a song.

👁 Read Judges 5 v 1–11

ENGAGE YOUR BRAIN

▶ *How many times is "the Lord" mentioned in these verses?*

▶ *Why do you think that is?*

▶ *What happened when the people deserted God? (v8)*

Deborah is singing about how tough life had been — it wasn't safe to travel on the roads (v6); the Israelites couldn't defend themselves (v8). Then God rescued them and their lives changed dramatically. That's why the Lord gets so many mentions.

👁 Read verses 12–23

▶ *Who fought alongside Deborah and Barak?*

▶ *And who wimped out and stayed at home?*

▶ *What "good" reasons do you use to avoid doing what God wants?*

Verse 20 probably means that God used the skies to defeat the enemy. He caused rain and a flooded river (v21) to drown them. God was the real hero here.

👁 Read verses 24–31

▶ *Jael did something horrifically violent — so why was she praised so highly?*

▶ *What two things did Deborah pray? (v31)*

PRAY ABOUT IT

Will you pray that God's enemies are defeated? And how about praying for Christians you know, that they'll serve God more and more.

THE BOTTOM LINE

God rescues His people.

Sing His praises.

118 Invaded

Yesterday we saw the Israelites singing God's praises, but after a while they were singing the same old tune and forgetting the Lord. So their singing would turn to cries again.

⊙ Read Judges 6 v 1–6

▷ How impressive was the Israelites' enemy this time? (v5)

▷ What did they do to Israel? (v3–4)

▷ What were God's people reduced to doing? (v2)

▷ What did they eventually get around to doing? (v6)

Imagine this invasion, destruction and terror for seven years in a row. But it was exactly what they deserved for turning away from God. Eventually, they turned back to Him for help.

⊙ Read verses 7–10

▷ Did God send a judge immediately to rescue His people?

▷ What had God done in the past for them? (v8–9)

▷ What had He asked the Israelites to do? (v10)

God's people asked for a rescuer, but instead He sent a prophet to tell them off. They needed more than just a quick fix — their sin problem was long term. They needed to realise they were suffering because they'd turned their backs on God.

We often bring a shopping list of requests to God in prayer, and yet forget our responsibilities in living for Him. One of the kindest things God does for us is to show us exactly how we're messing up. With His help, we can put things right and start living for Him again.

PRAY ABOUT IT

Don't forget to listen to what God is teaching you. Ask Him to show you your sin and how to sort it out. And then bring your other requests to God. Try it now.

119 Mighty weakling

Today we meet a mighty warrior. But if he's so mighty, why does he claim to be the least important person from the weakest family? And why is he hiding in a winepress?

👁 Read Judges 6 v 11–16

ENGAGE YOUR BRAIN

▶ *How did the angel, representing God, greet Gideon? (v12)*

▶ *What was Gideon's less than friendly answer? (v13)*

▶ *How have verses 8–10 already answered this?*

▶ *So how would God rescue Israel this time? (v14)*

▶ *How could weakling Gideon possibly do that? (v16)*

Gideon has loads of questions and many doubts. But God has just one answer for him: *"I will be with you"* (v12, 16). This great promise will help us keep going through many bad times. God doesn't answer all of Gideon's questions or fill in all the details. Faith in God, knowing that He will be with us, should be enough.

👁 Read verses 17–24

▶ *What impressive thing did the angel do? (v21)*

▶ *Why was Gideon terrified? (v22)*

Gideon realised he was in the presence of all-powerful, almighty God. Sometimes we forget how impressive and terrifying God is. This is the Creator of the universe. No wonder Gideon freaked out. Yet the Lord promised to keep Gideon safe.

PRAY ABOUT IT

This is the God we serve. This is the God who's on our side. He is awesome and loving and powerful and forgiving. When you talk to God, do you give Him the respect He deserves? Why not start right now?

THE BOTTOM LINE

Almighty God is with His people.

120 Choosing sides

God has chosen nervous Gideon to rescue His people. Yesterday we saw Gideon build an altar for God. But the town already has an altar — to the false god Baal.

👁 Read Judges 6 v 25–32

▶ What was God's first task for Gideon?

▶ Is Gideon looking like a mighty warrior yet? (v27)

▶ What did the locals think of Gideon's demolition job? (v28–30)

▶ What was Gideon's dad's brilliant answer to this murderous mob? (v31)

God commanded Gideon to tear down the altar used for worshipping other gods such as Baal. God's message to Israel was this: you can't worship both me *and* other gods. If you want to be my people, you must be totally devoted to me.

Gideon had to show whose side he was on. He may have done the deed at night, but everyone soon knew he was on God's side. The idea of being a secret Christian is a ridiculous one. To be a Christian means to be committed to God above everything else — and this should be obvious to everyone who knows you.

GET ON WITH IT

What are you devoted to as much as (or more than) God?

What will you do about this?

Do people around you know you're a Christian?

How should your life reveal your faith more boldly?

PRAY ABOUT IT

Talk through these issues with God, asking Him to help you take a stand for Jesus, being more devoted to Him.

THE BOTTOM LINE

We must all choose sides and wear our team shirts with pride.

121 Give fleece a chance

Not long ago, the Abiezrites had wanted to kill Gideon for trashing their altar to fake god Baal. Now they're going to follow him into battle.

👁 Read Judges 6 v 33–35

ENGAGE YOUR BRAIN

▶ *Who were attacking God's people? (v33)*

▶ *Who were fighting alongside Gideon?*

▶ *But who was behind Gideon and the Israelites? (v34a)*

God gave Gideon His Holy Spirit to supply him with the courage and ability to fight for God. All Christians have God's Spirit in them, giving them the courage and ability to stand up for God.

👁 Read verses 36–40

▶ *What had God promised Gideon? (v36)*

▶ *But what did Gideon want from the Lord? (v37, 39)*

▶ *Incredibly, what did God do? (v38, 40)*

It's as if Gideon's heart was failing him — he knows God's will, but can't bring himself to face it. Maybe the problem isn't that we don't know God's will for us — it's that we don't like it and would rather avoid it. But look at the way God deals with Gideon — tremendous patience, great tenderness. God was going to teach Gideon to trust Him more, but just now Gideon needed reassurance.

GET ON WITH IT

Is there anything you know God wants you to do but you're trying to avoid it?

What will you do about it?

PRAY ABOUT IT

Praise God for His great kindness and patience despite our reluctance and weakness. Ask Him to give you the courage and ability to do what He wants you to.

122 God's 300

The Midianite armies are all over the plain like a swarm of locusts, ready to destroy the Israelites. Surely Gideon will need a massive army to fight them. But God has other ideas.

◉ Read Judges 7 v 1–8

▶ *How many men did Gideon start with? (Work it out from verse 3.)*

▶ *How many did God leave him with? (v7) Why? (v2)*

God often uses the weak in His plans. We shouldn't get big-headed when God uses us to serve Him. It's a great privilege to be a part of God's plans, but it doesn't mean we're extra brilliant — it's all down to God.

◉ Read verses 9–15

▶ *How did God encourage Gideon? (v9–11)*

▶ *How large was the enemy army? (v12)*

▶ *What were this powerful army scared of? (v14)*

◉ Read verses 15–25

▶ *What did the 300 men do? (v20)*

▶ *What did God do? (v22)*

There's no mention of Gideon and his men even having weapons with them! This was a stunning victory against a huge enemy, using only trumpets, clay jars and flaming torches. But there was no doubt that it was God's victory. He used this small group of weaponless warriors to defeat a terrifying enemy.

PRAY ABOUT IT

Nothing is impossible for God. No one is more powerful than Him. And He often uses surprising methods and weak people in His perfect plans. None more surprising than Jesus' death to rescue us. Spend time thanking God for these mind-blowing truths about Him.

THE BOTTOM LINE

God wins.

123 Catch some Zs

God had given Gideon and the Israelites an astonishing victory over the Midianites. But the job wasn't finished yet. Gideon was still pursuing the enemy, but some of his own people were getting in the way.

👁 Read Judges 8 v 1–3

ENGAGE YOUR BRAIN

▶ *What annoyed the Israelite tribe of Ephraim? (v1)*

▶ *How would you describe Gideon's reply to them? (v2–3)*

The Ephraimites were annoyed that Gideon had started the fight without them. They were more interested in grabbing glory for themselves than for God. Gideon could have exploded with anger. Instead, he replied politely and humbly.

GET ON WITH IT

▶ *Who really bugs you? How can you be more humble and gentle in the way you handle them?*

👁 Read verses 4–21

▶ *How did the people in Succoth and Peniel respond to Gideon's request for help? (v6, 8)*

▶ *What happened to them? (v16–17)*

▶ *What had Zebah and Zalmunna done to Gideon's brothers? (v19)*

▶ *So what happened to Z & Z? (v21)*

▶ *How did Gideon show his cowardice again? (v20)*

The people of Succoth and Peniel didn't trust God to give Gideon the victory so they played it safe. But this meant they sided with Israel's enemies and so were punished as Israel's enemies.

THINK ABOUT IT

Ever turn against other Christians? Or get in the way of people serving God? Or cause arguments? Or say stuff behind people's backs? Say sorry to God now for specific times you've done these things.

124 Not again...

Weak Gideon had become strong because he trusted in God. But it's funny how power often corrupts people. Well, more tragic than funny.

👁 Read Judges 8 v 22–27

ENGAGE YOUR BRAIN

▶ *What did the Israelites get wrong? (v22)*

▶ *What did Gideon get right? (v23)*

▶ *But what did he get badly wrong? (v24–27)*

The Israelites made Gideon their hero, seeming to forget that God was behind all their victories. So Gideon let them know that God was in charge (v23). After saying such a brilliant thing, Gideon messed up big time. He said God should rule Israel but then made a gold ephod (special tunic worn by priests) which the people worshipped instead of God! It's easy to say the right, godly thing but then let God down immediately.

👁 Read verses 28–35

▶ *What was the good news? (v28)*

▶ *What was the very bad news? (v33–35)*

Yet again, God's people failed to learn their lesson. They didn't remember all the unbelievable things God had done for them, and they refused to let Him rule them. They went chasing after false gods again. Tragic.

THINK ABOUT IT

What things do you worship? What do you make more important than God?

PRAY ABOUT IT

Talk to God about what you give too much time or respect to. Ask Him to help you to stop trying to be the boss of your life. If you genuinely mean it, tell God you want Him to be King.

THE BOTTOM LINE

Put God first in your life.

125 | Trees tease

Gideon (also known as Jerub–Baal) died. He left the Israelites spiralling back into sin and idol worship. He also left 70 sons and a bloodthirsty power struggle.

👁 Read Judges 9 v 1–6

ENGAGE YOUR BRAIN

▷ *Who did the people of Shechem choose as leader? How would you describe him from these verses?*

▷ *What terrible thing did he do? (v5) But who escaped?*

👁 Read verses 7–15

This story has confused people for years. Jotham seems to be accusing the people of choosing a useless thornbush (Abimelek) to be their king, instead of someone good and godly.

👁 Read verses 16–21

▷ *What had Gideon/Jerub-Baal done for the people? (v17)*

▷ *But how had they treated his family? (v18)*

▷ *What would happen to them because of their actions? (v20)*

Despite his confusing tree tale, Jotham is talking sense. God's people should take care in choosing leaders. And they should treat their leaders (and families) properly.

THINK ABOUT IT

▷ *Are you careful about who you follow and listen to?*

▷ *What are the qualities of a good Christian leader? And a bad one?*

▷ *How well do you treat Christian leaders you know? How will you treat them better?*

PRAY ABOUT IT

Thank God for the people who lead your church/youth group. Ask Him to help you be wise in who you listen to and let influence you.

THE BOTTOM LINE

Follow good, godly leaders.

126 Abimelek abolished

Gideon's (Jerub-Baal's) son, Abimelek, killed all his brothers except one. Jotham escaped and told Abimelek and the people of Shechem that, because of their treachery, they'd destroy each other.

👁 Read Judges 9 v 22–25

ENGAGE YOUR BRAIN

▶ *How did the people in Shechem treat Abimelek? (v25)*

▶ *Why? (v23–24)*

👁 Read verses 26–41

▶ *What did Gaal want? (v29)*

▶ *What did Zebul do? (v30–33)*

▶ *What was the outcome? (v39–41)*

👁 Read verses 42–57

▶ *What did Abimelek's army do to Shechem? (v45)*

▶ *What else? (v49)*

▶ *How did Abimelek meet his end? (v53)*

▶ *Why did all of this happen? (v56–57)*

These weren't merely two groups of evil people destroying each other.

God was behind it all (v23–24, v56–57). The people of Shechem had foolishly chosen an ungodly leader and had worshipped idols. Abimelek had murdered his own brothers in his hideous pursuit of power. So God punished them by letting them destroy each other.

Sometimes it seems as if evil rules the world. So many horrible things on the news. But God is still in control. His plans are still working out. In the end, God gets the victory. He sent Jesus to win the battle against evil once and for all. Never forget that.

PRAY ABOUT IT

Thank God that He's in control and always acts for the good of His people. Pray that you will trust Him more.

THE BOTTOM LINE

God is the perfect judge.

127 Daniel: Beast behaviour

Time for the second half of Daniel. It often gets missed out as it's, well, weird, and full of wild dreams and visions. But God uses Daniel's visions to teach us some incredible things about Him.

👁 Read Daniel 7 v 1–8

▶ *How would you describe Daniel's dream?*

▶ *Where do the winds come from?*

In the Bible, the "sea" is often code for the rebellious and chaotic world fighting against God. Despite the chaos below, notice that the winds come from heaven — God is still directing events.

▶ *These beasts represent different powerful kingdoms. How would you sum up the first three beasts/ kingdoms? (v3–6)*

▶ *But what suggests that these kingdoms are still under God's control? (v4–6)*

▶ *What is different about the fourth beast? (v7)*

This kingdom seems unstoppable. Do you ever look at the world, particularly certain parts of it, and worry that some evil is unstoppable? Perhaps when you see corrupt governments letting their people starve, or oppressive regimes torturing and executing their opponents? But take heart. As we've already seen, God is 100% in control.

PRAY ABOUT IT

Remember it's God's world! Why not spend some time now praying for His will to be done, "on earth as it is in heaven" — pray specifically for places or situations you know where people are rebelling against their Creator.

THE BOTTOM LINE

The world seems chaotic, but God is still the King.

128 | Throne zone

Daniel's wild vision continues. Don't worry — we'll get the interpretation of it next time, but for now, the action shifts to a courtroom.

👁 Read Daniel 7 v 9–14

ENGAGE YOUR BRAIN

▶ *How is God described? (v9)*

▶ *What does this name tell us about Him?*

▶ *How is God's throne described? And his court? (v9–10)*

▶ *What does this remind us about Him?*

▶ *How does God treat the beasts? (v11–12)*

God's judgment is absolute and totally just. He judges all humans, kings and regimes.

▶ *How does that make you feel when you look at today's world rulers?*

▶ *Who else is present in the court? (v13)*

▶ *What does the Ancient of Days give to Him? (v14)*

▶ *How does the world respond to Him? (v14)*

▶ *What is His kingdom like? (v14)*

Does that title "son of man" seem familiar? Yep, when Jesus chose it to refer to Himself, He was fully aware of this bit of Daniel!

▶ *What does Daniel 7 v 13–14 remind us about Jesus?*

PRAY ABOUT IT

Spend some time worshipping Jesus for who He was, is and will be eternally, using verses 13 and 14.

THE BOTTOM LINE

God's kingdom lasts for ever and Jesus is God's perfect King.

129 Victory insight

Daniel was freaked out by the first vision, so he asked one of the court officials to fill him in on the true meaning.

👁 Read Daniel 7 v 15–28

ENGAGE YOUR BRAIN

▶ What did the four beasts represent? (v17)

▶ But what's the great news for God's people? (v18)

▶ What is Daniel particularly concerned about? (v19–20)

▶ What will God's enemies do? (v23–25)

▶ But what will happen in the end? (v26)

"Saints"/"Holy people" = God's people: all of them, not just super holy folk with beards and sandals. If you're a Christian, you're a saint!

▶ What is the great future for the people of God? (v27)

▶ But what will the short term involve? (v21, 25)

Maybe that's why Daniel was so shaken by this vision (v28). Before God's ultimate victory and the wonderful future ahead of us, God's people will suffer. You only have to look around you to see this is true today.

PRAY ABOUT IT

Pray for Christians suffering around the world, that they would know the truth and comfort of verses 18, 22 and 27.

Check out www.opendoorsuk.org/pray/ for more prayer ideas.

THE BOTTOM LINE

God's people will suffer but they are on the winning side.

130 Vicious attack

Another scary vision, two years later. Belshazzar is still king, so things are still really messed up.

👁 Read Daniel 8 v 1–14

ENGAGE YOUR BRAIN

▶ Who is the first character that Daniel sees in his dream? (v3–4) What is he like?

▶ What is the next character like? (v5–8)

▶ What happens to the ram?

▶ Then who appears? (v9)

▶ How is this character powerful?

This all seems pretty weird, but the themes are the same as the last vision: power, conflict and victory. Notice, as before, that the target for all these powerful characters is God's people (v12).

▶ What is the enemy doing in verse 11? ("Prince of the host"/"commander of the army" = God)

God's enemy goes straight for the temple, the place where God met His people. It's like those disaster movies where aliens blow up the White House — it's a symbol of the centre of power. Jesus' death was the ultimate sacrifice. So believers no longer need the temple and sacrifices — we can go straight to God. But Jesus' followers still have an enemy.

TALK IT OVER

Peter tells us that the devil "prowls around like a roaring lion looking for someone to devour". How can we stand firm in our faith? Read 1 Peter 5 v 8–9 and Ephesians 6 v 10–18 with another Christian, then chat and pray together about what you've read.

PRAY ABOUT IT

Ask God to keep you strong and safe in your faith.

THE BOTTOM LINE

Be on your guard.

131 Vision explained

Daniel needed supernatural assistance to understand this vision (us too!), and so God sent his messenger, Gabriel, to explain it.

👁 Read Daniel 8 v 15–27

ENGAGE YOUR BRAIN

▶ *What time period is Daniel's vision about? (v17, 19)*

▶ *Who do the ram and the goat refer to? (v20–21)*

This "end time" starts with the Persian Empire, then Alexander the Great, and after that some more kings…

▶ *What is the king in verse 23 like?*

▶ *How will he exert his influence? (v24)*

▶ *Just how big is his ego? (v25)*

These verses are probably talking about a chap called Antiochus IV Epiphanes, who persecuted the Jewish people (v10) in Judah (v9) in 170BC. It's not hard to see who's behind him, though, is it?

▶ *What time period is this vision also about? (v26)*

Rebellion against God and persecution of His people is nothing new; it's a pattern that will continue until Jesus returns and puts a stop to it for ever. The devil was defeated at the cross but he is not yet destroyed.

▶ *Why do you think Daniel was devastated by this vision and explanation?*

PRAY ABOUT IT

Rebellion against God is ugly and we are all guilty of it. Say sorry to God for your own sin and thank Him for Jesus, who took the penalty for it. Pray for those who are still in angry rebellion against God, that He would have mercy on them and help them to see Jesus' rescue.

THE BOTTOM LINE

All rebellion against God is ugly and won't go unpunished.

132 Pray as you learn

Today's Daniel bit happened during King Darius' reign (he threw Dan into the lions' den). Remember, God's people are still exiles in Babylon and far from God's temple and the promised land.

👁 Read Daniel 9 v 1–3

ENGAGE YOUR BRAIN

▷ *What gives Daniel new hope? (v2)*

▷ *Why could this be good news for Daniel and the rest of the exiles?*

▷ *What is Daniel's response? (v3)*

The visions Daniel had had were pretty mind-blowing, but it's reading God's promises in His word that really gets Daniel excited. How about you?

👁 Read verses 4–16

▷ *Why did Daniel think God might answer his prayer?*
v4:
v7:
v9:

God's people had consistently rebelled against Him — that's why they'd been exiled in the first place — but since then they had still failed to turn back to Him and live His way. It didn't look as if God's promise to bring them home had any chance of coming true.

👁 Read verses 17–19

▷ *What is Daniel most concerned about? (v17, 19)*

▷ *Why is this the only way to pray?*

Daniel prays like Moses and other Bible greats — not on the basis of their own good deeds (or lack of...) but on the basis of what they know God is like — loving, righteous, merciful and forgiving. And Daniel wanted God to get the glory and honour He deserves.

PRAY ABOUT IT

When we come to God in prayer, it's only because of Jesus that we can call Him "Father" and know that He will hear our prayers. Spend some time doing that now, praying that God will get the glory He deserves.

133 Number cruncher

Dan prayed for Jerusalem to be restored, as God had promised. But there was more to understand about this promise. Cue Gabriel — who gives Dan a totally mind-boggling maths lesson.

Read Daniel 9 v 20–24

ENGAGE YOUR BRAIN

▶ *How quickly did the angel arrive? (v21, 23)*

▶ *How would Gabriel's words have encouraged Daniel? (v22–23)*

▶ *What God will do for His people and their city, Jerusalem? (v24)*

▶ *How long will it take? (v24)*

God is going to act to put a stop to His people's sin, to restore their relationship with Him, to pay for their wrongdoing and make them "at one" with Him. He's also going to anoint — mark out as special — His holy one. Gabriel says this will take "seventy sevens" aka seventy weeks. But it's not literal — seven is the number of perfection in the Bible, so it's more like saying "in God's perfect timing".

Read verses 25–27

▶ *Who is on His way? (v25)*

▶ *What will happen to Him? (v26)*

▶ *What will he do? (v27)*

▶ *Who might this be talking about?*

Daniel didn't see the full picture, but we do. Jesus has always been at the centre of God's plan to deal with His people's sin and bring them close to Him again. We might not follow all the details here but the big truth is awesome: *Jesus saves.*

PRAY ABOUT IT

Don't get bogged down in the detail — thank God for the eternal truth that Jesus came to deal with our rebellion and bring us back into relationship with our loving, all-powerful Creator.

134 Shining example

Here's what's happening. King Cyrus has taken over from Darius and has let some of the Jews go back to Jerusalem (yay!) where they are rebuilding the walls and temple (double yay!); but they're also facing opposition (boo!).

👁 Read Daniel 10 v 1–6

ENGAGE YOUR BRAIN

▷ *Just how upset is Daniel? (v2–3)*

▷ *Who does he see in his vision, and what is he like? (v5–6)*

▷ *Remind you of anyone? (Hint: Revelation 1 v 13–18.)*

Our God is incredibly holy. Daniel's vision here and John's vision of Jesus show us a glimpse of how majestic, powerful, awesomely holy and, yes, totally terrifying He is.

👁 Read Daniel 10 v 7 – 11 v 1

▷ *How does Daniel react in verses 8–10 and 15–17?*

▷ *What is it about God that makes him react like this?*

▷ *How did Daniel see himself in relation to God? (v17)*

▷ *What did God do to encourage him? (v18–19)*

▷ *Why did He do this for Daniel? (v12)*

Life might look impossible, but God is awesomely powerful and in complete control. More than that, He cares for and strengthens His people.

PRAY ABOUT IT

"Peace! Be strong now; be strong," God says to Daniel (v19). Thank Him for His promise to you in Jesus: "In me you may have peace. In this world you will have trouble. But take heart! I have overcome the world" (John 16 v 33).

THE BOTTOM LINE

Jesus is our peace and our strength.

135 | War stories

Think about the last 100 years of your country's history. Imagine writing a quick summary of it without using any names of the key people involved. Confusing? You bet. Well, that's what this next part of Daniel is like.

👁 Read Daniel 11 v 2–35

ENGAGE YOUR BRAIN

▶ What do these kings and military leaders have in common? (v3, v5, v11, v12, v14, v16, v21, v27, v28, v30, v32)

•

•

•

▶ Look at these characteristics. How are they like what we've seen in previous visions (and even in the kings of Babylon/Persia etc)?

▶ What is the outlook for God's people? (v30–35)

Bible historians have suggested various matches for all these characters, but rather than getting bogged down in the detail, what is the big picture? Yep, arrogant human kings setting themselves against the heavenly King. Same old story.

▶ Can you see this attitude in any countries or world leaders today?

And just as God's people were persecuted here (v30–35), it's the same today. If we stand up for God, and tell people about Jesus, we will suffer. But it's a true privilege to serve God. Jesus went through far more pain and suffering for us, so that one day we will live with Him in perfect peace for ever, with no more suffering!

PRAY ABOUT IT

Read Psalm 2 and use it to shape your prayers today.

THE BOTTOM LINE

The LORD is King.

136 Rise and fall

Daniel is learning about a future king who would become Public Enemy Number One for God's people.

👁 Read Daniel 11 v 36–45

▷ *What is this king's ruling philosophy (v36)?*

▷ *Is that usually a good way to live?*

If you are familiar with the book of Judges, you might remember the repeated line: "In those days Israel had no king; everyone did as they saw fit" (Judges 21 v 25). The result was total depravity and disaster. Humanity has a nasty habit of making a mess of everything.

▷ *What will the outcome be for Israel (aka the Beautiful Land) and its inhabitants? (Daniel 11v41, v45, and look back to v31)*

▷ *What would eventually happen to this king? (v45)*

This king might be a nasty piece of work, but he's just being up-front about what all human sin is — wanting to get rid of God and be God ourselves. Adam and Eve began it; we're all guilty of it.

PRAY ABOUT IT

Thank God for Jesus, "who, being in very nature God, did not consider equality with God something to be used to his own advantage; rather, he made himself nothing by taking the very nature of a servant, being made in human likeness. And being found in appearance as a man, he humbled himself by becoming obedient to death — even death on a cross!" (Philippians 2 v 6–8)

THE BOTTOM LINE

We wrongly exalt ourselves, but Jesus humbled Himself.

137 The end?

A slow zoom out now for Daniel, past the immediate future, and the kingdoms to come, to the end of time and the only kingdom that will last for ever.

👁 Read Daniel 12 v 1–4

ENGAGE YOUR BRAIN

▶ What must God's people expect before the end? (v1b)

▶ But what will God do for His people? (v1a)

Michael is like a heavenly bodyguard, protecting God's people — they will always face opposition and hardship in this world, but…

▶ What will God's people ultimately be delivered from? (v2)

▶ What will their future be? (v2–3)

▶ How about those people who set themselves up against God? (v2)

A wonderful future — everlasting life and shining righteousness. Or everlasting shame and contempt. There's no middle way — you're either with God or against Him.

▶ How will we know who God's true people are? (v1)

Revelation 21 v 27 calls this book "the Lamb's book of life". It's Jesus' book and our eternal destiny is all down to how we respond to Jesus. Accept Him as Saviour and Lord, or dismiss Him?

PRAY ABOUT IT

Talk to God now about people you know who reject, dismiss or ignore Him. Plead with Him to turn their lives around.

TALK IT OVER

Why is it good news that God will judge the earth? Chat it through with an older Christian.

138 Wise and fall

We've already seen what will happen when the world ends, but how will the book of Daniel end? By reminding him (and us) how to live in the meantime.

👁 Read Daniel 12 v 5–13

▷ *What are the two men discussing? (v5–7)*

▷ *Does Daniel get what's going on? (v8)*

▷ *What is he told to do? (v9, 13)*

▷ *What is the encouragement for him (and us if we're following Jesus) in verse 13?*

▷ *What are we reminded about life before Jesus returns? (v10)*

Don't take the numbers literally (v7, 11). They simply tell us that God's in charge. Not just of *what* happens, but *when* too. The end will come at the time God chooses.

So how do we live now? Like Daniel, we must keep on following God. That's what it means to be wise (v10). It's wise to live your life in the light of what is to come. Even when it's unbearably hard, as Jesus warned us.

The end will come with the return of Jesus Christ. Daniel didn't know that. We do, from the New Testament. And God's prepared a great future for His followers. We get ready for it by following Jesus now.

PRAY ABOUT IT

Thank God for purifying you and making you spotless (v10) through Jesus' death and resurrection. Thank Him for refining you as you trust Him every day through the good times and the hard times. Pray for Him to have mercy on those who are currently rebelling against Him. Pray for specific people you think of.

THE BOTTOM LINE

There is a great future for those who follow Jesus.

139 Romans: Authority figure

Back to Romans. For a reminder of what it's all about, run back to page 107. What's your first response to the word "authority"? Boring? Government? Dictatorship? Do you ever think of it as a good gift from God?

👁 Read Romans 13 v 1–7

ENGAGE YOUR BRAIN

▶ *Who is ultimately behind all governments and authorities? (v1, 2, 4, 6)*

▶ *How are authorities supposed to behave? (v3–4)*

▶ *What authorities are there in your life? Teachers? Parents? Police?*

▶ *What is your attitude towards them? Do these verses change anything?*

This kind of teaching was pretty radical at the time. Most non-Roman religions would not accept the right of foreign authorities to rule over them. But Paul is concerned that Christians live in peace with those around them (look back to 12 v 18) and recognises that all things are ultimately under God's control. The Roman government was at times very hostile to Christians, even executing them in large numbers, but Paul doesn't tell them to respond with lawlessness or armed revolution.

TALK IT OVER

How far do we, as Christians, have to obey our authorities and governments? Are there any instances when it's OK to break the law? Discuss this with an older Christian.

PRAY ABOUT IT

Most of us live in a democracy, where we're able to protest and vote if we disagree with our governments. Think for a moment about Christians in countries where they do not have that freedom. Pray that they would be able to live out Romans 13 v 7 in very difficult circumstances.

THE BOTTOM LINE

God is our ultimate authority.

140 | Wake up! Get dressed!

At the beginning of chapter 12, Paul urged us to look BACK to God's mercies. At the end of chapter 13 we're looking FORWARD to Christ's return; so how does that affect the way we live now?

👁 Read Romans 13 v 8–14

ENGAGE YOUR BRAIN

▶ Look back at verse 7. What was Paul's opening instruction? How does verse 8 continue this idea?

▶ How does love fulfil the law, and, in this case, the Ten Commandments? (v8–10)

▶ What do we need to understand about the present time? (v11–12)

"The day" in the Bible talks about the day of Christ's return. How exciting that it's closer now than when we first believed! So wake up from your slumber! Don't live like the rest of this dark world — it's nearly daytime!

▶ If we need to wake up, what are we to wake up from? (v13)

▶ Can you put these things into everyday language? What do they look like in your situation — at school, college, work?

▶ Once we've woken up, we need to get dressed. What do we put on? (v12, 14)

▶ What will that involve? What should we be thinking about and not thinking about? (v14)

Armour might not be as comfortable as pyjamas but let's not forget that we are fighting a battle. Read Ephesians 6 v 10–18 for some ideas on what the armour of light might involve.

PRAY ABOUT IT

Thank God that Jesus is coming back and will deal with all the darkness of this world for good.

THE BOTTOM LINE

The day is nearly here — wake up and get dressed!

141 Weak and strong

You might think the issue in these next verses is all about the pros and cons of vegetarianism, but it's about much more than that.

👁 Read Romans 14 v 1–4

ENGAGE YOUR BRAIN

▶ *What is the wrong attitude towards someone with a "weaker" faith?*

▶ *What is the right attitude?*

▶ *Why should we treat people this way? (v3–4)*

▶ *Are you ever tempted to look down on other Christians?*

👁 Read verses 5–9

▶ *How does Paul want us to think about living as a Christian? (v5)*

▶ *What should typify the way we live? (v6–8)*

▶ *Does this sum up your life?*

👁 Read verses 10–12

▶ *What is the big reminder here of why we shouldn't judge others?*

PRAY ABOUT IT

Ask God's forgiveness for the times when you have passed judgment on another Christian — maybe they haven't joined in with something and you've thought they were seriously uncool, or perhaps they do things *you* think are unacceptable (even though the Bible doesn't say so) for a so-called Christian. Recognise that God is the Judge, not you, and say sorry.

GET ON WITH IT

Do you live, work, eat, drink, party, watch TV and so on *"to the Lord"*? Think about your week ahead — how can you do this more? Don't forget to ask God's help.

THE BOTTOM LINE

God is Lord and Judge. Live for Him.

142 Meaty matters

Is it OK to eat meat? In Rome, meat from a butcher had often been sacrificed in honour of pagan idols before it made its way to the shop window — was that really OK for Christians to munch on?

👁 Read Romans 14 v 13–23

ENGAGE YOUR BRAIN

▶ What does Paul remind us was the point of the last section (v13)?

Now he moves on to the nitty-gritty of the issue itself.

▶ What is Paul's take on the whole veggie issue? (v14)

▶ And his take on the "weaker" Christians?

▶ So what are the implications for someone of "stronger" faith? (v15, v20–21)

Whatever the ins and outs of a particular debate, it's important to remember the bottom line — Christ died for sinners, to give us His righteousness and peace and joy by His Spirit. Anything outside of this is a secondary matter.

▶ Put more positively, how should we live? (v19)

TALK IT OVER

Chat with an older Christian about how we decide whether something is of primary or secondary importance — use these verses to help you. Consider the following examples:

1) Someone who says Christians shouldn't drink alcohol.

2) Or who says Christians shouldn't watch horror movies.

3) Someone who denies the resurrection actually happened.

4) Or who says that Jesus isn't the only way to God.

GET ON WITH IT

Is there anything which you do which might cause a "weaker" Christian to stumble? Don't do it around them!

143 Plea to please

"Go on then, please yourself!" Ever had this said to you when someone's fed up with you not agreeing with them? Paul ends this bit on how we should treat those of weaker faith by explaining why we shouldn't please ourselves...

👁 Read Romans 15 v 1–6

ENGAGE YOUR BRAIN

▶ *What reason (v3) does Paul give for his instructions in verses 1-2?*

If Christ allowed Himself to be insulted for our sake, then we shouldn't get so uptight about our "rights" — think of the needs of others instead. The second half of verse 3 is a quote from Psalm 69 v 9, which reminds Paul how the Old Testament pointed forward to Jesus.

▶ *Find three reasons to be thankful for the Old Testament. (Rom 15v4)*

▶ *What is our unity based on, and who gives it? (v5)*

▶ *What is the ultimate purpose of Christian unity? (v6)*

👁 Read verses 7–13

Another set of reasons to bear with one another now as we look at what God is like.

▶ *What do we learn about God in verses 7–12?*

Back in Genesis 12, God promised Abraham that, through his offspring, the whole world would be blessed. In Christ that promise became reality — it wasn't just the Jews who got to enjoy God's presence and love, but also the Gentiles, the outsiders.

THINK IT OVER

Bearing in mind God's character, how should that affect the way we treat each other — weak or strong, Jew or Gentile, cool or uncool?

PRAY ABOUT IT

Why not use Romans 15 v 13 as a basis for your own prayers for yourself and your church or youth group?

THE BOTTOM LINE

God unites us as we follow Christ.

144 In summary

Paul is getting near to the end of his seriously heavy letter and now explains why he's written to the Roman Christians.

👁 Read Romans 15 v 14–22

ENGAGE YOUR BRAIN

- ▶ *What is Paul's take on the Romans Christians? (v14)*

- ▶ *So why has he written to them? (v15–16)*

- ▶ *How does he sum up his job? (v16, 18–19)*

- ▶ *What's his big desire? (v20–22)*

PRAY ABOUT IT

Ask God to give you that same desire to share the good news about Jesus with people who currently don't know Him.

SHARE IT

Preach the gospel today where Christ is not known!

👁 Read verses 23–33

It seems that Paul was probably in Corinth when he wrote this letter.

- ▶ *Where are his three intended destinations? (v24, 25, 28)*

- ▶ *Why the big detour? (v25–26)*

- ▶ *Why did Paul see this task as so important? (v27, 31)*

- ▶ *How might this have challenged the church in Rome (think again of their background)?*

- ▶ *How does Paul want the Roman Christians to pray for him? (v30–32)*

THE BOTTOM LINE

See if you can sum up Paul's reasons for writing the book of Romans.

145 Paul's pals

What's your first impression when faced with the list of names in Romans 16? Be honest. Tempted to skip it? Think again, because although we don't know these people, it's really encouraging for us to read!

👁 **Read Romans 16 v 1–16**

ENGAGE YOUR BRAIN

Phoebe (mentioned in verse 1) would probably have delivered this letter to the people Paul mentions here.

▶ *How does Paul describe Phoebe?*

▶ *Write down what we find out about the people Paul sends greetings to:*

Priscilla & Aquila:

Epenetus:

Mary:

Andronicus & Junias:

Ampliatus:

Urbanus:

Stachys:

Apelles:

Aristobulus & co:

Herodion:

Narcissus & co:

Tryphena & Tryphosa:

Persis:

Rufus & his mum:

Asyncritus, Phlegon, Hermes, Patrobas, Hermas & co:

Philologus, Julia, Nereus and his sis, Olympas & co:

▶ *Spot any recurring comments?*

▶ *How would you like to be described by Paul?*

▶ *Did you notice where these early Christians met? (v5)*

PRAY ABOUT IT

Thank God for Christians who have encouraged you.

THE BOTTOM LINE

God gives us the gift of other Christians.

146 Final thoughts

It's been a long letter — well done in getting to the end! Some closing thoughts from Paul now...

👁 Read Romans 16 v 17–20

ENGAGE YOUR BRAIN

▶ *What is the key thing Paul wants his Roman brothers and sisters to watch out for? (v17-19)*

▶ *In what two ways does Paul encourage the Romans? (v20)*

Hold on to the teaching you have learned — don't leave the gospel behind! Remember what you were, what Christ did, the diverse people He has united to Him, and how He wants you to live with the help of His Spirit.

GET ON WITH IT

Remind yourself of these truths today (and every day!).

👁 Read verses 21–27

More greetings, this time from those with Paul, including his secretary Tertius (v22).

▶ *What does Paul remind us about the awesome gospel in verses 25–27?*

Remind yourself of Romans 1 v 16–17.

PRAY ABOUT IT

Thank God for His wonderful plan of salvation in Jesus. Thank Him that it's for everyone — Jew and Gentile. Thank Him for how He has acted in your life.

THE BOTTOM LINE

Never forget the glorious gospel message.

147 Matthew: Follow the leader

As we return to Matthew's Gospel, Jesus is in a serious mood. He sets His sights on people who are standing on the sidelines, criticising and passing comment on others rather than following Him.

👁 Read Matthew 11 v 20–24

ENGAGE YOUR BRAIN

▶ Why is Jesus so angry with Chorazin, Bethsaida and Capernaum? (v20)

Tyre and Sidon were notorious, idol-worshipping cities. As for Sodom, well, its wickedness was legendary. In fact, in the Old Testament, God destroyed it with a rain of sulphur!

👁 Read verses 25–30

▶ So if Jesus is unhappy with those who criticise and fail to repent, who is it that will be blessed? (v25–26)

▶ What is Jesus offering? (v28–30)

▶ What must we recognise about ourselves?

▶ What will Jesus give us?

▶ What sort of a master is He?

▶ Why is rest so attractive?

▶ In what way are people weary and burdened in life?

It's been God's choice and plan all along (v26). The way of Jesus isn't within reach of proud, religious know-it-alls; it's only for those prepared to come to God in total dependence (v25). What a great invitation (v28) — people then felt weighed down by all the religious demands placed on them. Jesus offers release from that. And, in the future, there will be eternal rest. For now, life won't be easy following Jesus (v29) but it's the best life there can be!

PRAY ABOUT IT

Have you ever accepted Jesus' offer in verses 28–30? Do you need to come back and receive His rest again?

148 Sabbath scandal

All this stuff about resting on the Sabbath seems a bit heavy. Remember that keeping the Sabbath special was one of the Ten Commandments and was a big deal to the Jewish leaders. But as usual they've missed the point.

👁 Read Matthew 12 v 1–14

ENGAGE YOUR BRAIN

▶ *What were the disciples doing wrong? (v1–2)*

Technically, they were *working* as they were "harvesting" the grain. I know, talk about being picky! The Pharisees were clearly looking for any excuse to attack Jesus.

▶ *How does Jesus defend the disciples in verses 3–4?*

▶ *What does He point out in verse 5?*

▶ *What does He say they've misunderstood? (v7)*

▶ *What two things does He say about Himself? (v6, 8)*

Remember the whole point of God's law in the Old Testament? It revealed God's character and what it would mean for His people to live in perfect relationship with Him. Back in Matthew 5 v 17 Jesus told His disciples He had come to fulfil the law and the prophets. He is the temple — the place where God meets humanity. He is the Lord of the Sabbath — the one in whom we find rest.

▶ *Is God pleased by picky rule-keeping?*

▶ *What sort of heart does God want? (12v7)*

▶ *How do verses 12–14 show Jesus' true character and that of the Pharisees?*

GET ON WITH IT

Do you secretly think that as long as you're doing the right things — reading your Bible, praying, going to church/youth group, not swearing or getting drunk — God will be pleased with you? Stop thinking like that and re-focus your eyes on Jesus.

THE BOTTOM LINE

God wants a relationship, not just rule-keeping.

149 Devil's advocate

Plotting to kill Jesus is bad enough but the Pharisees go one further now and condemn themselves. Oops.

⊙ Read Matthew 12 v 22–37

ENGAGE YOUR BRAIN

▶ *What miracle does Jesus perform in verse 22?*

▶ *What do the people ask themselves? (v23)*

They're not just asking if Jesus is a descendant of David but if He is THE son of David — the promised King and Messiah.

▶ *Shockingly, what is the Pharisees' verdict? (v24)*

▶ *How does Jesus defend Himself using common sense? (v25–29)*

▶ *What amazing event have the Pharisees missed? (v28)*

▶ *What is Jesus' terrible warning in verses 30–37?*

Some Christians worry that they have somehow committed this unforgivable sin (v31–32), but Jesus is quite clear. If you say good is evil and that the work of God is the work of the devil, how on earth can you be saved? You're rejecting the very one who can save you!

So blasphemy against the Spirit is refusing to submit to Jesus and become a Christian. Look again at verse 32 — even those who speak against Jesus can be forgiven. Remember how on the cross Jesus even prays for those who crucified Him? (Luke 23 v 33–34)

PRAY ABOUT IT

By nature our hearts are wicked. It's only by Jesus' death on the cross and by the Holy Spirit coming to live in us that they can be clean. If you've never asked God to do that for you, do it now — don't delay! And if you have, give great thanks to Him and pray for those who are currently facing God's punishment.

150 Something fishy

Yesterday we read about a great healing, a false accusation and a fierce reply. But the Pharisees hadn't finished with Jesus yet.

👁 Read Matthew 12 v 38–45

ENGAGE YOUR BRAIN

▶ *What do the Pharisees demand? (v38)*

▶ *What is Jesus' response? (v39)*

▶ *Why do you think He reacts like this?*

▶ *What sign does He offer them?*

▶ *What does Jesus mean by the sign of Jonah? (v40)*

▶ *What did the men of Nineveh do that these Jewish leaders won't? (v41)*

▶ *What image does Jesus use to show how bad these unbelieving Pharisees are? (v43–45)*

It's hard to process the fact that these Pharisees had Jesus Christ, the Son of God, right there in front of them and yet failed so spectacularly to see who He was. Or did they? We're not just talking about incomprehension here, but real hostility. Perhaps they did grasp who they were dealing with but didn't want Him as their king.

It's a terrible thought.

👁 Read verses 46–50

▶ *What amazing truth does Jesus reveal about those who follow Him? (v46–50)*

▶ *So what does that mean to YOU?*

PRAY ABOUT IT

Thank God now for the amazing privilege of being able to call Him "Father" and of having Jesus as your perfect older brother.

151 Hide and seed

A very famous parable today, but it may not be quite what you were expecting...

👁 Read Matthew 13 v 1–17

ENGAGE YOUR BRAIN

▶ *How does Jesus teach the crowd — what style does He use? (v3)*

▶ *Why does He use it? (v10–17)*

▶ *Who is "in" and who is "out"? (v11)*

▶ *Does verse 15 shock you?*

▶ *Why / why not?*

If you always thought parables were illustrating a moral through an easy-to-understand story, then verse 13 may have come as a bit of a shock. Jesus is using parables so people *don't* understand what He's talking about.

Confused? Well look at verse 11 and verse 16. Jesus' followers can understand because Jesus opens their ears and helps them to grasp God's truths.

SHARE IT

We cannot convince anyone to follow Jesus. He has to open blind eyes.

But that doesn't mean we don't need to share the good news — it just takes the pressure off needing to get a result — that's all down to God!

PRAY ABOUT IT

Ask Jesus to be merciful to your friends and family who aren't following Him, to open their eyes and help them to understand that He is the King.

THE BOTTOM LINE

Only Jesus can open our eyes and help us to see.

152 Seeds revealed

Like a magic-eye picture or invisible ink, the hidden meaning of this parable is now made plain...

👁 Read Matthew 13 v 1–9, 18–23

ENGAGE YOUR BRAIN

Fill in the table below using today's Bible bits.

Where the seed fell	What it reminds us of	What it means

PRAY IT THROUGH

Ironically, as Jesus told this parable, it was coming true at the same time — some would have listened but not understood, others would have seemed to respond but given up later, and still others would have heard, understood and been fruitful. Pray that you would be that last kind of soil and ask God to help you sow the seed of the gospel around you today.

153 Weed it and reap

Another parable today. Profound truths, but hidden from everyone except Jesus' followers.

👁 Read Matthew 13 v 24–30

ENGAGE YOUR BRAIN

▶ *What did the man sow?*

▶ *What happened to the field?*

▶ *What were the owner's orders?*

👁 Read verses 36–43

▶ *What is Jesus [the Son of Man] doing in the parable? (v37–38)*

▶ *So what can we say about the world around us now? (v38)*

▶ *Who is in charge throughout events? (v37, 41)*

▶ *What happens to the enemy — the devil? (v41–42)*

▶ *What are we all heading towards? (v39–43)*

"Whoever has ears let them hear." There is a warning here for those who listen to Jesus and want to understand His words. People's responses will only become fully clear to everyone else when God judges, dividing everyone into two groups. For now, the growth of God's kingdom is mostly hidden. The true size of it will only be seen when Jesus returns.

PRAY ABOUT IT

One judgment. Two outcomes. It's both a terrifying and a glorious prospect. Talk to God now about your reactions.

SHARE IT

Ask Jesus to help you share the good news about Him with someone today. Remember Jesus does the sowing — it's all under His control.

THE BOTTOM LINE

There will be no escaping God's day of judgment.

154 Cutting the mustard

Can you think of anything tiny that has a huge influence? Maybe a microchip or a virus from a killer disease?

👁 Read Matthew 13 v 31–35

ENGAGE YOUR BRAIN

▶ What is key about the mustard seed? (v32) What is key about yeast? (v33)

▶ What are we supposed to learn about the kingdom of heaven (living with Jesus as King) from these parables?

▶ Do you feel that your church is weak or insignificant? Do these parables shift your perspective?

"Here is a man who was born in an obscure village, the child of a peasant woman. He worked in a carpentry shop until He was thirty. Then for three years He was a travelling preacher. He never owned a home, never wrote a book, never had a family, never travelled two hundred miles from the place He was born. He didn't do any of the things that usually accompany greatness. He had no credentials but Himself. While still a young man, the tide of popular opinion turned against Him. His friends ran away. One of them denied knowing Him. He was turned over to His enemies and was nailed upon a cross between two thieves. While He was dying His executioners gambled for the only piece of property He had – His coat. When He was dead, He was laid in a borrowed grave through the pity of a friend. Twenty long centuries have come and gone, and today He's the centrepiece of the human race. All the armies that ever marched, all the parliaments that ever sat and all the kings that ever reigned, put together, have not affected the life of people on this earth as powerfully as that one solitary life." (Adapted from an essay by Dr James Allan Francis)

PRAY ABOUT IT

Thank God for how His amazing plan was put in place before creation (v35) and how it changed the world.

155 | True treasure

Three more short and sweet parables to help broaden our understanding of what God's kingdom is like.

⊙ Read Matthew 13 v 44–52

ENGAGE YOUR BRAIN

▶ *What do the parables in verses 44–45 tell us about God's kingdom?*

▶ *Does this differ from your attitude to Jesus and living for Him?*

▶ *Would you give up everything to follow Christ? If not, why not?*

PRAY ABOUT IT

The apostle Paul writes that "to live is Christ and to die is gain" (Philippians 1 v 21). Can you honestly say that? Ask God to give you that wholehearted love that treasures Jesus above everything.

GET ON WITH IT

What is standing between you and living all out for Jesus? Non-Christian boyfriend or girlfriend? Making academic or sporting success an idol? Internet porn? Wanting to be in with the cool crowd? Get rid of it!

▶ *Why is it so important to understand the parable in Matthew 13 v 47–50?*

▶ *What should understanding lead to? (v52)*

The previous parables have all been about what the kingdom of heaven (life with Jesus as King) is like, but this last one is about every teacher who has been instructed by Jesus. The treasure that Jesus has shown us — the treasure of the kingdom — needs to be brought out of the storeroom and put on display.

SHARE IT

How can you display the treasure of the good news about Jesus today?

THE BOTTOM LINE

Christianity isn't just a lifestyle choice — it's life or death.

156 Roots of rejection

Ever get sneered at by people who knew you before you were a Christian? Maybe your friends or parents think you'll grow out of this "religious phase"? Take heart, you're in good company!

👁 Read Matthew 13 v 53–58

ENGAGE YOUR BRAIN

ⓓ *Where does Jesus head to next? (v54)*

ⓓ *What sort of a reception does he get? (v54–57)*

ⓓ *How does Jesus react? (v57)*

ⓓ *What is the verdict on his old neighbours? (v58)*

As we look back with the benefit of hindsight, it seems incredible that people had Jesus right there in front of them and yet didn't have faith.

But God knew all along that this would happen.

The first chapter of John's Gospel tells us that: *"He was in the world, and though the world was made through him, the world did not recognise him. He came to that which was his own, but his own did not receive him. Yet to all who did receive him, to those who believed in his name, he gave the right to become children of God"* (John 1 v 10–12).

ⓓ *What great promise had Jesus made in Matthew 12 v 49–50?*

PRAY ABOUT IT

It can be really disheartening when the people closest to us are the least interested in Jesus. But take heart, Jesus knows what that feels like.

Talk to Him now about it.

THE BOTTOM LINE

When our human families and friends reject us, we have a heavenly Father.

157 Murder in mind

Back in chapter 12 we saw the Pharisees plotting to kill Jesus. In chapter 13 we saw stubborn unbelief, and now we get the first grim example of the opposition that Jesus and His followers will face.

👁 Read Matthew 14 v 1–12

ENGAGE YOUR BRAIN

▶ *Why do you think Herod has this opinion about Jesus? (v2)*

▶ *What had happened to John the Baptist? (v3, 10)*

▶ *Do you think Herod felt guilty? (v1–2)*

This Herod was the son of the child-killer from chapter 2 of Matthew's Gospel, and he was just as sinful and obsessed with his position as his father. As tetrarch (official ruler in the north) he thought he could get away with anything, so he illegally divorced his wife to illegally marry his sister-in-law, and then illegally had John the Baptist beheaded without a trial because he had pointed out that what Herod was doing was wrong. Nice guy. Not.

▶ *Why was John imprisoned? (14v3–5)*

▶ *Why was he killed? (v6–10)*

Herod hated John for pointing out his sin but he was too afraid of the people to kill him immediately. Then, when he does eventually kill John, it's because he is worried about what his guests will think about him.

PRAY ABOUT IT

Ask God to help you to fear Him and His opinion of you rather than what other people might say or think.

THE BOTTOM LINE

God's people will face murderous opposition.

158 | Bread role

Ah, the miracle of the picnic lunch.
Think you know all about it? Think again.

👁 Read Matthew 14 v 13–21

ENGAGE YOUR BRAIN

▶ *Why has Jesus headed for a bit of peace and quiet? (v9–13)*

▶ *Considering all that had recently happened, would you expect Him to welcome a huge crowd?*

▶ *What does this show us about Jesus? (v14)*

▶ *Is the disciples' reaction in verse 15 understandable?*

▶ *Is Jesus' answer? (v16)*

▶ *How many people were in the crowd? (v21)*

Clearly the disciples wouldn't have been carrying enough food for so many people — well over 5,000 (v21) — so why does Jesus ask them to feed the crowd? He's testing them. They've seen Jesus do amazing things before; will they turn to Him in faith now?

Why are the events of verses 17–21 so amazing? List them:

▶ *Who is the only one who can create something out of nothing?*

▶ *So who is Jesus?*

PRAY ABOUT IT

Ask Jesus to help you trust Him and turn to Him in every circumstance. Thank Him for His care and compassion for His people.

THE BOTTOM LINE

Jesus cares and Jesus creates.

159 Focus on Jesus

Another famous miracle today. Before you read it, ask God to help you see it with new eyes. Ask Him to teach you new things.

👁 Read Matthew 14 v 22–36

ENGAGE YOUR BRAIN

▶ *After the mass catering of verses 13–21, Jesus heads for some time out again. Why? (v22–23)*

▶ *Is the disciples' reaction in verses 25–26 understandable?*

Well, yes and no. It was certainly out of the ordinary. But think about what they had witnessed Jesus doing only a few hours earlier.

▶ *What does Jesus say to calm them? (v27)*

Jesus isn't just saying: "Hello, it's me". He's saying: "It is I" or more exactly "I am". Ring any bells?

This is the great "I AM", the God of Israel speaking (Exodus 3 v 14).

▶ *Why should Jesus' words help the disciples not to be afraid?*

▶ *What does Peter's experience show us?*

▶ *Should we be trying to copy him?*

The point is not to try and be like Peter, as some people would tell us, but to realise where he goes wrong. Keep looking at Jesus, keep trusting in Him, don't be put off by looking at anything else.

▶ *What does Peter cry out in Matthew 14 v 30?*

▶ *How quickly does Jesus respond?*

▶ *How do the disciples react? (v33)*

PRAY ABOUT IT

Thank Jesus that we know who He is and that if we ask Him to save us, He will. Thank Him for how much more we can see from this point in history than the disciples understood at that moment in the boat. Pray that He would help us to keep our eyes fixed on Him.

160 Judges: Heroes and zeros

Remember the circle pattern in Judges? The Israelites turn to other gods — God lets their enemies defeat them — Israelites cry out to God — God sends a judge to rescue them — Israelites turn to other gods... Well, it's back.

👁 Read Judges 10 v 1–5

▶ *What are we told about Tola?*

▶ *And Jair?*

We know virtually nothing about these judges, but they led Israel for 45 years. We're told that Tola "saved Israel" after evil Abimelek had tried to destroy it. He's unknown nowadays, but God used him to save His people! All we know about Jair is his 30 sons on 30 donkeys in 30 cities. God chooses all kinds of people to serve Him — famous, unknown, big, small, male, female, shy, confident. That means He can use you to serve Him in a big way. Will you let Him?

👁 Read verses 6–16

▶ *Spot the circle pattern again*
v6:
v6–8:
v10:

▶ *But how did God answer the Israelites' cries?*

▶ *How did the Israelites show they really meant it? (v15–16)*

God was fed up with rescuing His people over and over only for them to abandon Him for fake gods. So He said: Go to those useless gods for help, I won't save you any more. God won't tolerate sin and rejection for ever. And yet He's still so loving. Verse 16 is amazing: "He could bear Israel's misery no longer." God hates to see His people suffer. Even though they'd abandoned Him again and again, He would rescue them once more.

PRAY ABOUT IT

Thank God for His fairness, His hatred of sin and His unbelievable love for His people. Ask Him to help you turn away from false "gods" and live for Him wholeheartedly.

161 Judge Jephthah

God gave Israel another judge to rescue them. Check out how the Israelites treat Jephthah in the same way we saw them treat God yesterday — rejecting him and then turning to him for undeserved help.

👁 Read Judges 10 v 17 – 11 v 11

ENGAGE YOUR BRAIN

▶ What promises did Israel's leaders make? (10 v 18)

▶ Who did they ask to save them from the Ammonites?

▶ Why was this a surprise? (11 v 1–2)

▶ What were they doing right this time? (v10–11)

Here's another unlikely hero. Jephthah was rejected by his own family and living in exile with a band of adventurers. But God uses the most surprising heroes to save His people. Jesus, too, was despised by many and had to flee His home, but God used Him to bring the ultimate rescue to His people.

👁 Read Judges 11 v 12–28

▶ Why did the Ammonites attack Israel? (v13)

▶ What three answers did Jephthah give to the Ammonites' claims?
v15:
v23:
v26–27:

▶ How did the king respond? (v28)

Even though the Ammonites were being ridiculous with their claims on the land, Jephthah tried hard to make peace with them, rather than go to war immediately. But our first reaction to injustice is often to attack, rather than to make peace.

GET ON WITH IT

Who have you fallen out with? How can you try to sort things out in a peaceful way?

PRAY ABOUT IT

Ask God to help you to be calm like Jephthah as you talk to that person. Ask Him to help you to make peace.

162 | Tragic victory

The Ammonites wanted to kick God's people out of their own country. So the Israelites made Jephthah their leader, hoping he'd rescue them and defeat the Ammonites.

👁 Read Judges 11 v 29–33

ENGAGE YOUR BRAIN

▶ *How was Jephthah able to lead the Israelites? (v29)*

▶ *What had he promised God? (v30–31)*

▶ *What did God enable Jephthah to do? (v32–33)*

God gave His Holy Spirit to help Jephthah (as He does to all believers); Jephthah trusted God and made a serious promise to Him; God gave Israel a huge victory. Sounds great, but this story had a tragic ending.

👁 Read verses 34–40

▶ *What shock awaited Jephthah as he arrived home in victory? (v34)*

▶ *Why was this happy event actually so tragic? (v30–31, 35)*

▶ *What was brilliant about his daughter's response? (v36)*

▶ *What was her final request? (v37)*

Heartbreaking. God gave Jephthah and the Israelites a great victory over their enemy, but celebration was short-lived. Because of a rash promise Jephthah had made, he lost his only daughter. Truly tragic.

THINK ABOUT IT

▶ *Do you ever make promises you can't keep?*

▶ *Ever speak before you think?*

▶ *Will you think twice before saying stuff that may have a bad effect in the future?*

PRAY ABOUT IT

Thank God that He gives Christians His Spirit to help them serve Him. Ask Him to help you think before you speak and not make foolish promises.

163 Give God the glory

God rescued His people from their enemies yet again, with Jephthah leading them to victory. But because of a rash promise, he lost his daughter. And now some fellow Israelites are causing trouble.

👁 Read Judges 12 v 1–7

ENGAGE YOUR BRAIN

▶ What was the problem for the Israelite tribe of Ephraim? (v1)

▶ How did Jephthah answer them? (v2–3)

▶ Then what did Jephthah and his men do?

The Ephraimites and the Gileadites were all Israelites — God's people. Yet they attacked each other because of the pride of the Ephraimites. They wanted to be in control; they wanted to get the praise.

THINK ABOUT IT

Do you always want to be the one who's seen to be serving God? Are you prepared to serve God behind the scenes as well as in the limelight? Christians should want God to get the glory, not themselves.

👁 Read verses 8–15

▶ What do we learn about these leaders of Israel?
Ibzan:
Elon:
Abdon:

Some judges have loads written about them. Others (like Ibzan, Elon and Abdon) are barely mentioned. But it doesn't really matter. The book of Judges is all about God, not these people. It's great that God used these men and women to lead His people. But it was God who rescued them. It's God who is in control. And it's God who should get all the praise from His people!

PRAY ABOUT IT

Spend time thanking and praising God for who He is. And for what He's done for His people by sending Jesus to rescue them.

164 Angel delight

Yet again the Israelites turned away from God. This time He punished them by letting the Philistines rule them oppressively for a whopping 40 years. But God is going to give His people another rescuer.

👁 Read Judges 13 v 1–5

ENGAGE YOUR BRAIN

▶ What was the bad news for Manoah and his wife? (v2)

▶ What surprising news did God's angel bring? (v3)

▶ What specific instructions did she have to follow? (v4–5)

▶ What's special about him? (v5)

Yet again, God used someone surprising in His plans. This time it was Manoah and his wife (who was unable to have kids). But the angel of the Lord had news for her, as well as a programme to follow before and after the birth of her miracle baby. We don't even know her name, but God included her in His rescue plans. So never think you're too insignificant for God.

This baby was not allowed to have his hair cut. It was a sign that he was special — set apart to serve God. He would begin to rescue Israel from the Philistines (v5). This baby would grow up to be a saviour of God's people, but he'd only begin the job. David would complete the rescue from the Philistines. This boy, Samson, is only a partial saviour, but he points us to the perfect Saviour — Jesus Christ. Jesus finished the job for good. By His death and resurrection, Jesus offers complete rescue from sin and death.

PRAY ABOUT IT

Ask God to give you the confidence and ability to serve Him, even if you don't understand why He'd ever use you in His plans. Thank Him for sending Jesus, the perfect Saviour, who offers rescue to anyone who trusts in Him.

THE BOTTOM LINE

Samson began to save; Jesus saves completely.

165 Flame and fortune

The angel of the Lord visited Manoah's wife and told her she would miraculously have a baby who she must set apart to serve God. When Manoah heard about it, he wanted to know more.

👁 Read Judges 13 v 6–18

ENGAGE YOUR BRAIN

▶ *What did Manoah ask God? (v8)*

▶ *What did the angel tell him? (v13–14)*

▶ *How much of this was new info?*

▶ *What had Manoah not yet understood? (v16–18)*

The angel of the Lord speaks God's exact words. Manoah and his wife are with God Himself. But they've not realised that yet. They think the angel is just a messenger.

Manoah wanted more instructions about how to bring up their son. But the angel merely repeated the original orders. Sometimes we want to know more from God, but what we really need to hear is what He's already told us. There's no point asking God for more if we're not obeying what He's already taught us.

👁 Read verses 19–25

▶ *What amazing thing happened?*

▶ *How did Manoah react? (v22)*

▶ *But what did his wife know? (v23)*

▶ *What was the happy outcome? (v24–25)*

Manoah realised how awesome and powerful God is. He didn't think he could survive being in God's presence. He was terrified.

We rarely give God the respect He deserves. He's awesome, mighty and terrifying.

PRAY ABOUT IT

Thank God that Jesus has made it possible for us to safely approach Him. Ask Him to help you treat Him with the respect and awe He deserves.

166 | Roars, riddles and relatives

Baby Samson was chosen to serve God in a special way. The scene now switches to Samson as a young man. Time to fight a lion and find a wife.

👁 Read Judges 14 v 1–7

ENGAGE YOUR BRAIN

▶ *What was surprising about Samson's choice of wife? (v2–3)*

▶ *But what did Samson's parents not realise? (v4)*

▶ *Where did Samson's devastating strength come from? (v6)*

The Philistines were ruling over the Israelites oppressively. God's people were not supposed to marry people from other godless nations. But Samson liked the look of a Philistine girl and God used this in His plans to defeat the Philistines. Already we can see the Holy Spirit at work in Samson, giving him the power to kill a lion with his bare hands.

👁 Read verses 8–20

▶ *What did Samson's bet lead to? (v15–17)*

▶ *How did Samson get the clothes needed to pay the winners? (v19)*

▶ *What happened to his bride? (v20)*

This isn't the last time we'll see Samson give in to nagging with disastrous consequences. It seems unfair that Samson killed 30 random people for their clothes, but it was all part of God's plan to punish the Philistines and rescue the Israelites from them. Samson and the Philistines now hate each other. Sparks will fly. More tomorrow.

PRAY ABOUT IT

Weird things happen in this chapter, but God is using all of them in His great rescue plan. Thank God that even in the chaos and confusion of life, He is in complete control, putting His big rescue plan into action.

167 Fox tails and donkey jaws

God's plan to rescue His people from the cruel Philistines is under way. Samson has already fallen out with some Philistines, killed some others and lost his wife to one. He's not happy...

👁 Read Judges 15 v 1–8

ENGAGE YOUR BRAIN

▶ *What provoked Samson's anger against the Philistines? (v1–3)*

▶ *In what bizarre way did he take revenge? (v4–5)*

▶ *How did the Philistines retaliate? (v6)*

▶ *And Samson? (v8)*

👁 Read verses 9–20

▶ *How did the locals react to Samson hiding from the Philistines in their territory? (v11)*

▶ *How did Samson use the situation to his advantage? (v12–15)*

▶ *Yet what nearly killed him? (v18)*

▶ *How did God save him? (v19)*

An even bigger shock than Samson using a donkey jaw as a weapon was Judah's cowardice. This Israelite tribe had always been ready to fight God's enemies (see Judges 1 v 1–4), but here they seemed happy to be ruled by the Philistines! But Samson wasn't happy, and God's Spirit gave him the strength to kill 1,000 enemies.

Samson knew that God had given him this victory. But the hero who'd killed 1,000 enemies was thirsty, weak and near death. So again he had to rely on God to save him. And God miraculously gave Samson the water he needed. If even brave, heroic Samson turned to God for help, then we should do the same. We should rely on Him for the strength to fight against the sin in our lives.

PRAY ABOUT IT

Ask God to give you the strength to serve Him. The strength to fight the sin in your life.

168 Strength and weakness

As part of His rescue plans, God gave Samson the strength to defeat his enemies. But Samson also had weaknesses.

👁 Read Judges 16 v 1–3

ENGAGE YOUR BRAIN

▶ What was Samson's weakness? (also 14 v 1 and 16 v 4)

▶ What danger did it lead to? (v2)

▶ How did he escape? (v3)

Samson was a Nazirite — someone set aside to serve God with His life. But he wouldn't give his whole life to God. Sex was too big a temptation for him and it got him into trouble. But God didn't take Samson's strength away from him and he showed his power once again (v3). Tomorrow we'll see Samson fall for another woman and get into far worse trouble.

THINK ABOUT IT

▶ Do you find sex or porn or sexual temptation too hard to resist?

▶ Do you tend to fall for people who don't share your faith?

"The Philistines were obviously against God, but this non-Christian girl/guy is so nice…" Thinking this way is too dangerous. So many people are slowly enticed away from their love of Jesus by people who may be lovely but don't love Jesus. If you're a believer, rule out the possibility of a relationship with them. Samson's service of God was wrecked, and the devil can do the same to you.

"But there's no harm in being friends… I won't get too involved… I know when to stop…" Don't kid yourself. Playing with temptation is a very dangerous game — as Samson was going to find to his cost.

PRAY ABOUT IT

Talk to God about anything He's challenged you about today. Be honest with Him. Ask for His help. Then take steps to deal with it.

169 | Hair today, gone tomorrow

Samson was the strongest man around. But his strength came from God. His weakness for the opposite sex would get between him and God and make him as weak as a kitten.

👁 Read Judges 16 v 4–14

ENGAGE YOUR BRAIN

▶ *What persuaded Delilah to betray Samson? (v5)*

▶ *What three strength-sapping lies did Samson devise?*
v7:
v11:
v13:

▶ *What did Delilah do each time? (v9, 12, 14)*

Surely, Samson isn't going to give in to Delilah. He knows full well that her design is to hand him over to the Philistines. But Samson was indulging his weakness for women.

👁 Read verses 15–22

▶ *How did Delilah break down Samson's defences? (v15–16)*

▶ *What took away Samson's strength? (v19–20)*

▶ *What did the Philistines do with him? (v21)*

▶ *But what began to happen? (v22)*

As a Nazirite, Samson was set apart to serve God, and showed his devotion by never cutting his hair. Once his hair was cut, the vow was broken, and he was no longer a Nazirite. And God would no longer give him great strength. Samson was supposed to be set apart for God, putting God first in everything. But he put Delilah first, forgetting God. So God left him.

THINK ABOUT IT

Do you put God first when living your life? What could you change so that your life is given to God?

PRAY ABOUT IT

Talk to God about your weaknesses and what gets between Him and you.

170 | Temple of doom

The Philistines have captured weak, baldy Samson and gouged his eyes out. It's time for them to celebrate and thank their god, Dagon, with Samson providing the entertainment.

👁 Read Judges 16 v 23–31

ENGAGE YOUR BRAIN

▷ *Who did they think was behind Samson's downfall? (v23–24)*

▷ *What was Samson's last request? (v26)*

▷ *And his final prayer? (v28)*

▷ *What did this final push achieve? (v30)*

Samson had messed up big time. He'd put women before God and had let his enemies overpower him. Instead of God getting the glory for Samson's strength, this fake god Dagon was being praised.

But Samson hadn't forgotten the Lord and called out to Him one last time. Even when we've let God down, we can still turn to Him. He still listens to us. Even though we disobey Him, God gives us far more than we deserve.

God answered Samson's prayers. Even if Samson's motives were not pure (v28), God's plans were still fulfilled — to punish His enemies and restore glory to His name.

Samson's death brought a sort-of rescue for Israel. Christians now look back to Jesus' death, which achieved a far greater rescue from the enemy, Satan, and his power.

PRAY ABOUT IT

Say sorry to God for specific times you've let Him down or brought disgrace to His name. Thank Him for forgiveness through Jesus and ask Him to use you in His plans despite your weakness.

171 Spiralling out of control

Remember the circle pattern in Judges?

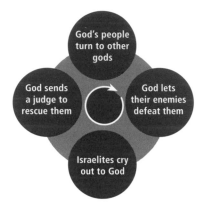

God's people turn to other gods

God sends a judge to rescue them

God lets their enemies defeat them

Israelites cry out to God

👁 Read Judges 17 v 1–6

ENGAGE YOUR BRAIN

▶ *Spot the mistakes...*
v1–2:
v3:
v4:
v5:
v6:

These were God's chosen people, but they were all living for themselves, not for God (v6). And when that happens, things can only get worse, as seen in this little story. Micah and his mother were not trusting in God; they were trusting God *and* manmade idols.

👁 Read verses 7–13

▶ *What offer did Micah make to this young Levite? (v10)*

▶ *What wrong assumption did Micah make? (v13)*

This whole story is a mess. Micah stole. His mum dedicated money to God but then used it to make an idol to worship. And Micah made other stuff to worship and bring him luck. And he thought paying a priest to live with him would put him right with God. This all happened because the Israelites had no godly leader, so everyone did what they wanted (v6).

PRAY ABOUT IT

Without proper guidance, it's easy to stray away from God and think we know best. We don't. Say sorry to God for anything that's an idol in your life. Ask Him to help you to listen to Christian leaders and live God's way, not your own.

172 Idol behaviour

A man called Micah was trying to do religion his own way — making his own idols and employing a Levite to be his live-in priest.

Read Judges 18 v 1–13

ENGAGE YOUR BRAIN

▷ What are we constantly reminded in this part of Judges? (v1; 17 v 6)

▷ What did these warriors seem to do right? (18v5–6)

The Israelites had no king. God should have been their King but they were living for themselves, not for Him. They wanted His blessing (v5) and stayed religious, but it was false religion, worshipping idols and not obeying God. The tribe of Dan had gone against God's orders and failed to conquer Canaan (Judges 1 v 34), so went elsewhere to find somewhere easy to conquer.

Read verses 14–21

▷ What did they do at Micah's place? (v17)

▷ What did the priest choose to do? (v19–20)

Read verses 22–31

▷ What was Micah relying on? (v24)

▷ Describe the Danites? (v25–27)

▷ Who did they worship? (v31)

The Danites must have felt smug — they now had their own territory, their own idols and their own priests. They probably thought God was on their side, yet theirs was false religion, not living God's way at all.

The hardest people to get through to with the gospel are the religiously satisfied. People who think they've done their bit, that God is pleased with them, yet they're not really serving God at all.

PRAY ABOUT IT

Pray for people you know who've created their own religious ideas but haven't turned to Jesus. Ask God to open their eyes and also to give you opportunities to share the gospel.

173 A moral mess

The last few chapters of Judges show just how far God's people had spiralled away from Him — doing things their own way, not His.

👁 Read Judges 19 v 1–21

ENGAGE YOUR BRAIN

▶ *What are we reminded of in verse 1?*

▶ *How does the Levite's dad-in-law show great hospitality? (v3–9)*

▶ *Why didn't they stay in Jebus?*

▶ *Was Gibeah more friendly? (v15)*

▶ *Who gave them a place to stay?*

👁 Read verses 22–30

▶ *What shocking thing happened? (v22–25)*

▶ *What disgusting response did he make to the girl's murder? (v29)*

▶ *How did people react? (v30)*

It seems unbelievable that such a horrific series of events could occur in Israel, among God's chosen people. They should have been living with Him as their King, but they ignored God and indulged in all kinds of sin. That's what happens when people refuse to live with God in charge.

It's easy to be blinded by the horrific nature of this story and miss the point it's making. These were God's people, and they were sinning against Him, because they were living for themselves, not Him.

GET ON WITH IT

In what ways do you refuse to let God be the boss? What sin do you need to kick out? How will you make sure God is your King every day, in every area of your life?

PRAY ABOUT IT

Talk to God about what's really nagging at you today.

THE BOTTOM LINE

When God's not your boss, everything falls apart.

174 Brother against brother

**Yesterday we read the disgusting story of...
actually, I'll let the Levite himself remind
you of what happened.**

👁 Read Judges 20 v 1–17

ENGAGE YOUR BRAIN

▶ *Who was there to hear the story?
(v1–2)*

▶ *How did the Israelites respond to
the Levite's story? (v10–11)*

▶ *What did they demand of the
Israelite tribe, Benjamin? (v13)*

▶ *How did the Benjamites reply?
(v13–14)*

▶ *How did the two armies
compare? (v15–17)*

The unity of Israel here is impressive
— gathering as one army to punish
the people of Gibeah in Benjamin.
But it's tragic that they were uniting
to fight against another Israelite
tribe. God's people were at such a
low point that they were fighting
each other.

The Benjamites stuck up for the
people of Gibeah. They were vastly
outnumbered but they would be
no pushovers, with their 700 left-
handed stone-slingers, causing
havoc among those who weren't
used to attacks from that angle.

👁 Read verses 18–25

▶ *What did the Israelites do right?
(v18, 23)*

▶ *What were the surprising results?
(v21, 25)*

It seems that God was punishing
both Benjamin and the rest of Israel
for rejecting Him. Even though the
Israelites had turned to Him for
guidance, the Benjamites came out
on top in the first two battles. This
reminds us that God's timing isn't
the same as ours: things may not
instantly go our way. But we can be
sure His plans will work out.

PRAY ABOUT IT

Talk to God about any Christians
you're in conflict with.

175 Leave me alone

The people of Gibeah (who were Benjamites) committed rape and murder, so the whole of Israel went to get revenge. Despite being hugely outnumbered, the Benjamites won the first two battles. Round three...

👁 Read Judges 20 v 26–48

ENGAGE YOUR BRAIN

▶ *What did the Israelites do differently this time? (v26)*

▶ *What was there with them? (v27)*

▶ *What did God promise? (v28)*

▶ *What was the result?*

▶ *Who was behind it all? (v35)*

This time, the Israelites showed they were serious about obeying God and needing His help — they fasted and offered sacrifices to God. Maybe after the first two defeats, Israel was repentant for its disobedience, pride and false religion. We're not told why their response was different and why God gave them victory this time, so we can only guess.

The Israelites had the ark of the covenant with them. The ark was the symbol of God's presence with His people. Despite all the setbacks and all their rebellion, God was still with them. But God wasn't with the Benjamites. That was the biggest punishment of all — God leaving them on their own.

Many people choose to be their own boss and ignore God. So the Lord gives them what they want and leaves them to ruin their own lives. There is no greater punishment than God leaving you. That's what hell is — eternal separation from God.

PRAY ABOUT IT

Pray for friends and family who choose to go their own way, not God's. Ask Him to show them the hopelessness of life without Him.

THE BOTTOM LINE

People who continue to reject God get what they ask for — eternity without Him.

176 Edge of extinction

The Israelites attacked the Benjamites and wiped out most of them. But their fury against Benjamin soon turned to sorrow for losing one of the twelve tribes of Israel.

👁 Read Judges 21 v 1–14

ENGAGE YOUR BRAIN

▷ *What had the Israelite men promised in an oath? (v1)*

▷ *Why was this a problem? (v7)*

▷ *How did they solve the problem? (v11–14)*

▷ *But… what? (v14)*

The Israelites tried to wipe out Benjamin for its sin, but now they regretted it and were worried the Benjamites would die out completely. But they couldn't supply the Benjamites with wives because of the oath they'd made. The people of Jabesh-Gilead had refused to fight on the side of the Israelites, so they were punished — killing the men and capturing the female virgins for the Benjamites. Hideous, but they still didn't have enough wives.

👁 Read verses 15–25

▷ *What was their next solution? (v20–21)*

▷ *What are we reminded at the end of Judges? (v25)*

In the last few chapters of Judges, we've seen God's people doing whatever they wanted (v25), rather than living God's way. They deserved to be wiped out by Him, but He was still with them. Unbelievable patience and love from God. Verse 25 reminds us they had no king. In the next book of the Bible, 1 Samuel, they get one…

PRAY ABOUT IT

How have you treated God badly recently, "doing as you see fit"? Admit these things to God. Thank Him for His incredible patience with you and ask for His help in living with Him as King of your life.

177 Psalms: Cross-eyed

Ever been in an exam where it's all going wrong? Ever tried talking to yourself to calm yourself down? (It's the first sign of madness apparently; the second is standing in your garden with custard-filled pants.)

👁 Read Psalm 27

ENGAGE YOUR BRAIN

This psalm is like eavesdropping on David as he tries to calm down by shouting out great truths about God. Find them and list them below:

God is magnificent. Yet He is not distant. He can be found. He uses His power to save, shelter and protect those who seek Him.

GET ON WITH IT

Don't panic! Remember God. Learn verse 1 now — it's a great stress-buster.

Check out verse 3. Facing military action? Probably not. Change the words to fit your life at the moment eg: *"Though arguments with family besiege me…"*

Now, personalise verse 4: *"One thing I ask from the LORD…"*

How did your one request compare to David's? God-centred like his, or self-centred? Despite the carnage surrounding him, David's looking towards God and eternity.

▶ *Is God reliable during troubles? (v5)*

▶ *Is He a good God? (v13)*

PRAY ABOUT IT

God is always reliable, but don't take Him for granted. God would be fully justified in turning us away because of His anger at our sin (v9). We need to be like David, begging for mercy (v7). We need to remember the cross, where God's mercy is poured out through Jesus. Do that now.

178 ⌐ The shield ¬

What gives you the confidence to come to our all-powerful God in prayer? If you're not sure, Psalm 28 should give your prayers a confidence-boost.

👁 Read Psalm 28 v1–2

ENGAGE YOUR BRAIN

▸ *What does David ask for?*

▸ *If God stays silent, what would David be like?*

David can cry out to the Lord because He's approachable. David is lost without God guiding him.

👁 Read verses 3–5

▸ *What's David's shockingly honest request in verse 4?*

▸ *If we ignore God's works, what will happen?*

David's very blunt! When reading stuff like this, remember that David's job, as king, also made him a judge.

God will justly punish evil. However, punishment is escapable. Not through being good, but by respecting God's works. God's ultimate work was Jesus' death in the place of sinners.

👁 Read verses 6–7

▸ *How do verses 6–7 give hope and comfort?*

Realising that God is a fair Judge can be terrifying. The only shield we have against God's judgment is… Him (v7). He hears our cry for mercy, offering protection through Jesus' death. Does that make your heart leap for joy? (It should!) Thank God now.

👁 Read verses 8–9

▸ *How is God described here?*

David's final focus is on God's strength and compassion, leaving no doubt that God will protect His people for ever.

PRAY ABOUT IT

God is approachable and He hears. Make the most of it! Pray about areas where you need help.

179 Stormin' Stuff

How do you picture God? A grandfather figure in white robes and a beard, floating on a cloud? An invisible force? Something else? Let's read Psalm 29 for a reality check.

👁 Read Psalm 29 v 1–9

ENGAGE YOUR BRAIN

▶ *Why should God be given glory? (v2)*

▶ *How would you describe God after reading these verses?*

▶ *What's the only right response to this awesome God? (end of v9)*

David seems to have written this psalm in the middle of a huge and terrifying storm that reminded him of how powerful and terrifying God can be.

"Ascribe" (v1–2) means "give credit where credit's due". And the heavenly beings (v1) are probably angels. These verses point to how incredibly powerful and fearsome God is. He deserves glory and worship for who He is. We should give it to Him.

👁 Read verses 10–11

▶ *How great is God? (v10)*

▶ *People often ask "Where is God?" What's the answer? (v10)*

▶ *How gracious is God? (v11)*

God is so glorious that David's human praise is inadequate. He must call on angels to help worship this God who shakes the earth simply by the power of His voice.

PRAY ABOUT IT

Spend time praising our awesome, fearsome, yet gracious God. And pray verse 11 for Christians in the world's disaster zones.

1 TIMOTHY

Holy housework

Hi Tim!

Having a fantastic time on our hols. Place is lovely. Dad's got sunburn — already! Sorry, forgot to stock up on cat food before we left. Can you get some? (Sardine and trout's her favourite.) Oh, and make sure you tidy up the house before we get back. Right, I'm off to the pool…

Love, Mum x x x

Oh brilliant. They get a suntan while you're grovelling under the sofa, hoovering up cat hairs.

You're getting the flavour of Paul's first letter to Timothy, a young-ish Christian leader who's in charge of a church that has problems. But Paul's not writing to tell Tim about his suntan. He's got more urgent matters in mind, which will involve some pretty tough work for Tim.

Here's how Paul put it:

"Although I hope to come to you soon, I am writing to you with these instructions so that, if I am delayed, you will know how people ought to conduct themselves in God's household." (1 Timothy 3 v 14–15)

Paul had a job for Timothy to do — to sort the house out. Or, to be precise, to sort God's household out. To get the church in order. To get its members behaving and relating to each other as God wants.

Like vacuuming out the cat hairs, it would be a painfully testing job. Tim would have to confront people, challenge them and sometimes tell them off. He'd make enemies. Paul told Timothy it would be like a fight. But it had to be done because the church is God's household — it must live in line with God's truth.

Christians are all part of God's family, the church. So Paul's words matter to us too. Get ready for some spring-cleaning…

180 | False start

Ever talked with someone from a cult? They quote from the Bible and seem to know it better than we do. But it's dangerous: they pick bits from the Bible, and use them wrongly. It's not a new problem; Paul had it in his day too.

👁 Read 1 Timothy 1 v 1–2

ENGAGE YOUR BRAIN

▶ Who appointed Paul to his role as an apostle?

▶ How did he describe his relationship with Timothy?

Paul was an apostle — someone sent out by God to teach people about Jesus. In his letter to Timothy, Paul makes it clear that he's the boss. It's packed full of fatherly advice, commands and encouragement.

👁 Read verses 3–7

▶ What did Paul tell Tim to do? (v3)

▶ What did Paul think of these false teachers? (v6–7)

It was vital that Timothy stuck with this church and stood against the false teachers. Their teaching was based on myths and family trees, not on Jesus and God's word. It led to controversy, not faith.

▶ What does true, godly teaching lead to?

This false teaching was preventing love in the church — love for God and love for each other. Paul said that love comes from:

– a pure heart (made clean by Jesus)

– a good conscience (obeying God, avoiding sin)

– a sincere faith (not just on Sundays).

PRAY ABOUT IT

Ask God to help you stand up to people whose teaching isn't based on God's word and doesn't promote love. Ask Him to help you develop a pure heart, a good conscience and sincere faith in Jesus.

THE BOTTOM LINE

Truthful teaching leads to love.

181 Point of law

How many of the Ten Commandments can you name off the top of your head? (Jot them down, then check in Exodus 20 v 1–17.) What's the point of Old Testament law, such as the Ten Commandments?

👁 Read 1 Timothy 1 v 8–11

ENGAGE YOUR BRAIN

▶ *What does Paul say about the Old Testament ("the law")? (v8)*

▶ *Who is the law really for? (v9–10)*

▶ *So what's the point of Old Testament law?*

The Old Testament isn't there to merely give us brilliant, exciting and gory stories. It's not there for self-righteous teachers like the ones Paul's been warning us against (v7). It is for sinners — ordinary people like us. God's law is God's perfect standard for living, and it shows up our sinfulness. It makes us realise we need to change our ways.

▶ *What's the test for right teaching? (v10–11)*

The Old T shows us God's perfect standards and leads us to the gospel — what God has done for us through Jesus (v11). We can't meet God's sinless standard by ourselves.

Only Jesus dying in our place can make us right with God.

GET ON WITH IT

How can you make sure you read and know more of the Old Testament? Maybe you could ask a leader at church to find you a plan for reading through the whole Bible. Or make one yourself.

PRAY ABOUT IT

Read the Ten Commandments in Exodus 20 v 1–17. Talk to God about the sins you really struggle with.

THE BOTTOM LINE

Hold on to the Old Testament — it points us to Jesus.

182 Amazing grace

Are you excited about the gospel — the truth of what God has done through Jesus? Try to talk about the gospel, non-stop, for one minute. Go on. Paul was massively excited about Jesus Christ...

👁 Read 1 Timothy 1 v 12–14

ENGAGE YOUR BRAIN

▶ *How would you describe Paul's life before he came to know Jesus? (v13)*

▶ *What did he recognise had happened to him? (v14)*

Paul was thrilled to talk about Jesus and what He'd done. Paul knew that before meeting Jesus he'd been a nasty piece of work — hunting down and persecuting Christians. But He'd seen God transform his life, through the faith and love of Jesus.

👁 Read verses 15–17

▶ *Why did Jesus come into the world? (v15)*

▶ *Why did God choose to save someone as evil as Paul? (v16)*

Amazing stuff. Jesus Christ, God's own Son, became human to save disgusting sinners like us! He even forgave an enemy of God like Paul. By doing this, God showed how incredibly gracious, patient and forgiving He is. If Paul can be changed by God, anyone can. Yes, ANYONE. They just have to believe in Jesus and receive eternal life (v16).

PRAY ABOUT IT

Pray for people you can barely imagine becoming Christians. Ask for Jesus to transform their lives through His grace, love and forgiveness.

Then use verse 17 to give God the praise He deserves.

THE BOTTOM LINE

Christ Jesus came into the world to save sinners.

183 Fighting Talk

Yesterday, Paul distracted himself a little, getting all excited about the gospel and the amazing way Jesus had changed his life. But now he's back to telling Tim what the deal is.

👁 Read 1 Timothy 1 v 18–20

ENGAGE YOUR BRAIN

▶ What did Timothy have to live up to? (v18)

▶ How did Paul describe Timothy's difficult task? (end of v18)

We don't know what the *prophecies* about Timothy were. But we know that there was expectation on his shoulders. People expected him to serve God and fight against God's enemies — especially false teachers who led people away from Jesus.

▶ What must Tim do? (v19a)

▶ What happens if we let go of our faith and our obedience to God? (v19b)

Paul urged Tim to hold on to his faith and to keep a good conscience by living in a way that pleased God. To let go of these two things would be disastrous for his faith.

It was vital that Timothy stuck to his task, and it's vital that Christians today do the same. It's difficult in a world full of so many distractions and temptations. But we're in a battle, and we need to make sure we're fighting for the right side. God's side.

PRAY ABOUT IT

1. Pray for Christian friends — that they'll keep on fighting, holding on to their faith, and living God's way.

2. Pray for anyone you know whose faith has been shipwrecked.

THE BOTTOM LINE

Fight the good fight.

184 | Pray for everyone

In Timothy's church, it seems people were teaching the lie that the gospel — the truth of God's great rescue — was only for certain people. Paul was going to blow that theory out of the water.

👁 Read 1 Timothy 2 v 1–2

ENGAGE YOUR BRAIN

▶ *What does Paul urge Timothy to pray? (v2)*

▶ *Who should he pray this for?*

Paul says to pray "for all people". Bring variety into your prayers — pray for specific needs, general problems, with thanksgiving… Pray for all people — everyone needs to be saved.

PRAY ABOUT IT

Paul also encourages us to pray for "all those in authority." Make a prayer list and pray for at least one of these people/groups every day.

👁 Read verses 3–7

▶ *Why pray for everyone that they'll come to know Jesus? (v3–4)*

Paul gives us stacks of reasons to pray for people:

1. It pleases God that we pray (v3).

2. He wants *all people* to be saved (v4)

3. There's only one God (v5); people need to know this.

4. There's only one way to God — through Jesus (v5).

5. Jesus died for *everyone* (v5)

6. Paul preached to Gentiles (non-Jews) as well as Jews. The gospel is for *everyone*.

GET ON WITH IT

The great news of Jesus is for everyone, so tell them. And get praying for them — for friends, family, enemies, teachers, presidents, plumbers — everyone. Start praying right now. Use verses 1–2 to help.

THE BOTTOM LINE

Pray for everyone — they all need Jesus.

185 ¦ Controversial stuff

Are you more likely to get on your high horse with your opinions or dive under a table to dodge an argument? Paul has something controversial to say. Especially if you're female.

👁 Read 1 Timothy 2 v 8–10

ENGAGE YOUR BRAIN

▶ *What are men to do? (v8)*

▶ *In what ways should women aim to be attractive? (v10)*

Paul's not saying that prayer is only for men. Or that only women need to do good deeds. Paul is saying that *everyone everywhere* must pray. They should pray about difficult situations instead of resorting to anger, arguments and aggression (v8). And *everyone everywhere* should live attractive lives rather than trying to impress others with their appearance.

👁 Read verses 11–15

▶ *What is not a woman's role in church, according to Paul? (v12)*

▶ *What reasons does he give? (v13)*

These women wouldn't accept the teaching of the church's leaders and pushed themselves forward.

Paul says it's not right for women to teach men in church. It would reverse God's created order (v13). Paul isn't saying women have no contribution to make in church — He's saying that men and women should stick to their God-given roles.

It's not all negative! Paul says: *"A woman should learn."* This was controversial too, as many Jewish leaders wouldn't let women be taught from God's word at all.

TALK IT THROUGH

▶ *How does today's teaching make you feel? Why?*

Write down any questions you have and ask an older Christian.

THE BOTTOM LINE

Ask God to help you understand anything that has angered or confused you. Ask Him to help you trust Him and obey His word.

186 Leading example

What do you look for in church leaders? What do you expect them to be like? What do you expect them not to do? Circle the ideas below that match your own.

Church leaders should be:

godly   guitar-playing   cool
single   married   male   female
bearded   middle-aged   under 30
parents   preachers   Christian
kind   suit-wearing   organised
full of Bible knowledge   hospitable

Church leaders should NOT be:

under 30   ugly   rude
new Christians   old Christians
male   female   cool
untrained   out of touch
argumentative
lacking in Bible knowledge

👁 Read 1 Timothy 3 v 1–7

ENGAGE YOUR BRAIN

- ▶ *How does Paul describe the job of a church leader? (v1)*

- ▶ *What must leaders be like? (v2–7)*

- ▶ *Why do they need a good reputation outside the church?*

In the New Testament, church leaders are called "overseers" or "elders" or "pastors". Different names, same job. Paul was clear on what they should be like: responsible, respectable, self-controlled, hospitable, good teachers, with a good reputation. Not violent, argumentative, hard-drinking, money-chasing, proud or brand new Christians.

That's a long list. No wonder Paul says that anyone who sets their heart on church leadership "desires a noble task" (v1). These guys deserve our respect and support.

PRAY ABOUT IT

Pray for your church and youth leaders. Ask God to help them keep going and to help them with the things they really struggle with.

187 | Serving suggestions

Timothy's church had a problem with false teachers. So Paul's been telling Tim what to look for in his leaders. Now he turns to deacons — others who serve in the church.

👁 Read 1 Timothy 3 v 8–13

ENGAGE YOUR BRAIN

🔽 What must those who serve in church do? (v9)

🔽 What are the great benefits of serving the church? (v13)

It's important that those who serve Jesus in their church live a godly life. They must be people who deserve respect, not heavy-drinkers or self-promoters. OK, they will mess up sometimes, but they must strive to live lives that please God.

GET ON WITH IT

🔽 How will you serve in your church?

🔽 Is there anything you need to change in your life, so you can serve God even better?

👁 Read verses 14–16

🔽 Why did Paul write all these instructions?

🔽 How does he describe the church? (v15)

🔽 How does he describe Jesus?(v16)

The church (all Christians) are "God's household" — God's family. They are the "foundation of the truth." Did you realise you were part of something so amazing and important? The church holds on to and spreads the great truth about Jesus (v16).

PRAY ABOUT IT

Ask God to help you get involved in serving the church — other Christians. Ask Him to help you with anything that's getting in the way of you serving Him well.

188 Don't eat that; don't marry him

Heard any weird ideas about what it means to be a true Christian? Anyone told you that you need to do (or stop doing) certain things to be accepted by God? Paul stomps on such wrong teaching...

👁 Read 1 Timothy 4 v 1–2

ENGAGE YOUR BRAIN

▶ *How does Paul describe false teachers? (v2)*

▶ *Where does such misleading teaching really come from? (v1b)*

These guys were calling themselves Christians but were teaching seriously wrong views that were leading people away from Jesus, eventually abandoning their faith. Such false teaching and lies are evil and must be stamped out, says Paul.

👁 Read verses 3–5

▶ *What were they teaching?*

▶ *What's around today that's like this teaching?*

▶ *How does Paul answer this negative teaching? (v4–5)*

By saying "Don't get married" or "Don't eat this", these guys were saying "You get saved by what you do and don't do." Complete rubbish.

Only faith in Christ can make us right with God. If anyone says you have to do this or not do that to be a Christian, they're lying. Yes, we want to do what's right and live God's way, but that's a sign of gratitude and obedience to God. It doesn't save us. Only Jesus can do that.

PRAY ABOUT IT

Spend time praising God for some of the great things He's created (including tasty food and marriage!). Ask Him to help you not to be misled by wrong teaching.

THE BOTTOM LINE

It's not down to what you do or don't do. It's all down to Jesus.

MATTHEW

King of controversy

Many people picture Jesus as a laid-back, gentle hippy. Always preaching love and tolerance. Always being nice. Never being controversial or offensive. But that's not the Jesus Matthew tells us about.

MEET JESUS

As we immerse ourselves in Matthew's story, we'll meet a Jesus who regularly clashes with religious authorities, offends "holy" people and points out hypocrisy. We'll meet a Jesus who goes against what society expects — he meets with and accepts those whom "respectable" people shunned and avoided.

We'll meet a Jesus who conquered demons. We'll meet a Jesus who said unpopular and controversial things about religion, divorce, and heaven and hell.

We'll meet a Jesus who didn't come to be warm and fuzzy all the time. We'll meet a Jesus who said shocking things and made people feel uncomfortable — whom people hated because His words were hard to swallow. We'll meet a Jesus who came to die.

As Matthew takes us into the intimate life story of Christ, we won't meet a wishy-washy do-gooder. We'll meet the all-powerful, Satan-slaying Son of God. This is someone we must take very seriously. Because, if you let Him, Jesus will change your life.

189 | Blind faith

The Pharisees thought they were the true leaders of God's people. They thought they were God's favourites. But Jesus was about to show them up for who they really were. The controversy kicks off immediately.

⊚ Read Matthew 15 v 1–9

ENGAGE YOUR BRAIN

▶ What accusation was made? (v2)

▶ How did Jesus respond? (v3)

▶ How were these men being hypocritical? (v4–6)

▶ What was the sad truth about their religion and teaching? (v8–9)

Jesus pointed out how the Pharisees made up ridiculous rules that actually stopped people from serving God and honouring their parents! He showed up their "religion" for the sham it was — they were all talk and their hearts were not devoted to God (v8).

⊚ Read verses 10–20

▶ What were the disciples worried about? (v12)

▶ How did Jesus describe the Pharisees? (v14)

▶ What did Jesus say makes people unclean? (v18–20)

The Pharisees were focusing on man-made rules. But they weren't concerned about their hearts, their thoughts or their words — the important stuff. These supposedly holy leaders were like the blind trying to lead the blind, and the result would be spiritual disaster.

THINK IT OVER

▶ In what ways do you concentrate on keeping rules or appearing good rather than dealing with your evil thoughts?

▶ What specific stuff do you need God's help to deal with?

PRAY ABOUT IT

Talk to God about these things. Thank Jesus for coming into the world to deal with the problem of our hearts.

190 Gone to the dogs

More controversy today. A woman comes up to Jesus, begging him to heal her demon-possessed daughter. What do you think Jesus' response will be?

👁 Read Matthew 15 v 21–28

ENGAGE YOUR BRAIN

▶ *Where was this woman from? (v21–22)*

▶ *What was surprising about Jesus' response? (v23)*

▶ *And the disciples' response? (v23)*

▶ *Why wouldn't Jesus heal her daughter? (v24)*

▶ *What do you think verse 26 means?*

▶ *And what was the women's brilliant answer? (v27)*

▶ *What happened in the end? (v28)*

Jesus was now in a Gentile (non-Jewish) area. The Jews were God's chosen people. So when this Gentile woman asked Jesus for help, His answer was simple — *I came for the Jews, not Gentiles.* But the woman seemed to know Jesus' mission was far wider reaching than to just the tiny Jewish nation.

The message of Jesus is for everyone. All types of people from every kind of background can get to know God through Jesus. His death made it possible for anyone to be part of God's chosen people.

GET ON WITH IT

▶ *If Jesus' message is for everyone, what does that mean for you?*

▶ *For people you see regularly?*

▶ *What should Christians do?*

▶ *What will YOU do, exactly?*

PRAY ABOUT IT

Thank God for the people who told you about Jesus. Now talk to God about your answers to the above four questions.

THE BOTTOM LINE

The message of Jesus is for everyone.

191 Sign language

Today's story sounds very familiar. Jesus had recently fed over 5,000 Jewish people with a few loaves and fish. This time, He does the same thing for Gentiles.

👁 Read Matthew 15 v 29–39

ENGAGE YOUR BRAIN

▶ What did Jesus do on the mountainside? (v30)

▶ How did these Gentiles react? (v31)

▶ What did this show about Jesus? (v32)

These non-Jews saw Jesus' miracles and were amazed. They even praised the God of Israel! Unheard of! As we saw yesterday, Jesus' message is for everyone. He has compassion (v32) for everyone.

👁 Read Matthew 16 v 1–4

▶ What did the Jewish leaders demand? (v1)

▶ How did Jesus ridicule their request? (v2–3)

▶ How did He describe them? (v4)

▶ What sign would He give them?

The Pharisees were the ultra-religious group who made up loads of extra rules to live by. The Sadducees were another Jewish group, who said there was no life after death. The Pharisees and Sadducees were opposed to each other's teaching but they were united in hating Jesus.

Jesus had done so many incredible things already — seeing one more miracle would not have caused these stubborn men to accept Jesus. They were out to get Him. But Jesus saw through their demands. The only sign they would see would be Jesus dying and rising again three days later.

PRAY ABOUT IT

These men were seen as holy and religious yet they rejected Jesus. Instead, Jesus would save many outsiders. Thank God that Jesus came for outsiders like us. Pray that you won't assume you're good enough for God.

192 | Stale bread

The disciples had seen Jesus feed thousands of people with just a tiny amount of bread (and fish). Twice. And they'd seen the Pharisees and Sadducees fail to believe Jesus. But the disciples still missed the point...

👁 Read Matthew 16 v 5-7

ENGAGE YOUR BRAIN

▶ *What mistake had the disciples made? (v5)*

▶ *What did Jesus warn them? (v6)*

▶ *But what were they more worried about? (v7)*

It's like a sitcom joke. These twelve guys had just witnessed two incredible food miracles, with basketfuls of bread left over. And what do they do? Leave their packed lunch at home!

So Jesus takes this opportunity to warn them about false teaching. But the disciples miss the point. Again.

👁 Read verses 8-12

▶ *Why didn't they need to worry about having no food? (v8-10)*

▶ *What should they be more concerned about? (v11-12)*

Yeast is used in baking bread, to help dough rise. You add a little bit of yeast and it spreads through the whole batch of dough. In the same way, wrong teaching, from religious leaders who refused to recognise Jesus' identity, was getting everywhere. See how Jesus sadly had to describe the disciples (v8).

THINK IT OVER

▶ *In what areas of life do you need to trust Jesus more?*

▶ *Do you believe everything you're taught about Christianity and spirituality?*

▶ *How can you check that what you're being taught is true?*

PRAY ABOUT IT

Ask God to help you trust in Him to provide for your needs. And pray that you won't fall for false teaching that leads you away from God.

193 Jesus jigsaw

Since the beginning of his book, Matthew has been building up a picture of who Jesus is. Like a jigsaw — slotting the different parts of the picture together. But the disciples couldn't put the picture together. Until now.

👁 Read Matthew 16 v 13–17

ENGAGE YOUR BRAIN

▶ What was the public opinion about Jesus ("the Son of Man")? (v13–14)

▶ What did Peter realise? (v16)

▶ What did Jesus think of this answer? (v17)

Peter realised that Jesus was both God and human in one person. God's chosen Messiah was in town: the Rescuer and Ruler who God had promised. This is the one the Old Testament had pointed to; the one everyone was waiting for!

👁 Read verses 18–20

▶ What did Jesus say about Peter and about the church? (v18)

▶ What surprising thing did Jesus say to His disciples? (v20)

Verse 18 means Jesus will build His church on the apostles' (Peter and co) true teaching about Jesus. And the church will never be destroyed by the devil!

Peter finally realised who Jesus is but Jesus told His disciples not to tell anyone. The Jews expected the Christ to be a mighty warrior who'd free them from the Romans. Imagine what would have happened if word got out that the Christ was here! But Jesus wasn't that kind of Messiah. The disciples had to learn why Jesus had come before they could start talking about Him. That comes tomorrow.

PRAY ABOUT IT

Tell Jesus your own reply to verse 15. Don't just repeat the "right" words, tell Him everything. Ask Him to help you understand.

THE BOTTOM LINE

Jesus is the Christ, the Son of the living God.

194 Cross words

Peter must have been feeling great — he'd finally realised that Jesus is God's Son, the Christ. And Jesus gave Peter a great job. But there was loads Peter still hadn't grasped about Jesus. Vital stuff.

👁 Read Matthew 16 v 21–23

ENGAGE YOUR BRAIN

▶ What had Jesus come to do? (v21)

▶ What do you think of Peter's reaction?

▶ What did Jesus think of it? (v23)

Earlier, the devil had tried to tempt Jesus to abandon His mission. This mission required Jesus to die for sinners like us. It's understandable that Peter didn't want his friend and master to suffer and die. But Peter wasn't seeing the big picture. Jesus came to die on the cross. It was essential and would be glorious.

👁 Read verses 24–28

▶ What does Jesus expect of His disciples? (v24–25)

▶ Why is it vital to make the right decision about believing and following Jesus? (v27)

Back then, if you saw someone carrying a cross, you knew they were heading towards their death. "Denying yourself" means exactly that: giving up the right to live. Being prepared to live for Jesus, whatever the cost. Even if that means suffering or death.

There's no other way to follow Jesus. He went to the cross and He expects us to give everything for Him. It's the route to life; true life.

PRAY ABOUT IT

Maybe it's time to ask God's forgiveness, and to ask Him to help you realise who Jesus really is. And to get back to making Jesus everything you live for. Talk to God about it right now.

THE BOTTOM LINE

If anyone would come after me, he must deny himself and take up his cross and follow me.

195 Mountain tension

Chapter 16 was a rollercoaster for the disciples. A real high point was realising who Jesus is. A downer was when they learned what He'd come to do. Then the twist of what it would mean to follow Him. Now for more thrills and spills.

👁 Read Matthew 17 v 1–8

ENGAGE YOUR BRAIN

▶ *What amazing thing did Peter, James and John witness? (v2)*

▶ *Who else was present? (v3)*

▶ *What did God the Father say about Jesus? (v5)*

▶ *And what must Jesus' followers do? (v5)*

Jesus was "transfigured": His whole appearance changed (v2). Ever looked directly at the sun? That's how Jesus was — dazzlingly pure, glorious, unique. And then they heard God's voice, confirming that Jesus really was His Son. So they should listen to Him. And so should we.

👁 Read verses 9–13

▶ *What did Jewish law experts claim? (v10)*

▶ *What was Jesus' answer to this? (v11–13)*

The Jews believed (from Malachi 4 v 5) that Elijah would return before the arrival of God Himself. Jesus says that John the Baptist was the "Elijah" who prepared the way for Jesus. Most of the people didn't realise his importance, just as they rejected Jesus and would kill Him (Matthew 17 v 12).

GET ON WITH IT

▶ *How can you make sure you don't make the same mistake and ignore Jesus?*

▶ *How will you make sure you listen to His words?*

▶ *Which of his commands do you need to take more seriously?*

PRAY ABOUT IT

Talk to God about your answers.

196 Demon disarray

Peter, James and John are walking down the mountain with Jesus, having just seen something amazing. But they're soon brought back to earth with a thump.

👁 Read Matthew 17 v 14–18

ENGAGE YOUR BRAIN

▷ *What was the double problem?*
v15:
v16:

▷ *What was Jesus' reaction to His disciples' inability to heal the boy?*

▷ *Was it a problem for Jesus? (v18)*

A high spiritual experience is often followed by a crashing low. Here, Jesus came down the mountain to see His disciples in a mess.

👁 Read verses 19–21

▷ *Why couldn't they drive out the demon?*

▷ *What can real faith in God achieve?*

The disciples should have trusted Jesus' power and authority. Even a little faith can move obstacles that seem immovable. God can do great things through us if we trust Him to.

👁 Read verses 22–23

▷ *What did Jesus tell His disciples again? How did they react?*

It's incredibly sad that Jesus was betrayed and had to suffer and die. But we don't need to be grief-filled like the disciples. We know that Jesus died to rescue us and He was raised back to life (v23) and rules in heaven!

PRAY ABOUT IT

Say sorry to God for the times when you've shown no faith in Him. Ask Him to increase your faith and trust in Him so you can serve Him better. And thank Him for Jesus' death and resurrection.

THE BOTTOM LINE

Real faith can move mountains.

197 Fishy funds

Ever heard people complain about paying taxes? Maybe you pay them yourself and you notice the huge chunk they take out of your wages. At least that's something Jesus, God's Son, doesn't need to bother with. Well, actually...

👁 Read Matthew 17 v 24–26

ENGAGE YOUR BRAIN

▶ *What did the tax collectors quiz Peter about? (v24)*

▶ *What's the answer to Jesus' strange question? (v25–26)*

▶ *Any idea what point Jesus was making?*

Of course kings don't collect taxes from their own sons. That would be crazy. Jewish people had to pay temple tax. The money was used to look after God's temple. Jesus was God's Son, so it was ridiculous to ask Him to pay taxes for His Father's temple. But most people didn't believe Jesus was God's Son.

👁 Read verse 27

▶ *How did Jesus get the money to pay the tax?*

▶ *Why did Jesus pay the tax?*

The money that Jesus paid would go to the temple and to the Jewish leaders who would eventually torture and kill Him. Jesus was contributing towards His own death. But He knew He had to die as part of His Father's perfect plans. And He paid the taxes so as not to offend anyone. Sometimes we have to give up our rights if it helps God's work.

THINK IT OVER

▶ *Do you sulk or put up a fight when it comes to paying money you owe?*

▶ *Or what about doing chores?*

▶ *How does your attitude affect how others view your faith?*

PRAY ABOUT IT

Ask God to help you make wise decisions and not cause unnecessary trouble or offence. And thank Him for Jesus' great wisdom and power.

198 Who's the greatest?

Jesus talked last time about tax, where big guys in authority grab money from little people. Maybe that's what nudged the disciples to ask about authority — who are the big guys in God's kingdom?

👁 Read Matthew 18 v 1–4

ENGAGE YOUR BRAIN

- ▶ *What surprising thing did Jesus do when they asked this big question? (v1–2)*

- ▶ *What's shocking about Jesus' words? (v3)*

- ▶ *So who's the greatest? (v4)*

Children were unimportant in that society: to be looked after, but not to be looked up to. Jesus' action (v2) was shocking, His teaching (v3–4) even more so. Disciples should be like children — insignificant, unimpressive, willing to be nobodies.

Such a change isn't just for those who already follow Jesus. It's the only way to become a Christian — realising you're nothing without Jesus.

👁 Read verses 5–6

- ▶ *So what should we do for humble Christians? (v5)*

- ▶ *But what's the big warning? (v6)*

Christians shouldn't put themselves first. They must be welcoming towards other believers, not leading other Christians astray.

GET ON WITH IT

Write down specific ways you can…

a) show more humility

b) be more welcoming and inclusive

c) stop doing stuff that causes others to sin

PRAY ABOUT IT

Only you know what you need to talk to God about today.

THE BOTTOM LINE

Be childlike — humble, welcoming, and innocent.

199 Cut it out

More controversial teaching from Jesus. He's not used many picture stories recently. But today we've got arm chopping, eye gouging and sheep chasing!

👁 Read Matthew 18 v 7–9

ENGAGE YOUR BRAIN

▶ *If something in your life causes you to sin, what should you do with it?*

▶ *Why?*

Hacking legs off and throwing them in the river sounds drastic! But Jesus isn't saying we should actually chop off body bits! He's saying we must try to *cut out* the things in our life that cause us to sin.

GET ON WITH IT

▶ *What do you read/watch/listen to that you shouldn't?*

▶ *Which friendships lead you towards sin?*

▶ *What exactly will you do to cut sin out of your life?*

👁 Read verses 10–14

▶ *What should be our attitude towards younger/weaker Christians? (v10)*

▶ *Why? (v14)*

Sometimes we're also tempted to look down on and gossip about Christians who are wandering away from God. But God never gives up on them (v14), so neither should we. Pray for such people and think of ways to bring them back.

PRAY ABOUT IT

Ask God to help you to cut out from your life those things that cause you to sin. Then spend time praying for younger Christians you know, that they'll grow as believers. And for friends who are wandering away from God's way.

200 Clashing Christians

Would you forgive a Christian friend if they... a) wore embarrassing clothes in your company? b) borrowed and broke your phone? c) upset your closest friend? d) humiliated you publicly? e) apologised for any of these?

How big is your forgiveness? Jesus talked last time about care for "little ones" — ordinary Christians. Now He says what to do when they mess up and commit sin.

👁 Read Matthew 18 v 15–18

ENGAGE YOUR BRAIN

▶ *If another Christian wrongs you, what should you do first? (v15)*

▶ *And if that fails? (v16)*

▶ *And if that fails? (v17)*

Don't rush up to others to retaliate. Our main concern shouldn't be for revenge or getting what's best for ourselves. We should want to help other Christians when they sin, so that they keep living God's way. If you talk over your differences and the other person continues sinning, only then should you bring in other people. We must pray about the situation too...

👁 Read verses 19–20

▶ *What's the great promise here?*

▶ *How does verse 20 transform small Christian meetings?*

Presumably, the two or three were meeting to pray for the wrongdoer. But the principle goes wider — where a handful of Christians gather in Jesus' name, agree and pray, then He is with them. And God will answer!

We can sometimes get down if our youth group or school Christian meeting only has a few people in it. But even in tiny groups, Jesus is there with His followers!

PRAY ABOUT IT

Pray for any Christian friends you've fallen out with. Ask God to help you deal with the situation in a godly way. And pray for Christian groups and meetings you attend. That you'd remember Jesus is with you.

201 Don't forget to forgive

How forgiving are you? If someone wrongs you or upsets you, how willing are you to forgive them? And what if someone repeatedly lets you down?

👁 Read Matthew 18 v 21–22

ENGAGE YOUR BRAIN

🅓 *How many times should we forgive someone?*

Jesus doesn't mean literally that number of times. It's hard to forgive people who've upset us or treated us really badly. Especially if it happens again and again. But Jesus says we should forgive them over and over, without end. And here's why.

👁 Read verses 23–35

🅓 *How big was the cancelled debt?*

🅓 *What punishment should he have received? (v25)*

🅓 *What did the man do with his own debtor? (v28–30)*

🅓 *What should he have done? Why? (v32–33)*

🅓 *So what happened to him? (v34)*

🅓 *What's the message to us? (v35)*

It seems crazy. This guy is let off a staggeringly huge debt that would have led to him losing his family. But when someone owes him a small amount, he goes bananas.

This is a picture of Christians. They deserved death and hell but, because of Jesus, God forgives them completely. When people wrong us or upset us, it's nowhere near as bad as how we've treated God. So we should forgive them, just as God forgives us. Over and over again.

GET ON WITH IT

Who do you need to show forgiveness to? Which broken relationship do you need to mend?

PRAY ABOUT IT

Thank God for His incredible forgiveness. Ask Him to help you show His attitude of forgiveness when people mess you around.

202 | The D-word

"There are two sides to every argument and they're usually married to each other." Sadly, for many, marriage is no laughing matter. Many marriages are in trouble or end in divorce. It can tear families apart.

👁 Read Matthew 19 v 1–6

ENGAGE YOUR BRAIN

▶ *What did the Pharisees want to know? (v3)*

▶ *How did Jesus answer them?*

The Pharisees were hoping Jesus would disagree with Old Testament teaching and get Himself in trouble. Jesus simply pointed out God's plan for marriage — a husband and wife are joined together and shouldn't be separated.

👁 Read verses 7–9

▶ *What was their next question, and Jesus' answer? (v7–8)*

▶ *What controversial thing did Jesus say about divorce? (v9)*

The Pharisees claimed that Moses commanded divorce. Jesus replied: *Not at all. He'd only reluctantly permitted it.* Like it or not, God's principle is that marriage is for life.

Anyone who gets divorced thinking there's an escape clause is wrong. Jesus only allows divorce if your partner commits adultery.

👁 Read verses 10–12

▶ *What conclusion did the disciples come to? (v10)*

▶ *Did Jesus agree?*

Jesus says marriage isn't for everyone — so we shouldn't obsess about finding a husband/wife. Some people will serve God better if they stay single. Others will serve Him in their marriages.

PRAY ABOUT IT

Pray for people who are suffering because of family break-up (maybe that's you). Ask God to be at the centre of their lives. And pray for married couples you know — that they will never want to give up.

203 Money talks

"What must I do to get eternal life?" "If I keep the Ten Commandments, will that get me into heaven?" How would you answer these questions? Let's check out Jesus' answers.

👁 Read Matthew 19 v 13–22

ENGAGE YOUR BRAIN

▶ What's wrong with the man's question? (v16)

▶ How did Jesus answer him? (v17–19)

▶ What did the guy claim? (v20)

▶ How did Jesus pull the rug out from under his feet? (v21)

▶ What was this man's main problem? (v22)

This young man rates himself highly — he rolls up thinking what good deed he can do to gain eternal life. Jesus' reply (v17): *You want to know about good and bad? Try God's standards then — to be good enough for Him means keeping the Ten Commandments. Can you do that?*

Jesus then gives him commandments 5–9 and a summary: "Love your neighbour as yourself."

▶ Could he have kept all these?

▶ Could you?

None of us is good enough to earn eternal life. We've all sinned, and sin stops us being good enough. Only Jesus can help us, if we turn to Him for forgiveness, coming to Him like a little child who has nothing to offer (v13–15).

This man actually seems to believe he's kept God's commands. But Jesus knows better: *You want to be perfect? Then cut your love of money by giving it away and set your heart on following me.*

Money, relationships, job, sport, studies — none of these should get in the way of your love for Jesus.

PRAY ABOUT IT

Talk to God honestly about anything He's put on your heart today.

204 Mission possible

Yesterday we met a young guy who seemed to have it all — he was rich and lived a good life. But he wouldn't put Jesus first. Sad. Jesus now has more to say on wealth and what He expects from His followers.

👁 Read Matthew 19 v 23–26

ENGAGE YOUR BRAIN

▶ *What controversial thing did Jesus say? (v23–24)*

▶ *How did the disciples react? (v25)*

▶ *And what other incredible truth did Jesus speak? (v26)*

The common view was that if you were rich, it must be because God liked you. But money can take over people's lives and become more important to them than God. That doesn't mean rich people *can't* become Christians. **Nothing** is impossible for God. But we can't earn our way into heaven (with money or living a good life). Only Jesus can rescue us.

👁 Read verses 27–30

▶ *What does Jesus expect from His followers? (v27, 29)*

▶ *What will be their reward? (v29)*

▶ *When will they receive it? (v28)*

Being a Christian is costly. Sometimes we'll lose friends because we love Jesus. We also have to turn away from the things that used to be more important to us than Jesus. But one day, when Jesus returns, we'll be rewarded far more than we could ever imagine! The Christian life isn't easy, but it's definitely worth it.

THINK IT OVER

▶ *Do you care too much about money and possessions?*

▶ *What can you do to make sure God is more important to you than other stuff?*

▶ *In what situations will it help to remember that nothing is impossible for God?*

205 | 1 Timothy: Holy Housework

Back to 1 Timothy, where Timothy had to deal with false teachers in his church. A tough task. Like all of us who are trying to serve God, Timothy needed encouragement and a shove in the right direction.

👁 Read 1 Timothy 4 v 6–10

ENGAGE YOUR BRAIN

- ▶ *How does Paul describe the wrong teaching? (v7)*

- ▶ *Why should Tim drive out these false teachers? (v6)*

- ▶ *Why is godly living even better than a good body? (v8)*

Superb encouragement and advice from Paul: If you want to be a good minister, Timothy, carry on teaching the truth. Have nothing to do with teaching that doesn't come from God's word — it's all old wives' tales.

Instead, train yourself to be godly. It will have a huge impact on your life, and unlike physical fitness, the benefits will last for eternity.

We have to work at it. It will be a struggle (v10a). But it's not all down to us — it's down to God, who saves those who put their hope in Him.

GET ON WITH IT

- ▶ *How hard are you working at living a godly life?*

Devise a **training routine** to help you grow. Set times when you'll read the Bible, pray, help out at church, meet with other Christians to read the Bible and pray together.

PRAY ABOUT IT

Have you planned your training routine yet? Do it now. And then talk to God about it, asking Him to help you stick at it.

THE BOTTOM LINE

Train yourself to be godly.

206 Too much too young?

Ever been looked down on by older Christians because you're young? Ever felt you're a bit too young to make a real impact as a Christian? Paul has some wise words for you.

Read 1 Timothy 4 v 11–12

ENGAGE YOUR BRAIN

▷ Should somebody's age get in the way of spreading the gospel?

▷ In which areas should you set an example for other believers?

When we're young, we can sometimes be uneven in our faith — concentrating on certain parts of our Christian lives, but neglecting others. Paul says: *Sort your whole life out, so that you're an example to others.* Then your age won't be an issue.

GET ON WITH IT

Speech – how do you need to change the way you talk?

Conduct – how could the way you live be a better example of godly living?

Love – do you show your care for others (not just close friends) in practical ways?

Faith — what do you need to trust God about? That you're saved? That He's with you? That He hears your prayers?

Purity — what parts of your life are not pure? What will you do about it?

Read verses 13–16

Paul's advice is for church leaders. But verse 16 applies to all of us: "Watch your life and doctrine (your beliefs) closely." We need to keep checking that we're living lives that please God. And we need to make sure that our beliefs are in line with God's word.

PRAY ABOUT IT

Look back at GET ON WITH IT. Talk through your answers with God.

THE BOTTOM LINE

Set an example in speech, conduct, love, faith and purity.

207 Family fortunes

Do you get on well with older Christians?
How do you treat people younger than you ?
What about the way you are with the opposite sex?

👁 Read 1 Timothy 5 v 1–2

ENGAGE YOUR BRAIN

▶ *How should you not treat older Christians?*

▶ *What should your relationship with older Christians be like?*

When you're young it's easy to tell people exactly what you think of them, or be a bit cheeky. Paul says: *Show older Christians proper respect.* Show them the same respect, politeness and love you should show your parents. If you think they've done wrong, don't tell them off in a disrespectful way.

▶ *How do your attitudes towards older Christians need to change?*

👁 Read verses 1–2 again

▶ *How should you treat younger Christians?*

▶ *What about members of the opposite sex?*

The church is a family. That means close relationships. It also means treating people with respect, as equals. It means not patronising, bullying or embarrassing younger kids. It means remembering that Christians of the opposite sex are your brothers and sisters in Christ, not eye-candy. Treat them with respect, and act towards them in a way that's pure and pleases God.

GET ON WITH IT

▶ *Which younger people do you need to treat better?*

▶ *How could your attitude towards the opposite sex be more godly?*

PRAY ABOUT IT

Talk to God about any issues raised.

THE BOTTOM LINE

Check the way you relate to Christians of all ages.

208 Widow of opportunity

Life as a church leader is tough — so many problems to deal with, people to look after and to teach. Paul has some more advice for Timothy and his church in Ephesus.

👁 Read 1 Timothy 5 v 3–8

ENGAGE YOUR BRAIN

▶ Who should look after elderly Christians? (v4)

▶ Why? (end of v4)

▶ What does Paul say to people who don't look after their families? (v8)

Yesterday Paul taught us to have respect for members of our church family, the church. But we should also look after the people who cared for us and brought us up (v4). Especially elderly relatives who can't care for themselves.

GET ON WITH IT

▶ Is there anyone in your family you can show more care to?

▶ Can you encourage other members of your family to look after elderly relatives?

ENGAGE YOUR BRAIN

▶ Who should the church care for? (v5)

It's the church's responsibility to look after widows who are left alone with no family. Especially the ones who put their hope in God and not in pleasure-seeking (v5–6).

GET ON WITH IT

▶ Is there anyone elderly and alone at your church you could help?

▶ What will you do for them?

PRAY ABOUT IT

Pray for people you know who are in need. Ask God to help you show more love and care to those left lonely and in need.

THE BOTTOM LINE

Look after the lonely.

209 Merry widows

Any idea what a "widows list" is? No, me neither. We're not sure exactly what the list is that Paul's talking about. But that doesn't matter — there's still loads from Paul's teaching that we can apply to our lives.

⊙ Read 1 Timothy 5 v 9–16

ENGAGE YOUR BRAIN

▶ *What did a widow need to do to qualify for the list?*

Whatever the list was, it's clear that if you were on it, the church would look after you. Only widows over 60 need apply. This group of older women served God and the church in a special way. They showed hospitality, washed other Christians' disgusting, dusty feet, and helped out those in trouble, as well as doing tons of good deeds.

We can often dismiss elderly widows as not much use. Or ignore them completely. But they can do so much to serve God and His people.

GET ON WITH IT

▶ *Which elderly ladies in your church can you talk to more and get to know?*

Write their names down and try to pray for them every week.

⊙ Read verses 11–16

▶ *What things got in the way of these women serving Jesus?*

It seems that some of the younger widows had pledged themselves to the Lord's work and not to marry.

But then other things — falling in love, gossiping — got in the way of their commitment to Jesus.

PRAY ABOUT IT

▶ *What things get in the way of you serving Jesus?*

Pray about these things, asking God to help you throw out stuff that stops you being committed to Him.

210 Double honour

What do you think of your church and youth leaders?
What good things do they do?
Do they get the respect and thanks they deserve?

👁 Read 1 Timothy 5 v 17–25

ENGAGE YOUR BRAIN

▶ *What do good leaders deserve? (v17)*

▶ *What should we do if we hear worrying rumours about our leaders? (v19)*

Paul gave Timothy advice on appointing leaders (v22) and disciplining them when they did wrong (v20–21). But since you're probably not in charge of a church, let's focus in on verses 17–19 and our attitudes towards our Christian leaders.

1. HONOUR THOSE IN AUTHORITY

Church leaders have a tough job. Responsibility isn't easy. These guys are serving God and deserve respect.

2. HONOUR THOSE WHO TEACH US

It's a huge privilege to learn from God's word. The Lord speaks to us through preachers and youth leaders.

They put loads of time into studying, understanding and teaching the Bible.

▶ *Do you ever thank them or talk to them about their talks?*

3. PAY LEADERS FAIRLY

This seems obvious. Yet many Christian workers are paid poorly, overworked and given little respect or thanks.

▶ *Is there anything you could do for a Christian worker you know who feels unappreciated?*

4. DON'T LISTEN TO RUMOURS

Christian leaders are always under attack. We sometimes don't realise all the hurtful things that are said to them or about them. Don't spread rumours and don't listen to rumours.

PRAY ABOUT IT

Spend five minutes praying for your church and youth leaders.

211 Work it out

Ever feel like a slave? Either in a job, at school or at home? How would you sum up your attitude towards your "boss" or "slave master"?

👁 Read 1 Timothy 6 v 1–2

ENGAGE YOUR BRAIN

▶ *What does Paul say our attitude towards our boss (or teacher or parent) should be? (v1)*

▶ *Why? (v1)*

We may not like it, but we've got to show respect to those who have authority over us. That means doing what they say, not talking back or making life difficult for them. Why? Because non-Christians notice the way Christians act. Showing disrespect to bosses, parents or teachers reflects badly on God — our ultimate boss.

▶ *Should we expect Christian bosses to be softer on us? (v2)*

▶ *What should be our attitude towards our Christian boss?*

▶ *Why? (v2)*

We can sometimes expect an easy ride from other Christians. But

Paul says: *Work even harder for Christians!* It's an opportunity to serve your Christian brother or sister. You're both working for God. So don't slack off.

GET ON WITH IT

▶ *How does your attitude to your "boss" and work need to change?*

▶ *How can you show them greater respect?*

▶ *How can you serve another Christian this week?*

PRAY ABOUT IT

▶ *What has challenged you today?*

Talk it over with God and ask Him to help you change the way you work.

THE BOTTOM LINE

Show respect to your boss.

212 Love of money

Do you think it's better to be rich or poor? What's your attitude to money? Would you like more? Why/why not?

👁 Read 1 Timothy 6 v 3–5

ENGAGE YOUR BRAIN

▶ *What were these men wrongly teaching? (end of v5)*

▶ *What five things did their teaching result in? (v4–5)*

Leaders in Timothy's church were greedily flattering and exploiting wealthy church members. They were not teaching the truth about Jesus. Paul said these men were robbing people of the truth. Teaching that godliness leads to wealth is nonsense. It results in envy, bitterness and arguments.

👁 Read verses 6–10

▶ *What's really worth having? (v6, 8)*

▶ *Why? (v7)*

▶ *What are the dangers of wanting to be rich? (v9–10)*

Whether we're wealthy or poor, we always want more. But God has already given us so much, and we should be content with that. We haven't earned the things we have — they're all given to us by God.

Love of money is the devil's trap. Once you start chasing money and possessions, you're never satisfied. You always want more cash, nicer clothes, better gadgets. It also leads to many other temptations and sins (v10) and even to wandering away from faith in Jesus. Read verses 9-10 again, taking them very very seriously.

PRAY ABOUT IT

▶ *What have you been challenged about today?*

▶ *What will you do about it?*

Tell God about it right now.

THE BOTTOM LINE

"Love of money is a root of all kinds of evil."

213 Fighting talk

What advice would you give to someone who wanted to be a man or woman of God? What should they aim for? Compare your ideas with Paul's...

👁 Read 1 Timothy 6 v 11–12

ENGAGE YOUR BRAIN

▶ What should the man/woman of God chase after? (v11)

▶ What does it mean to "fight the good fight of the faith"?

Flee from the love of money. It can pull you away from God.

Pursue right-living, godliness, faith, love, endurance, gentleness.

Fight the good fight of the faith. Keep going. Give your everything to living for God.

Take hold of eternal life. God has rescued you from sin. Live like someone who'll live for ever with God.

👁 Read verses 13–16

Is that the longest sentence you've ever read? Here's how *The Message* phrases it:

"I'm charging you before the life-giving God and before Christ, who took his stand before Pontius Pilate and didn't give an inch: Keep this command to the letter, and don't slack off. Our Master, Jesus Christ, is on his way. He'll show up right on time, his arrival guaranteed by the Blessed and Undisputed Ruler, High King, High God. He's the only one death can't touch, his light so bright no one can get close. He's never been seen by human eyes — human eyes can't take him in! Honour to him, and eternal rule! Oh yes."

Paul encourages Tim to stick at it — He's serving an awesome God.

PRAY ABOUT IT

Look back at **flee, pursue, fight, take hold**. Talk to God about how you're doing with these four things. Ask Him to help you with the ones you struggle with.

214 Real riches

Money was a big issue for Tim's church. Those with no money wanted to get rich quick but ended up giving in to temptation and sin. But the people who were well-off had problems too.

👁 Read 1 Timothy 6 v 17–19

ENGAGE YOUR BRAIN

▶ *What mistakes were rich people in the church making? (v17)*

▶ *Where should they put their trust and hope?*

People who have a comfortable life (that includes most of us) can become arrogant. They trust in their own abilities and their money to get them through life. Paul says: *Don't be so dumb — you can't put your trust in such uncertain things. Take your eyes off them and focus on trusting in and living for God. Then you'll really enjoy all He's given you.*

▶ *What positive things should we be doing? (v18)*

▶ *Why? What's at stake? (v19)*

If God has given you stuff, be generous and give to others. Share what you have. Do good things for others. Enjoy what God has given you and share it with people.

We shouldn't be looking to grab what we can in this life. We must serve God with what we've got, be generous, and enjoy the rewards and perfect life of eternity with God.

GET ON WITH IT

▶ *Who will you give to and what can you give to them?*

▶ *Who can you do good deeds for?*

PRAY ABOUT IT

Ask God to help you actually do these things. Ask Him to help you fix your sights on serving Him and on eternity with Him, not on getting what you can right now.

THE BOTTOM LINE

Give generously and trust in God.

215 Final words

Paul has reached the end of his long letter to Timothy. In it he has encouraged Tim to stand up to false teaching and to keep living God's way. Take it away Paul, one last time…

👁 Read 1 Timothy 6 v 20–21

ENGAGE YOUR BRAIN

▶ *Any ideas what Timothy had to guard?*

Paul was telling Tim to hold on to the truth of the gospel. To keep teaching people the truth about Jesus, especially as others were teaching lies. It's vital for Christians to know what they believe, to hold on to that truth and to share it with others.

GET ON WITH IT

▶ *How can you learn more of God's great truth and understand the gospel better?*

▶ *Who can you talk to about Jesus?*

ENGAGE YOUR BRAIN

▶ *What two things must Tim turn away from? (v20)*

▶ *What's the danger if he doesn't? (v21)*

Do you think Timothy has got the message yet?? One last time Paul urges him to turn his back on those who spread godless chatter. These guys claimed to have real knowledge but it was opposed to the truth of God's word.

Watch out for people who claim to have "real knowledge" or new understanding. Does what they say match up with the Bible?

PRAY ABOUT IT

Ask God to help you understand and hold on to the awesome truth of the gospel. Ask Him to help you recognise and stand against those who try to distort the truth.

RUTH

The big finale

Imagine your life edited into a 90-minute movie. In which Netflix category would you find it? Comedy? Romance? Thriller? The chances are, the true story of your everyday life wouldn't break records at the box office. Real life isn't often like the movies. You can't edit out the dull bits, and the plot is hard to follow.

That's why it's great to know there's another bigger story being told. God is steering the world through its dramas to a glorious climax. However entertaining or not our lives turn out to be, what matters is that we fully take up our part in His story.

RUTH, THE MOVIE

The story of Ruth wouldn't be out of place on the big screen. It's got it all: tragedy, romance, drama — and even a happy ending. (Why not read it through like a novel before starting the studies?) But God's

big story is also in view. The events described are more than just random happenings to ordinary people. Heaven's King is directing the details of their days.

Over the next eight studies, follow Ruth's story carefully, keeping these key questions in mind:

- How do her experiences and choices compare with mine?

- How has God stepped directly into the chapters of my life?

- Am I living my life like Ruth, to play my part in His plan?

Although God has a plan, there is a sense in which your future life remains unwritten. The choices you haven't yet made will shape the story ahead. Let Ruth inspire you to face every episode with faith.

216 | Who do you think you are?

Imagine life as a refugee. Imagine rolling into a town with no home or mates. Imagine just trying to survive where you don't know the language or customs. Imagine yourself in Naomi's shoes.

👁 Read Ruth 1 v 1–5

ENGAGE YOUR BRAIN

▶ *Why did they leave Bethlehem in the first place?*

▶ *Why was Moab a weird place to run to? (see Judges 3 v 14)*

In their ten years away, Naomi's family had been hit by multiple tragedies. As if losing her husband wasn't enough, her two sons were taken too. Whatever is to come in her story, it's clear that Naomi's past is no picnic.

👁 Read Ruth 1 v 6–13

▶ *Where does the conversation in verses 8–13 take place? (v7)*

▶ *What are Naomi's hopes for her daughters-in-law? (v8–9)*

▶ *How does she view their prospects if they follow her?*

In many ways, Naomi talks sense. Two foreign widows couldn't expect to get the pick of the available Jewish boys. But there's a hint that her logic has been coloured by her tragic past: *Why stick with me? God's against me* (v11,13).

PRAY ABOUT IT

Have tough times affected your confidence in God? Tell Him about your lowest moments. Then thank Him that circumstances don't change His death-defying love (John 3 v 16).

THE BOTTOM LINE

Even in your lowest moments, don't forget God's great love for you.

217 | Clinging on

"It just didn't work out." That's a common verdict on a failed romance. But is that it? Does love just sometimes run out of gas whether we like it or not, or can we keep it moving?

👁 Read Ruth 1 v 14–18

ENGAGE YOUR BRAIN

▶ What pulls Orpah back to Moab (according to Naomi)? (v15)

▶ In contrast, what parts of Naomi's future does Ruth promise to share? (v16–17)

▶ What part of Ruth's character convinces Naomi to stop persuading? (v18)

THINK IT THROUGH

Because life is unpredictable, the idea of being totally committed to anyone or anything for life can seem extreme. But Ruth, not thinking of herself, and knowing her responsibility to God, holds nothing back.

▶ Do you show that type of determination in your love?

👁 Read verses 19–22

▶ What kind of welcome do they receive in Bethlehem?

▶ Naomi means "pleasant". Which words mean the opposite?

▶ What hope is hinted at in verse 22?

Naomi's friends barely recognise her. Her ten-year ordeal has clearly left its mark. If Naomi is still clinging to the Lord, it's only just. But the author wants us to know it's not over yet.

GET ON WITH IT

Who do you know who's running on empty? How might you encourage them to cling to God, who is always good?

THE BOTTOM LINE

"For as high as the heavens are above the earth, so great is his love for those who fear him."
(Psalm 103 v 11)

218 Don't just sit there!

"It's Not Fair!" It's easy to feel that God does exciting things for others but never for you. Is it possible we need a change in our attitudes and actions?

👁 Read Ruth 2 v 1–13

ENGAGE YOUR BRAIN

▶ What attitude does Ruth hope to find among the harvesters? (v2)

▶ How does Boaz show that?

▶ What does Boaz expect God to do and why? (v11, 12)

THINK IT THROUGH

Ruth's mopping-up plan is not as cheeky as it seems on the surface. God's law commanded harvesters to be "deliberately careless" — leaving leftovers for poor foreigners. Even in simply receiving what she's entitled to, Ruth is experiencing the benefits of her choice to make Naomi's God her God (1 v 16).

👁 Read Ruth 2 v 14–16

▶ In what way has Boaz exceeded Naomi's expectations and rights? (v14)

▶ How does Boaz add to God's basic allowance? (v15–16)

Ruth's optimistic outlook and humble hard work are a far cry from Naomi's self-pity of chapter 1. As a result she starts to experience "over-the-top" favour, showing that God doesn't limit His care for the poor to just survival necessities. It also seems that Boaz is starting to take a shine to Ruth. God is blessing Ruth!

GET ON WITH IT

What do you really need? Tell God about it today! Now follow Ruth's simple action plan, showing that you trust God to provide.

1. Think about others too. Who can you work alongside who has the same need? (v2)

2. Be bold but humble. Who can you ask respectfully to help you? (v7)

3. Work hard. What effort can you put in towards your target? (v7)

219 Hold on to hope

What a difference a day makes. What might be different by this time tomorrow? The truth is, whatever you have planned, you really don't know what's just around the corner. Are you ready for the unexpected?

👁 Read Ruth 2 v 17–19

ENGAGE YOUR BRAIN

▶ Boaz was already impressed by Ruth's commitment. Which actions show she's determined and faithful? (v17–18)

▶ What makes Naomi so keen to ask questions about Ruth's day?

THINK IT THROUGH

An "ephah" was a container big enough to climb into — not bad for one day's leftovers! But given what we know about God, should we be surprised when he gives more than the bare minimum?

▶ How has He done this for you?

👁 Read Ruth 2 v 19–23

▶ Naomi's excitement explodes when she finds out who's helping Ruth. What is her view of Boaz's character?

▶ How does he show the extra-generosity of God? (v21)

▶ What does this offer mean for the two widows?

Between the ends of chapters 1 and 2 everything has changed. Bitter Naomi can now see a brighter future. It reminds us that with our loving and powerful God there is always hope. If you're in a hole, today could be the day things turn around.

PRAY ABOUT IT

Is there anything good you've given up hoping for? A friend or family member who rejects Jesus? An unfair situation that seems to be ignored? Bring it back to your Father today, and ask Him for the perseverance that keeps hope alive (Colossians 1 v 11).

220 Comfort vs commitment

How far would you put yourself out for your family? Do someone else's chores? Spend your savings on a gift for them? Marry someone for their benefit???

👁 Read Ruth 3 v 1–9

ENGAGE YOUR BRAIN

▶ *What is Naomi's hope for Ruth? (v1)*

▶ *Why do you think Ruth goes along with the scheme?*

▶ *Although strange to us, Ruth's request was a clear signal to Boaz. What did it mean? (See Ezekiel 16 v 8 for a clue.)*

Put yourself in ancient Israel. You're male and your married brother dies before having kids of his own. The law says you ought to marry his widow — become her "kinsman redeemer". To us, it might sound unfair, but God wanted His people to imitate His amazing covenant love. Commitment was to matter more than convenience.

👁 Read Ruth 3 v 9–18

▶ *What kindness had Ruth already shown? (2 v 11)*

▶ *What was her image among the town's people? (3 v 11)*

▶ *What freedom did she give up for her family?*

Right back at the start of our story, Ruth refused to opt for an easy life in her homeland. At every stage she has been more concerned with loyalty to Naomi than clinging to her rights. And now that she practically has her pick of eligible men, again she chooses what's best for her family.

Jesus surrendered His freedom in praying "not my will, but yours be done" (Luke 22 v 42). He calls us to the same attitude. The anguish He felt at Gethsemane reminds us that this is far from easy.

GET ON WITH IT

We are called to put commitment before comfort. In what way might following Christ this week mean giving up time, money, popularity?

221 New-look love

What's the most romantic thing imaginable? A candlelit dinner for two? Serenading your loved one by moonlight? An exotic holiday on a paradise island? Get ready for a new-look love.

👁 Read Ruth 4 v 1–6

ENGAGE YOUR BRAIN

▷ *Who witnessed Boaz's meeting?*

▷ *What was the relative's response to the offer of land? (v4)*

▷ *Why did he not want a wife? (v6)*

As we've already seen, Ruth was an attractive proposition! And the relative was not reluctant to buy the land. So why was the idea of marriage a deal breaker? Well, when you sign up as a "kinsman redeemer", your main role is to give the dead man an heir. That means you buy the land, but once you have a son, he gets everything you've paid for. For Ruth's relative, this deal would take a huge chunk away from the inheritance due to his own kids. But Boaz is ready to pay.

👁 Read Ruth 4 v 7–10

▷ *What does the custom of removing a sandal signify?*

▷ *How would you describe the mood of Boaz's summary speech?*

Becoming a kinsman redeemer costs. Yet Boaz seems to celebrate the deal. His speech says: *Ruth is mine and I don't care who knows it!*

PRAY ABOUT IT

The Bible's model for a husband's love is the self-giving love of Jesus. Not flowers and chocolates, but the commitment of the cross. Is that the kind of marriage you're aiming for?

Ask God to develop in you a love that shows something of His passion.

THE BOTTOM LINE

"This is love: not that we loved God, but that he loved us and sent his Son as an atoning sacrifice for our sins." (1 John 4 v 10)

222 The comeback king

The sprinter crosses the finishing line milliseconds before his big rival, and he wins the gold medal. As the world's media surround him, he just smiles and says: "Thanks, Dad!" In his finest hour, he wants someone else to get the glory. Do you?

◉ Read Ruth 4 v 11–15

ENGAGE YOUR BRAIN

▶ Who does the future of this new family depend on? (v11–13)

▶ Why might Ruth's age give new hope to Boaz?

Some people think you get what you deserve. So when things go well, we congratulate ourselves for our hard work. But we should really thank God. Right through the Ruth story, He has been at work, invisibly providing for each of our main characters.

◉ Re-read Ruth 4 v 9–10

▶ What had God provided for childless Naomi?

▶ How will Boaz change her life?

As kinsman redeemer, Boaz offers new hope to an old lady. His arrival does not just promise food on her table, but the descendants she

dreamed of. It's a small picture of the Great Redeemer, who just loves to turn our despair to joy.

THINK IT THROUGH

▶ How is God working behind the scenes of your own life?

▶ What situation has he redeemed?

▶ In what situation do you need new hope?

PRAY ABOUT IT

Take your thanks for the past and requests for the future to God, who specialises in the glorious comeback.

THE BOTTOM LINE

"You turned my wailing into dancing; you removed my sackcloth and clothed me with joy, that my heart may sing your praises and not be silent. Lord my God, I will praise you for ever." (Psalm 30 v 11–12)

223 History makers

Some people make history. Others end up being part of world-changing events by accident. Either way, just by living for Jesus you'll leave an everlasting legacy. Are you ready to change the world?

👁 **Read Ruth 4 v 16–22**

ENGAGE YOUR BRAIN

▶ *What role and relationship is Naomi given?*

As the story ends, we discover a bigger picture. God is using Ruth and Naomi in providing Israel with their greatest king, David. It's a reminder that even the seemingly small details of our humble days can be crucial to God's plans.

▶ *What country did David's great-grandma, Ruth, come from?*

▶ *Why might this have surprised some Jews?*

▶ *Who do you think is the main character in this story?*

THINK IT THROUGH

Ultimately, the Bible is one book, with God as its author. That means we can only really understand any part when we see how it fits into the whole. The storyline running throughout is this: Jesus, "Son" of David, and God's rescue through Him.

▶ *What have we learned about Jesus through Ruth?*

PRAY ABOUT IT

Without knowing it, Ruth has played a key role in God's eternal plan. We can't fully grasp how our actions today might affect future generations.

Bring before God your decisions and encounters of the next 24 hours.

Pray that He would use you in His mind-blowing purposes.

224 Matthew: King of controversy

We're back with Matthew's biography of Jesus. How are you feeling? Calm? Excited? Worried? Bored? Time for emotional aerobics now: this next controversial story could leave you shouting: "That's not fair!"

Read Matthew 20 v 1–16

ENGAGE YOUR BRAIN

▶ *How do you feel about this story?*

▶ *Is the landowner being unfair?*

Jesus said that this story explained a truth about His kingdom (v1) — life with Him as King.

▶ *What do you think that truth is?*

▶ *Who's who in the story?*

▶ *So is God being unfair?*

God calls people to live under His rule and to work for Him (living His way, telling others about Jesus). And they get what God promised them — eternal life, *whenever* they come to know Jesus. Awesome.

▶ *Did the last workers deserve a denarius?*

▶ *Did the first workers deserve to be hired?*

The landowner went back four times to hire new workers — that's how incredibly generous he was. It's ridiculous to be ungrateful and grumble at God for His compassion to others, when He's shown such amazing, undeserved love to us.

▶ *Does God give what He promises? (v13)*

▶ *Hasn't He the right to do as He wants? (v15)*

▶ *Is He generous to all His disciples? (v15)*

THE BOTTOM LINE

God's values are different from ours. This parable's a lesson in God's grace. So let's be thankful Christians working hard for Jesus, not grumbling grabbers after fame and status.

PRAY ABOUT IT

Thank God for His amazing grace. Pray that you'll grumble less at God and be more thankful.

225 Power serve

There's an old song about Jesus called "Meekness and majesty" — but the two don't seem to go together. How about "Meekness and being pathetic"? Or "Power and majesty"? But you can't mix the two, surely.

👁 Read Matthew 20 v 17–19

ENGAGE YOUR BRAIN

▷ What would have shocked the disciples about what Jesus said?

👁 Read verses 20–23

▷ What did James and John's mum ask for? (v21)

▷ How did Jesus answer? (v23)

"Can you drink the cup I'm going to drink?" means "Are you prepared to serve, suffer and be rejected as I will?" James and John said they were. And they did — both suffered loads as they spread the gospel. But only God the Father will decide who will have positions of honour in Jesus' kingdom.

👁 Read verses 24–28

▷ How did Gentile rulers act? (v25)

▷ How should believers be different? (v26–27)

▷ Why? (v28)

▷ Why did Jesus come into the world? (v28)

Greatness in the world's eyes is based on status, wealth and popularity. But greatness in God's kingdom is based on serving God and serving others.

It's not about having power and bossing people around. It's about enduring hard times and injustice without complaining or turning away from God. True leaders should get their hands dirty along with everyone else.

GET ON WITH IT

▷ How do you chase after status?

▷ How exactly will you be more of a servant this week?

226 Blind faith

Jesus and His disciples are on their way to Jerusalem, where Jesus has told them He will be tortured and killed. As they pass through Jericho, they're followed by a large crowd and are about to have a surprise interruption.

👁 Read Matthew 20 v 29–34

ENGAGE YOUR BRAIN

- ▶ Who shouted to Jesus?

- ▶ What did they call Him?

- ▶ What did they want?

- ▶ How did the crowd react?

- ▶ How did Jesus react?

- ▶ And what did the two men do then?

The crowd tried to silence these guys, but they shouted even louder to get Jesus' attention. They were blind, but could tell exactly who Jesus was. They called Him "Son of David". This is a name used in the Old Testament for the Christ — the King who would rescue God's people. They knew that Jesus was God's promised King.

And they knew He could heal them. Because they believed in Jesus, and because of His love for them, Jesus healed them. They followed Jesus.

THINK IT OVER

- ▶ Are you easily discouraged when people try to distract you from following Jesus?

- ▶ Are you determined to be a follower of Jesus?

- ▶ Do you truly believe that He's the King who can save you?

- ▶ Know anyone who's blind when it comes to Jesus?

- ▶ How can you follow Jesus more?

PRAY ABOUT IT

Use your answers to these questions to kickstart your prayer time today.

227 Royal visit

Donkeys. That's just the first surprise you'll get today. Jesus is on His way into Jerusalem, where His confrontation with those who refuse to accept His authority will continue. And boil over.

👁 Read Matthew 21 v 1–5

ENGAGE YOUR BRAIN

▶ What were Jesus' weird instructions? (v1–3)

▶ Why did this happen? (v4–5)

The Jews expected the Messiah to be a conquering hero arriving in style and force. But the Old Testament had promised that God's chosen Rescuer would be gentle and riding on a young donkey. Surprising.

👁 Read verses 6–11

▶ How was Jesus greeted by the people? (v8–10)

▶ What did they recognise about Him? (v9)

▶ How did others describe Him? (v11)

Jerusalem was packed with people ready to celebrate the Passover feast. They welcomed Jesus like royalty, praising Him. There was a huge buzz created by His entry — could this be the Messiah they'd been waiting for? Well, yes, He was! But Jesus wasn't the kind of King most people were expecting.

Hosanna means "Lord, save us". They were right that Jesus was their King who'd come to save them. But they thought He'd save them by fighting the Romans. They didn't realise that Jesus had come to die on the cross to save them from their sins.

A few days later, another crowd would be shouting for Jesus to be killed!

PRAY ABOUT IT

Spend time praising King Jesus.

Thank Him that He came as King to save His people from sin and punishment in hell.

THE BOTTOM LINE

Praise King Jesus! Welcome Him!

228 Tables turned

Jesus had arrived and was causing a big stir. He was doing loads of surprising stuff that fulfilled Old Testament prophecy about the Messiah. So people were amazed, yet many still refused to believe.

👁 Read Matthew 21 v 12–13

ENGAGE YOUR BRAIN

▶ *What surprising thing did Jesus do in the temple area?*

▶ *Why? (v13)*

He acted like it was His place. Actually, it was His Father's house and Jesus was furious with the way people abused it. The temple in Jerusalem was where people went to meet God. But instead of worshipping God, these guys used it to make money and scam people. They were also robbing God of the worship He should get in His house.

👁 Read verses 14–17

▶ *What kinds of people turned to Jesus? (v14–15)*

▶ *What about the religious leaders?*

▶ *How did Jesus answer them?*

Jesus was in Jerusalem, the city of God's chosen people. And everything He did pointed to His role as the promised one sent from God to rescue His people. Yet it was mostly outcasts and outsiders who realised who He was. Jesus was constantly showing from the Old Testament that He was the Christ, the Messiah. Yet the Scripture experts refused to believe it. Madness.

PRAY ABOUT IT

Pray that you won't make the same mistake as these leaders — knowing their Scripture, yet not getting to know Jesus. And pray that God will help you be accepting and encouraging towards believers who others look down on.

229 Withering words

Jesus' actions in the temple had got up the noses of the Jewish leaders. How dare He call the shots in God's temple? Who does He think He is? Well, what happened next clearly showed what Jesus thought of them.

👁 Read Matthew 21 v 18–19

ENGAGE YOUR BRAIN

▶ What point do you think Jesus was making, bearing in mind what's happened in verses 1–17?

There's more than just a branch-withering miracle here. In the Old Testament, God described His people as a "fig tree". He expected "fruit" from them, or they'd be punished. People in Jerusalem were like this fig tree. They were very religious, with a reputation for serving God. But underneath, there was no real love for God. No fruit. One day, these people would be punished.

So what's this got to do with us? Well, we may do religious stuff, like going to church and not swearing much… but God sees what our hearts are really like.

👁 Read verses 20–22

▶ What were the disciples more interested in? (v20)

▶ What was Jesus' surprising news? (v21-22)

Anything is possible in God's power. If we truly believe that God can answer our prayers, then he will answer them. We've got to have faith.

PRAY ABOUT IT

Ask God to help you truly live like one of his children. And ask Him to help you really believe that He will answer your prayers.

230 Question time

Jesus was in Jerusalem and had fallen out with the Jewish leaders. He'd pointed out their hypocrisy and they didn't like the way He'd thrown people out of their temple. They were out to get Him.

👁 Read Matthew 21 v 23–27

ENGAGE YOUR BRAIN

▶ What did the Jewish leaders want to know? (v23)

▶ How did Jesus answer? (v24–25)

▶ What was the problem? (v25–27)

These ruthless leaders tried to trap Jesus. If He said, "God gives me this authority", they could arrest Him for blasphemy and sentence Him to death. And if Jesus said, "No one has given me authority to do this", He'd be shown up to be a big fraud. So Jesus asked the leaders a trick question.

John the Baptist told people to get ready for Jesus, God's promised King. If these leaders said John's message came from God, they'd be admitting Jesus came from God too. But if they said it wasn't from God, they feared the crowds would turn against them. So they refused to answer the question — and so did Jesus.

👁 Read verse 28–32

▶ What point did Jesus make with this story? (v31)

Ouch! Jesus said corrupt cheats and prostitutes (people the religious leaders thought God would never accept) were being welcomed into God's kingdom. They'd seen the need to repent and trust. The religious leaders hadn't. So Jesus rejected them for rejecting Him — and turned to those who would accept and trust Him.

PRAY ABOUT IT

Rejecting Jesus outright is still a serious business. So is saying we follow Him and then doing nothing about it. Have you taken heart from the point of the story (v28–31)? Then talk to God about whatever's on your mind today.

231 Fruitless conversation

Jesus was challenged by the Jewish leaders to explain His authority. He refused point blank, saying that God was rejecting them for rejecting Him. And He's not finished yet, using another story to trap them.

👁 Read Matthew 21 v 33–41

ENGAGE YOUR BRAIN

▶ What did the owner want? (v34)

▶ But what did the tenants do? (v35–39)

▶ What did the Jewish leaders say should happen to the tenants? (v41)

In the Old Testament, God spoke of Israel as His vineyard. So God is the landowner in this story. The tenants are religious leaders. The servants are God's prophets. The son is Jesus. So the story is a brief history of God's people, Israel. The leaders were outraged by what the tenants did, failing to realise that they were exactly like the tenants!

👁 Read verses 42–46

▶ How did Jesus describe Himself? (v42)

▶ What would happen to Jewish people who rejected Jesus? (v43)

▶ How did the leaders react? (v45–46)

God's people Israel, and their leaders, had rejected God's prophets down the centuries. And now they'd rejected God's own Son. So God turned to those who *would* accept Jesus as the world's ruler and would live lives that produced fruit for God. They would now be God's true people.

THINK IT OVER

It's easy for us to criticise these Jews for rejecting Jesus. But let's not miss the truth for us: rejecting Jesus is serious. And we reject Jesus when we think we know better than God and live our own way, not God's.

▶ In what areas of life are you in danger of doing that?

Talk it over with God right now.

232 Wedding yells

Jesus told the religious leaders that they were no longer God's people — because they rejected Jesus and failed to produce fruit for God. Here He rams home the point with another clever story.

Read Matthew 22 v 1–7

This was the system: invitations were sent weeks in advance (and replies received). Then a second invitation (v3) was sent to inform guests when the banquet was ready. So the guests had already promised to come… and then didn't.

ENGAGE YOUR BRAIN

▶ *How did the guests respond to this second invitation? (v3–6)*

▶ *How did the king react? (v7)*

Read verses 8–14

▶ *After rejection, what did the king do? (v8–10)*

▶ *Why was one guy thrown out? (v11–13)*

▶ *What's the message? (v14)*

The story's point was sharp — God was rejecting the nation of Israel for rejecting Him. So He was now turning to those who would accept Him and His invitation. But they'd need to live a changed life for the Lord. God wants people who keep going with Him. Christians who last. When God judges, they'll be recognised as His chosen people.

THINK IT OVER

Make a list of excuses people give for not keeping going with God:

PRAY ABOUT IT

Pray for people you know who make those excuses (maybe yourself?), that they'll turn back to God. Thank Him for inviting you to His great heavenly feast. Pray that you'll remember this when life is tough, so you won't turn away from living for God.

233 Taxing question

The conflict between Jesus and the Jewish leaders had reached boiling point. They were furious at Jesus' claims that God would reject them for rejecting Him. They were out to get Jesus.

👁 Read Matthew 22 v 15–22

ENGAGE YOUR BRAIN

▶ *Who did the Pharisees enlist for help? (v16)*

▶ *How were they false? (v16)*

▶ *Why was their question (v17) a tricky one?*

▶ *How did Jesus answer them?*

▶ *How did the tricksters respond? (v22)*

The Pharisees were Jewish leaders who hated their Roman rulers. The Herodians supported Herod, the local Roman ruler. The two groups would normally be enemies but the Pharisees were so desperate to get Jesus, they teamed up.

With this question, there was no way Jesus could please both sides. If Jesus said, "Yes, pay Caesar's taxes", the Pharisees could accuse Him of siding with the Romans against the Jews. If Jesus said "No", the Herodians could claim He was breaking Roman law.

Jesus' answer was perfect. It's right to pay taxes and obey the government's laws. But there's also a higher loyalty. Humans bear the image of God — and so must give God the obedience He deserves.

GET ON WITH IT

▶ *In what ways do you disobey authority?*

▶ *In what specific ways can you give God what belongs to Him?*
time:
money:
abilities:
your life:

PRAY ABOUT IT

Talk your answers over with God, committing yourself to doing them.

234 Seventh question

People were still chomping at the bit to try and trick Jesus. This time it was the Sadducees — a group of rich Jewish leaders. They didn't believe in resurrection — eternal life with God. And they were out to trap Jesus.

👁 Read Matthew 22 v 23–30

▶ *How did the Sadd's try to trap Jesus?*

▶ *What was their problem? (v29)*

▶ *What had they failed to realise about life after death? (v30)*

It doesn't seem very likely, does it? One woman marrying seven brothers, one after the other? The Sadducees thought this bizarre question would beat Jesus. They even quoted what Moses had said (v24). Surely Jesus couldn't get out of this one. But Jesus didn't waste much time with the Sadd' guys' question.

Of course eternal life won't be the same as this life. We'll have brand new bodies. And we won't be married — we'll be living with Jesus. The Bible tells us that marriage is a picture of the close relationship between Jesus and His people.

👁 Read verses 31–33

▶ *What had the Sadd's failed to realise about God's people who had already died?*

The Sadducees claimed there was no life after death. Yet God had said: "I **am** … the God of Abraham, the God of Isaac and the God of Jacob" (Exodus 3 v 6). They'd been dead for ages, but God said He **is** their God. Abraham, Isaac and Jacob are alive and living with God in heaven!

SHARE IT

▶ *As a Christian, what can you say to friends who claim there is no life after death?*

▶ *What can you tell them about the hope you have of eternal life?*

PRAY ABOUT IT

Thank God for the great hope of a perfect future that Christians have, because of Jesus.

235 The greatest

Yep, Jesus' enemies are still trying to trip Him up. What would you say is the greatest commandment in the Bible? And why would you argue that it's the most vital one?

👁 Read Matthew 22 v 34–40

ENGAGE YOUR BRAIN

▶ Who was out to get Jesus now? (v34)

▶ Why was this question so tricky?

▶ What's the most important command according to Jesus?

▶ And the second?

▶ Why are these commands so important? (v40)

The Pharisees were hoping to get Jesus to say that some parts of the Old Testament weren't so important. No chance. And again, Jesus' answer was brilliant: *Give all of yourself to loving God.*

All your thoughts, words and actions should be for God! Christians still fail at times, but they really want to show their love for God. And part of the way we do this is by showing great love for people around us — not putting ourselves first all the time.

GET ON WITH IT

▶ *If you take verse 37 seriously, what do you need to start doing?*

▶ *And stop doing?*

Write down the names of six people you see regularly — some you like and some you don't. Then write down a specific way you can show God's love to them.

1.

2.

3.

4.

5.

6.

PRAY ABOUT IT

Read verses 37–39 again and then look at your answers to GET ON WITH IT. You should now have loads to talk to God about!

236 | One last question

Over the last week, we've seen Jesus' enemies ganging together, asking Him ridiculous questions, trying to trap Him into slipping up. They failed miserably. So now Jesus has a difficult question for them.

👁 Read Matthew 22 v 41–46

ENGAGE YOUR BRAIN

▶ *What was His question and how did they answer it? (v41–42)*

▶ *How does Jesus use Scripture to baffle them? (v43–45)*

▶ *How did these Old Testament experts respond? (v46)*

In Jesus' time, Jewish people were waiting for the Messiah (Christ) to rescue them. The Pharisees knew that the Messiah would be related to King David (v42). So they thought he was a man, and couldn't be God as well!

Verse 44 is something King David wrote in Psalm 110. By calling the Messiah "my Lord", David is saying that the Messiah is also God. The Jewish leaders hadn't worked this out.

But we know that Jesus is the Messiah, who rescues His people. And that He is God too!

Jesus had been called "Son of David", so the Jewish leaders knew He was challenging them to accept Him as the Messiah. They refused to, and next time they met, it would be to arrest Him.

THINK IT OVER

People still offer every excuse and argument possible to avoid accepting Jesus as King. Do you make that mistake too?

PRAY ABOUT IT

Thank God that Jesus is the Messiah — the perfect King who God sent to rescue us from the punishment we deserve for our sins. Ask God to help you get the message of Jesus across to those who refuse to believe. And pray that you'll live in a way that shows Jesus is King of your life.

JOB

Why me?

The young boy gets mercilessly picked on at school. He cries all the way home and sobs into his pillow. Why is life like this?

Cancer strikes a young mum. A happy personality is turned into a devastated shadow. The fear is crippling. Why did this happen?

The teenager never felt more lonely in a crowd. She'd never go to a party again. Not now she was in a wheelchair. Why is it like this?

Why do bad things happen to good people? And why do Christians sometimes seem to get a double dose? Doesn't God care? Or is He powerless to do anything about it?

MEET JOB

The book of Job doesn't provide any quick or easy answers to the problem of suffering. But it does lead us to God. And it's only in the awesome presence of God that we can begin to get a right view on life's hardships.

We'll stay with Job every step of his harrowing journey. From happy highs to miserable, painful lows. Through loss, sickness and unexplained suffering. We'll see him ask, "Why me?" We'll stand back amazed at his friends' responses. We'll even discover what true wisdom is. And then we'll see the Lord answer Job, and we'll bow down to His power and perfection.

Job is like no other book you'll read. It's heavy going but so rewarding. Stay the distance and see God pulling you into a more real relationship with Him.

237 | Satan's takeaway

Job is famous for being a man who went through times of incredible suffering. But life wasn't always bleak for him. Let's start at the beginning...

👁 Read Job 1 v 1–5

ENGAGE YOUR BRAIN

▶ *What did Job have going for him?*
v1:
v2–3:

Job was rich. But more importantly, he was close to God. He was so determined to live right for God that he made sure every possible sin of his children was forgiven (v5).

👁 Read verses 6–12

▶ *What was God's view of Job? (v8)*

▶ *What did Satan claim was the reason for Job being godly? (v10)*

▶ *What did God allow Satan to do? (v12)*

▶ *What limits did he put on Satan?*

Verse 9 is a key to the book — is Job only godly because God has given him loads of good things? See what's at stake? God's honour. Satan's suggesting: "People only

trust you, God, when you bless them. It seems you have to buy people's allegiance."

👁 Read verses 13–22

▶ *What did Job lose?*

▶ *What's surprising about Job's response? (v20–22)*

No blame. No wallowing in self-pity. Job knew that God had the right to do anything with him. It's a hard lesson to learn: God made us and is in charge of everything. He has every right to take things away from us.

PRAY ABOUT IT

Think about why you live God's way, and talk to Him about it. Thank Him for all He's given you. If you truly mean it, ask God to do whatever He wishes with everything you have. To use your life, talents and possessions for His glory.

238 A sore point

Satan wanted to prove that people only loved God when God gave the good stuff. So Job lost his wealth and his children, yet he still didn't turn against God. But Satan hadn't finished with Job.

👁 Read Job 2 v 1–10

ENGAGE YOUR BRAIN

▷ *What did Satan think would turn Job against God? (v4–5)*

▷ *How bad was it? (v7–8)*

▷ *What did Job's wife tell him to do? (v9)*

▷ *What point did Job make? (v10)*

Satan wouldn't accept defeat and continued to attack Job. All Job could do was sit in mourning, scraping at his horrible sores. Even his wife thought he should give up, blame God and wait for death. Job couldn't see why these disasters had happened, but he refused to blame God: we can't accept good times from God but not bad times too.

THINK IT OVER

▷ *Do you ever blame God when bad things happen?*

▷ *Do you thank Him enough for the good things He gives you?*

Talk to God about these issues now.

👁 Read verses 11–13

▷ *How did Job's friends react?*
v11:
v12:
v13:

This may not seem much, but this week-long silence was the best support they gave Job. Everything they said would undo this good work.

GET ON WITH IT

▷ *Who do you know who's suffering?*

▷ *How will you show sympathy and support to them?*

Ask God to comfort them and to help you be a good friend to them.

239 Happy deathday

"I wish I'd never been born!" "It would be better if I were dead." Ever heard someone say that kind of thing? Maybe you've felt like that yourself. Well, that's exactly the way Job was feeling and he wasn't ashamed to say it.

👁 Read Job 3 v 1–26

ENGAGE YOUR BRAIN

▶ What kind of questions did Job ask God?

▶ Why does he think dying in the womb would have been better? (v13, 17)

▶ How does death compare to Job's current situation? (v26)

Job was in so much pain and misery he wished his birthday was wiped from the calendar. That way he would never have been born, so he couldn't experience all this pain. He even wished a huge sea monster — Leviathan — would swallow his day of birth!

Let's face it, Job was far from satisfied, but he still refused to turn his back on God. Instead, in brutal honesty, he took all his difficult and indignant questions to God.

THINK IT OVER

▶ When life kicks you in the gut, do you sulk and blame God, or talk to Him about it?

▶ What in your life right now do you need to talk to God about?

PRAY ABOUT IT

It's OK to take your troubles to God. Tell Him all about them. You can be miserable with Him!

Be honest with God right now.

Tell Him how you feel. Tell Him what's getting you down or troubling you. Ask Him to help you trust Him through tough times. And thank Him for good things in your life too!

THE BOTTOM LINE

Take your troubles to God.

240 | The silence is over

When Job's friends heard of the tragedy in his life, they came to comfort him. They sat in silence with Job for a week. But now they're bursting with things to say to him. First up is Eliphaz.

👁 Read Job 4 v 1–11

▶ How does Eliphaz describe Job's situation? (v3–5)

▶ Why does he think Job should have hope? (v6)

▶ What big point does he make in verses 7–9?

▶ Do you agree with it?

👁 Read verses 12–21

▶ Where did Eliphaz claim his advice came from? (v12–16)

Eliphaz said that God doesn't punish innocent people. So Job must have sinned since he was suffering so much. Eliphaz even claimed his advice was given to him in a vision, so surely he must be right. But Eliphaz was wrong. We know that God wasn't punishing Job for sinning (see chapters 1 & 2). When bad stuff happens to us, it doesn't mean God is punishing us for a specific sin.

So how is it that we all have problems? Well, it *is* because of *sin*. Right at the beginning, Adam and Eve disobeyed God, and brought sin into the world. Sin has messed up our world, and we all suffer sometimes because of it. The ray of hope is that God often uses bad times to strengthen us and to make us rely on Him. And one day, all Christians will be gathered to the perfect place where there's no more sin or suffering.

SHARE IT

▶ If someone asked you why there's suffering in the world, how would you answer them?

PRAY ABOUT IT

When life is tough, don't blame God. And don't wallow, thinking it's because you're so sinful. Turn to God with your problems and ask Him to help you out.

241 Failing friends

Now it's Job's turn to speak. Chapters 1 & 2 made it clear that Job wasn't being punished by God for any sin he'd committed. Job protested his innocence. Sometimes to his friends (chapter 6) and sometimes to God (chapter 7).

👁 Read Job 6 v 1–13

ENGAGE YOUR BRAIN

▷ Which words would you use to describe Job's feelings in each of these sections?
v2–4:
v8–10:
v11–13:

👁 Read verses 14–30

▷ How does Job think his friends should act? (v14)

▷ But how do they act? (v15, 26)

▷ Why does Job think they're like this? (v21)

▷ What does he ask his friends to prove? (v28–30)

Job is certain he hasn't sinned and that God isn't punishing him for wrongdoing. He doesn't need his friends to turn against him and preach at him during such miserable times. He needs their support, devotion and comfort (v14). When people are suffering, they probably don't need us to preach at them. Or to say "I told you so!" They need our support, friendship, prayers and comfort. That often means shutting up and listening.

GET ON WITH IT

▷ Who do you need to apologise to for being too preachy?

▷ Who do you need to be more supportive to?

▷ How can you show them God's love, and comfort them?

PRAY ABOUT IT

Ask God to help you be a devoted, supportive friend.

THE BOTTOM LINE

Shut up and be supportive.

242 | Bildad blabbers

Job couldn't understand why God was letting him suffer so much. Eliphaz wrongly told Job it was his own fault. But would Bildad offer more helpful advice?

👁 Read Job 8 v 1–10

ENGAGE YOUR BRAIN

▶ What did Bildad think of Job's complaining? (v2)

▶ Why did he say Job's kids died? (v4)

▶ What did he say was Job's way out of misery? (v5–7)

▶ What else did he suggest? (v8–10)

Oh dear. Bildad is talking rubbish too. Job's kids didn't die because they'd committed terrible sins. God wasn't punishing them.

And it's not true that if Job lived a good life God would make everything perfect for him. The Bible tells us that believers *will* suffer sometimes (1 Peter 1 v 6–7). Our lives won't be perfect until eternal life with Jesus.

👁 Read Job 8 v 11–22

▶ What was Bildad's point? (v13)

▶ What pictures does he use to illustrate his point?
v11–13:
v14–15:
v16–19:

People who forget God often seem to do well, living their own way. But one day God will punish those who reject Him. Bildad was right about that.

And He was right that God won't reject people who live for Him (v20). But Bildad was dead wrong to assume that Job was an evil man just because God seemed to have left him. God was still with Job.

PRAY ABOUT IT

Thank God that He NEVER leaves those who trust Him. Ask Him to give you the courage and strength to trust Him when life is good and when life is tough.

243 | Job is right — and wrong

After Bildad's blabber, it's time for Job to reply. And he's got some big things to say about God.

👁 Read Job 9 v 1–10

ENGAGE YOUR BRAIN

▶ *How would you sum up Job's description of God? (v5–10)*

▶ *How do humans compare to God? (v2–4)*

👁 Skim-read verses 11–35

Job had lost almost everything. But he knew that God had every right to do all this and much more to him.

Job's got most things right so far, though not everything.

What Job got right

• All good things come from God, so God can take them away.

• God can do what He wants.

• Job is nothing compared with God, so he can't argue with God.

What Job got wrong

• God doesn't want to hear Job.

• God would hurt Job for no reason.

Job was wrong about these last two, and he still didn't understand why bad stuff was happening to him. Sometimes we just don't know exactly why bad things happen to good people. But the life and death of Jesus teaches us we can always trust God to do what's best for us.

PRAY ABOUT IT

Read Romans 8 v 28 and use it to praise God. And then use Job 9 v 5–10 to start you off praising God for His power and creation.

244 | Zophar so bad

Job's friends aren't being very supportive! Next up is Zophar. Will he be any different or will he give Job a hard time too?

👁 Read Job 11 v 1–6

ENGAGE YOUR BRAIN

▶ *What's Zophar's opinion? (v2–3)*

▶ *What does he want God to do? (v5–6)*

Zophar is even less subtle than Eliphaz and Bildad! He thinks Job is stupid to claim to be innocent. Zophar wants God to put Job in his place, and to show Job what true wisdom is. (Later in the book, God does exactly that — Job 28 v 28.)

👁 Read Job 11 v 7–12

▶ *What's the answer to verse 7?*

Zophar thinks Job is dumb to try and understand why God let him suffer so much. Zophar seems to think God is unknowable. It's true that there are many things our tiny brains can't understand about God. And we won't always understand why He lets certain things happen. But we *can* know God. We can have a close relationship with Him. For us, that's made possible by Jesus.

👁 Read verses 13–20

Job's friends think the solution is simple: if only Job would turn from his wicked ways and devote himself to God, then God would reward him with a bright future. But Job wasn't being punished for sinning. So Zophar had got it wrong too.

THINK IT OVER

▶ *Do you try to understand God?*

▶ *Do you want to be closer to Him?*

▶ *Do you live to please Him?*

PRAY ABOUT IT

Talk these issues over with God. Say sorry for your failings. Ask Him to help you seek Him more in the Bible; grow closer to Him through Jesus; and to give your life to serving Him.

245 Job fights back

Zophar was the latest of Job's "friends" to give him a hard time. As usual, Job replies to the accusations and then talks to God. Job's got loads to say this time, so get ready to speed-read!

👁 Speed-read Job 12 v 1–12

ENGAGE YOUR BRAIN

▷ *How does Job sum it up? (v4)*

▷ *What great truth does Job reveal about creation? (v10)*

👁 Skim verses 13–25

▷ *What does Job tell us about God?*
v13:
v14–16:
v23:

👁 Speed-read Job 13 v 1–12

▷ *What does Job think of his friends' "wisdom"? (v4–5, 12)*

▷ *What does Job want to do? (v3)*

👁 Read verses 13–19

▷ *What's surprising about Job's attitude towards God? (v15 16)*

Job's fed up with trying to convince his friends that he's innocent. They just won't listen. So he decides to argue his case with God. Job knows this may lead to destruction, but he also knows he can trust God to do what's right and fair (v15). It may even lead to him being rescued from his suffering and misery (v16). Later in the book we'll see what happens.

Pastor and author Christopher Ash puts it like this: *"Even in the depths of his suffering, Job doesn't give up. He loves God, so he says: 'I want to meet God. I want to be right with God. I want to be justified, vindicated… Though He may slay me, I will live in hope.' Job sets his hope in God for there's nowhere else he can turn."*

PRAY ABOUT IT

Thank God that whatever happens we can trust in Him. Thank Him for showing this by sending His Son to die in our place and rise again to rescue us.

246 | Who do you think you are?

Earlier, Eliphaz seemed almost gentle and sympathetic as he spoke to Job. Now he changes tone — letting his frustration out and ridiculing Job. Who needs enemies when you've got friends like these?!

👁 Read Job 15 v 1–13

ENGAGE YOUR BRAIN

▶ What does Eliphaz accuse Job of? (v4–6)

▶ Who does he think Job should listen to? (v10)

"Who do you think you are, Job, to get angry with us? We were only speaking the truth and trying to console you. God is speaking through us to you so you're really raging against God!"

But their words were not comforting or even true. And definitely not from God. They'd falsely accused Job of sinning — no wonder his eyes flashed with anger (v12)!

GET ON WITH IT

▶ Do you ever hurt people by "just being honest" or "trying to help"?

▶ Who do you need to be more sympathetic to?

▶ How will you do it?

👁 Quickly read verses 14–35

Eliphaz claims that wicked people suffer throughout their lives. They are tormented by fear and guilt. As usual, there's a grain of truth in Eliphaz's words. But only a grain. Some people do suffer because of their sin. But many people do wrong all their lives and hardly suffer or feel guilty at all. And many godly people suffer loads. But we can trust that God is faithful and always does what is right.

PRAY ABOUT IT

Ask God to help you to be more sympathetic and understanding in the way you deal with people. Pray for friends who don't seem to care about the sin in their lives. Ask God to show them their need for Jesus' forgiveness.

247 | Who's on my side?

How do you react when life seems unfair? Do you lash out at those around you? Do you question God? Do you humbly turn to Him in prayer? Do you trust that God's in control? Well, Job did all those things...

👁 Read Job 16 v 1–14

ENGAGE YOUR BRAIN

▶ *What's Job's complaint against his friends? (v2–3)*

▶ *How would he have acted differently in their shoes? (v5)*

▶ *Who does Job know is behind his suffering? (v7, 9, 11)*

Job describes God as a wild animal attacking him. Yet again he questions why so many bad things have happened to a servant of God like him. Has Job finally flipped and turned against God?

👁 Read verses 15–21

▶ *How does Job respond to his suffering? (v15–16)*

▶ *Has he turned against God? (v17)*

▶ *Why does he still cry out to God for help? (v18–21)*

Amazingly, Job doesn't turn against God. Yes, he sulks and complains and feels sorry for himself. Of course he does — he's lost his children, his wealth, and he's in constant pain. But Job never reacts in violence and he still turns to God in prayer.

Job knows that his friends won't be able to persuade God to end his suffering. His only hope is that he has a friend in heaven who will plead with God on his behalf (v19–21). That friend is *Jesus*. If we turn to Him for forgiveness, He will plead with God for us — and our sins will be washed away. Jesus is on our side. Only He can put us right with God.

PRAY ABOUT IT

Talk to God about this and anything else that's on your mind.

THE BOTTOM LINE

Jesus is our friend and defender.

248 | A glimmer of hope

At first it seems as if today's chapters are the same old pattern — one of Job's friends (Bildad) giving him a hard time; then Job defending himself and complaining about his suffering. But there's a glimmer of hope for Job!

👁 Read Job 18 v 1–21

ENGAGE YOUR BRAIN

▶ *What's Bildad's jibe at Job this time? (v1–4)*

▶ *What's Bildad's view of what happens to wicked people?*

Bildad claims that all sinful people will be punished in their lifetime. But life doesn't always turn out like that. Sin has made our world unfair. Sinners might not suffer in this life. But they *will* be punished when Jesus returns as Judge.

👁 Skim-read Job 19 v 1–22

▶ *How does Job answer Bildad? (v1–6)*

▶ *Choose three words that describe Job's view of his life:*

👁 Carefully read verses 23–29

▶ *What's the irony of verses 23–24?*

▶ *What's incredible about Job's words in verses 25–27?*

Job seems to be sinking to new depths of despair (v1–22) only to rise to new heights of faith and hope! This is a turning point for Job. He's been searching for reasons for his suffering. He's not found any but he comes to a remarkable conclusion: *I can trust God; He will vindicate me when I see Him face to face.*

Unlike Job, we live after Jesus' death and resurrection. Our Redeemer does live — Jesus Christ, who has snatched us from the clutches of death!

PRAY ABOUT IT

I hope you're praising and thanking God already…

THE BOTTOM LINE

"I know that my Redeemer lives." (Job 19 v 25)

249 So unfair

"Life's not fair!" Have you ever felt like screaming that at the top of your lungs? Job had. In fact, he seems to have been doing it a lot. But his friend Zophar disagreed strongly.

👁 Read Job 20 v 4–11

According to Zophar, if you reject God in this life, then you'll be punished in this life.

ENGAGE YOUR BRAIN

▶ Do you agree with that?

▶ What evidence in the world supports or disproves Zophar's theory?

👁 Read Job 21 v 7–16

▶ What does Job say about the lives of wicked people? (v13)

▶ What's their attitude to God? (v14–15)

▶ What don't they realise? (v16)

👁 Read verses 22–26

▶ What truth about this life does Job point out? (v23–26)

▶ What does he say to people who say that God is unfair? (v22)

The fact is: we live in an unfair world. It's been messed up by sin. Most people don't live God's way. So, of course life is unfair. Some "bad" people seem to have an easy life, and some "good" people seem to have misery piled on them. We often won't understand why.

But can we tell God He's wrong? Definitely not. He is the perfect Judge, who always does the right thing. It may baffle us sometimes, but we can be sure it's for the right reasons. And we can be sure that, at the end of this imperfect life, the wicked will be punished and God's people will go on to a new, perfect life with Him.

PRAY ABOUT IT

Talk to God about anything that's troubling you. Ask Him to help you respond in the right way when the wicked seem to be successful.

2 TIMOTHY

Letter from death row

Rome, Italy. A beautiful city of stunning buildings on the gorgeous River Tiber. There's the Colosseum, the Forum and some great cafes. But in the year AD 66, Paul wasn't sightseeing or sipping a cappuccino. He'd been chained up in prison by Emperor Nero, who hated Christians.

THE LAST WORD?

While on death row, Paul wrote another letter to his close friend Timothy. They had travelled across the Roman Empire together, spreading the gospel for 15 years. Now Timothy was leading a church in Ephesus (in Turkey), and Paul was alone, expecting to die soon.

2 Timothy may have been the last letter Paul ever wrote — so what would the great apostle say?

Would he make a will? Ask for another blanket? Beg for someone to get him out of jail?

SPREAD THE WORD

Well, the letter's got a number of touching personal requests, but they're just slipped in at the end.

Paul had one overriding concern in the letter. He simply wanted to make sure that the gospel of Jesus Christ would continue to spread once he was dead.

Paul wrote to urge Timothy to stand up for the gospel. If the gospel was to survive after Paul's death, Tim needed to do two things: (1) to carry on preaching it, and (2) to train other people to preach it and spread it.

2 Timothy has some big lessons for us, encouraging us to stick with the gospel, to stand up for it and to be prepared to suffer for it. Paul says, "Get stuck in!"

250 Fan the flame

How would you describe yourself in just a few words? Shy, quiet bookworm? Loud, colourful basketball player? Cheerful, prayerful Christian? Go on, give it a go. Be honest.

👁 Read 2 Timothy 1 v 1–5

ENGAGE YOUR BRAIN

ⓘ *How does Paul describe himself and then Timothy? (v1, 2, 5)*

Paul calls himself an *"apostle"* — someone sent out by God to tell people about Jesus. He's holding on to the promise of *"life ... in Christ Jesus"* — life now serving God, and eternal life with God once he's dead.

Paul feels fatherly towards younger Tim and this letter is packed full of wise advice. He also says that Tim has *"sincere faith"*, just as his mum and grandmother did (v5). And he has been constantly praying for Tim.

ⓘ *How many people do you pray for constantly?*

👁 Read verses 6–7

ⓘ *What does Paul encourage Tim to do? (v6)*

ⓘ *Why shouldn't Tim be timid when spreading the gospel?*

Paul says: *Don't hold back and don't be shy — the Holy Spirit will help you serve God and spread the message.* Christians have the Holy Spirit helping them to powerfully tell people about Jesus; to show love to people around them; and to be disciplined, fighting temptation.

SHARE IT

It can be terrifying to share your faith with people, but we're not alone. God has given us the Spirit to help us courageously share the gospel: He can overcome our lack of self-confidence!

PRAY ABOUT IT

1. Pray for Christians you know.

2. Thank God for His Holy Spirit.

3. Ask Him to give you the courage to spread the gospel this week.

251 No shame

Is there anything you're ashamed of? Maybe embarrassed to let your dad talk to your friends? Or ashamed that you play the flute or collect stamps? But are you embarrassed about your faith?

👁 Read 2 Timothy 1 v 8–10

ENGAGE YOUR BRAIN

▶ Why might Tim be ashamed of Paul or of the gospel?

▶ What did Paul ask Tim to do? (v8) Why? (v9–10)

In the first century AD, it was risky to preach about Jesus' death and resurrection. Paul was imprisoned for it and other Christians had been killed. Tim could easily have wimped out, but Paul called for Tim to suffer with him for the sake of the gospel.

1) God has saved you.

2) He's called you to live a holy life.

3) You didn't deserve to be saved.

4) You're part of God's plans.

5) He's been so gracious to you.

6) God's rescue plan has existed for ever.

7) Jesus died and rose again to destroy death.

8) He's given you eternal life!

That's why we shouldn't be ashamed of the gospel, of Jesus or of being Christians. In fact, we should be prepared to suffer for spreading the incredible news of Jesus. Just look at what God has done for His people.

👁 Read verses 11–12

▶ Why was Paul willing to suffer?

Paul knows why he's suffering. He knows that Jesus died in his place. And he's confident that one day he will live with Jesus eternally.

SHARE IT

How can those eight reasons help you share the gospel? What will you do?

PRAY ABOUT IT

Read verses 8–10, thanking God for all the things He's done. Ask Him to help you not to be ashamed of Him.

252 Right guard

Paul, the great gospel preacher, is in prison, facing death. He wants the gospel to keep spreading after he's gone, so he's writing to Timothy, encouraging him to be brave, to stand up for the gospel and to suffer if necessary.

👁 Read 2 Timothy 1 v 13–14

ENGAGE YOUR BRAIN

▶ *If gospel truth was to survive, what two things was Tim to do?*

▶ *What help would he have? (v14)*

Tim should stick to the pattern of sound, life-giving teaching that he'd heard from Paul. Even when people around him were imprisoned or killed for preaching the gospel, Tim must hold on to the truth about Jesus — with **faith** in Jesus, showing **love** even to those who hassle him.

Tim must guard the truth of the gospel by making sure it's taught accurately and well. Thankfully, the Holy Spirit would help Him.

▶ *What does the gospel need guarding against these days?*

👁 Read verses 15–18

▶ *Who stuck by Paul through the hard times? (v16)*

▶ *How was he a shining example?*

Onesiphorus was happy to be known as Paul's friend even though it was risky. He went to great lengths to find Paul in prison (v17, see 2v9) and helped him in loads of ways (1v18).

GET ON WITH IT

▶ *How can you help Christians who are suffering for the gospel?*

▶ *Which Christian leaders can you help out? How?*

PRAY ABOUT IT

Thank God for giving the Holy Spirit to help believers hold on to the truth. And pray for Christians you know of who suffer for their faith.

THE BOTTOM LINE

Guard the gospel, support gospel-spreaders.

253 | Pass it on

Chinese whispers: whispering a phrase into someone's ear to pass it down the line. "Don't be ashamed of the gospel" turns into "Dopey Jamie's frogs smell". Chinese whispers is what Paul DIDN'T want to happen to the gospel.

👁 Read 2 Timothy 2 v 1–2

ENGAGE YOUR BRAIN

▶ *What do you think verse 1 means?*

▶ *What's Tim to do with the gospel message?*

Paul's advice to Tim is: *Don't be ashamed of the gospel. Be strong. Rely on Jesus and what He's done for you — for forgiveness, power to keep going and hope for the future. And make sure you pass on what I taught you to people you trust to keep the truth of the gospel as they spread it.*

👁 Read verses 3–7

▶ *What could Tim learn from…*
a soldier? (v4)
an athlete? (v5)
a farmer? (v6)

The Christian life is tough. But Paul says be like a soldier; please your commanding officer — God. Don't get distracted from serving the Lord.

Athletes don't get gold medals if they cheat and take steroids. Paul says don't cut corners, don't just obey the Bible when it suits you. You won't receive the prize of eternal life if you're faking it.

A farmer works his fingers to the bone to produce good crops. The Christian life is hard work. Stick at it, and you'll be rewarded. Eternally.

PRAY ABOUT IT

The Christian life is long, hard and involves suffering. But the rewards will be mind-blowing. Talk to God about the tough times. Ask Him for strength and perseverance. Thank Him for the great gift of eternal life.

254 To die for

Paul is so enthusiastic about the gospel — the truth about Jesus, His death and resurrection — that he wants everyone to hear it and says it's even worth suffering for. Worth dying for.

👁 Read 2 Timothy 2 v 8–10

ENGAGE YOUR BRAIN

▶ What's at the heart of the gospel message? (v8)

▶ How is God's word different from prisoner Paul? (v9)

The core of the gospel message is Jesus — sent to the world as a man but raised from death to reign in heaven. Because of Jesus' death and resurrection, Paul was willing to "endure everything" for teaching the incredible truth to "the elect" — those God is going to save.

Paul could be chained up, but the gospel can't. God's word will continue to spread and transform lives.

👁 Read verses 11–13

▶ How do these verses show us that the gospel is worth suffering for?

▶ How do these words encourage people who are being persecuted?

This is probably an early Christian song. It's basically saying: Christians will suffer in this life, but God is faithful, so hold on for eternal life.

Christians no longer live for themselves: they now live for Christ and will live with Him for ever (v11). Those who stick at it will one day rule with Him! (v12) But Jesus will turn His back on those who don't (v12).

PRAY ABOUT IT

Read through verses 8–13 slowly. What do they make you want to say to God? What do you need to say sorry for? What can you praise Him for?

THE BOTTOM LINE

Jesus is worth suffering for.

255 Unashamed workman

Paul's thoughts switched from his prison to the church where Tim was leader. Tim needed to be able to deal with false teachers in the church who were threatening the gospel and leading people away from Jesus.

👁 Read 2 Timothy 2 v 14–16

ENGAGE YOUR BRAIN

▶ What did Tim need to do in the church? (v14–16)

▶ With so much dodgy teaching around, why was it crucial that Tim did what verse 15 says?

Loads of top advice here. Most of it for church leaders, but there's plenty we can take to heart too.

• Don't fall out over things that don't matter so much.

• Make sure you're working for God and, if you teach the Bible, make sure you get it right.

• Avoid ungodly talk; it will harm you.

GET ON WITH IT

▶ Which of these things do you need to deal with right now?

👁 Read verses 17–19

▶ What was the effect of this false teaching? (v18)

▶ Why won't such nonsense defeat the true gospel? (v19)

▶ What must Christians do? (v19)

The Bible says believers will rise from the dead and get new bodies when Jesus returns — that's what "resurrection" means here (v18). But these false teachers claimed it had happened already. Rubbish.

Tim was struggling with false teachers in his church, but God knows which people are truly His. They show a desire to obey Him and turn away from wickedness (v19).

PRAY ABOUT IT

Pray through verses 14–16, talking to God about any of these things you need to deal with. Ask Him to help you stand firm and not be fooled by false teaching.

256 Run away!

Go and open a random drawer in the kitchen. Which items in it are useful and which ones are useless? Why are you doing this??? Well, it links in with today's 2 Timothy talk.

👁 Read 2 Timothy 2 v 20–21

ENGAGE YOUR BRAIN

▷ What do you think Paul is waffling on about?

What's with all this talk of kitchen drawers and household objects? Remember reading yesterday about Tim's trouble with false teachers? Well, they are like objects used for common purposes, not special ones — God won't use them.

Instead, He seeks those who've been made holy, are useful to Him and are prepared to serve Him doing good stuff.

Next, Paul mentions two things God's people must do.

👁 Read verse 22

▷ What are some of the "evil desires of youth"?

▷ What kind of things should Christians chase after?

Strong words. We're not just told to ignore sinful desires, we must **sprint** away from them. If you find yourself in a tempting situation, get out of there; ditch those friends; block certain content on your laptop or phone; get yourself out of angry quarrels. Run away!

GET ON WITH IT

▷ What "evil desires" do you need to run away from and kick out of your life?

▷ What do you actually need to do to pursue righteousness, faith, love and peace?

PRAY ABOUT IT

You know what you need to talk to God about today.

THE BOTTOM LINE

Flee sin, chase after holiness.

257 Stupid squabbles

Ever had really heated arguments over pointless stuff? I once had a fiery squabble with someone about whether or not I was a cannibal! Ridiculous. Paul told Tim not to get drawn into stupid arguments.

👁 Read 2 Timothy 2 v 23–24

ENGAGE YOUR BRAIN

▶ *What exactly does Paul say about foolish arguments?*

▶ *What should God's servant do instead? (v24)*

Silly little quarrels are not only a waste of time but they can turn into bigger disputes and get in the way of spreading the gospel. It's easy to get drawn into arguments, especially when we feel wronged. Paul says avoid fights, show kindness during arguments and don't hold grudges.

👁 Read verses 25–26

▶ *How should Tim deal with people who oppose him?*

▶ *Why was it so important that Tim was gentle with such people?*

▶ *What was at stake? (v26)*

Yes, Tim should fight for the truth — but gently. When people argue with us, we want to win them over to the gospel, not beat them in pointless arguments. Getting fired up and aggressive won't help the gospel, but quietly opening your Bible with someone might.

Our arguments alone won't convince anyone to give their lives to Jesus — it is God who brings them to the truth (v25) so that they can escape the devil's clutches (v26).

GET ON WITH IT

▶ *How can you act differently during disagreements?*

▶ *Who can you gently introduce to the truth about Jesus?*

PRAY ABOUT IT

Ask God to help you conquer your anger and be gentle when people disagree with you. Ask Him to be working in the heart of the person you want to share the gospel with.

258 Terrible times

Paul is warning Tim about tough times ahead and false teachers spreading lies in the church. The "last days" he mentions means the time between Jesus' first coming and when He returns as Judge. That's right now.

👁 Read 2 Timothy 3 v 1–5

ENGAGE YOUR BRAIN

▶ *What are people like?*

▶ *Which of these things seem most relevant to our society?*

The beginning of verse 2 and the end of verse 4 sum up the whole list: "Lovers of themselves … rather than lovers of God". Putting yourself first before others leads to the other stuff — pride, boasting, abuse, disobedience to parents, lack of self-control and the rest. And God comes bottom of the list of priorities.

The really worrying bit is in verse 5 — many of these people call themselves believers! They go to church, say the right things, look the part but don't really live for God.

👁 Read verses 6–9

▶ *How are false teachers described? (v6–7)*

▶ *What will happen to them? (v8–9)*

Dodgy teachers claim to follow Jesus, but only love themselves. They prey on people who fall for their charms. Just like Pharaoh's magicians, Jannes and Jambres, who opposed Moses, they won't get far. People will soon see they have nothing genuine to offer.

PRAY ABOUT IT

Pray about people you know who refuse to put God first in their lives — maybe that's you. Pray for people you know who have been fooled by false religion, that God will open their eyes to the truth of Jesus.

THE BOTTOM LINE

Have nothing to do with false teachers.

259 God's great word

Most of us have older Christians we look up to — people who have had a big impact on our faith. For Timothy, it was Paul. He'd heard Paul preach the gospel and seen him suffer for it too.

👁 Read 2 Timothy 3 v 10–13

ENGAGE YOUR BRAIN

▶ *How does Paul's life differ from the false teachers'?*

▶ *What's the tough promise for Christians? (v12)*

Paul was a big influence on Tim's life. Tim could learn a lot from him — especially the way Paul was prepared to suffer for the gospel. That's the harsh reality of life as a Christian in a sinful world: we face persecution for our faith, while godless people go from bad to worse (v12–13).

👁 Read verses 14–17

▶ *What was Tim to do? Why? (v14–15)*

▶ *Where does the Bible (Scripture) come from? (v16)*

▶ *What should it be used for? (v16)*

▶ *What's the great result? (v17)*

This is how Christians can keep going despite persecution — living by God's word. The Bible comes to us straight from God. As you read the Bible, God Himself is speaking to you: teaching you, disciplining you, setting you straight and training you in right living. Equipping you to serve Him.

GET ON WITH IT

▶ *How do you treat the Bible?*

▶ *How can you make sure it impacts the way you live more?*

PRAY ABOUT IT

Thank God for Christians who've had a big effect on your life. Pray for them. And ask God to help you take His word more seriously and live by it.

THE BOTTOM LINE

All Scripture is God-breathed.

260 Fighting talk

Gospel heavyweight Paul took a hammering in his life. But he kept on fighting. And he wanted Tim to do the same.

👁 Read 2 Timothy 4 v 1–5

ENGAGE YOUR BRAIN

Paul's advice is particularly helpful to Christian leaders, but remember, "All Scripture is God-breathed" so there's bound to be stuff for us too.

▶ *What were Tim's orders? (v2)*

▶ *Why should they be taken seriously? (v1)*

▶ *How should Tim respond to false teachers? (v5)*

This is serious stuff — that's why Paul mentions God's presence and reminds Tim that Jesus will return as Judge. Tim better take this seriously: Preach God's word! Be prepared! Correct false teaching! Encourage! Keep your head! Stick at it!

PRAY ABOUT IT

Pray for Christian leaders, that they will follow Paul's instructions and teach God's word faithfully.

👁 Read verses 6–8

▶ *How was Paul a brilliant example to Tim? (v6–7)*

▶ *What's his prize?*

What an incredible description at the end of Paul's life. The hope of heaven and seeing Jesus face to face enabled him to keep fighting, keep sharing the gospel (even while in prison!) and to keep the faith. That should be our motivation too.

▶ *Do you long to see Jesus face to face? Why/why not?*

PRAY ABOUT IT

Thank God that Christians have the certain hope of eternal life with Him. Ask the Lord to help you stick at it, fighting for the gospel until your last breath.

THE BOTTOM LINE

Fight the good fight.

261 Getting personal

Paul is getting towards the end of his second letter to Timothy (I call it "Tim: Book Two"). He's getting personal, with a few words about people Tim knows — some good, some bad.

👁 Read 2 Timothy 4 v 9–13

ENGAGE YOUR BRAIN

▶ How do you think Paul was feeling as he wrote this? (v9–11)

▶ Why did Demas desert Paul?

Paul was feeling lonely. Crescens, Titus and Tychicus (great names!) were on gospel missions and Demas had run out on Paul. Like many people who seem to be following Christ, he was lured away from God by the temptations of the world. Only faithful Luke was still with Paul, so he asked that Tim and helpful Mark would join him before he died.

TALK IT THROUGH

▶ What kinds of things seduce people away from Christ?

▶ What steps can you take to avoid falling in love with the world?

▶ Who do you need to persuade to come back to living for God?

👁 Read verses 14–15

We need to watch out for people who oppose the gospel. We also need to watch our own reaction to them, making sure we don't become bitter and revengeful — we have to leave any punishment to God (v14).

PRAY ABOUT IT

1. Pray for people you know who "love the world".

2. Pray for Christians who are lonely.

3. Pray for Christians you know who quietly get on with serving God and other Christians.

4. Pray for people around you who hate Christianity.

5. Pray for yourself, that you won't be lured away by the temptations of the world.

262 Final Words

We've reached the end of Paul's letter to Tim. It's been packed with teaching, warnings and encouragement to keep spreading the gospel, whatever it costs.

👁 Read 2 Timothy 4 v 16

ENGAGE YOUR BRAIN

▶ *What was Paul's attitude towards those who'd deserted him?*

▶ *How do you react when people let you down?*

Paul had been in court, accused by the Romans, who wanted him dead. No one had showed up to support him, yet Paul didn't hold it against them. Amazing. It's so easy to hold grudges against people who let us down, but Paul encourages us to follow his example!

▶ *Who do you need to forgive and treat better? (v16)*

👁 Read verses 17–22

▶ *What was the great news when Paul was alone?*

▶ *What did God enable him to do? (v17)*

▶ *What could Paul be confident of?*

None of Paul's friends had been with him, but the Lord was at his side, giving him the strength he needed to shout the truth about Jesus (v17).

He was completely confident that God would rescue him and keep him safe. Not necessarily physically, as Paul knew he might be killed for preaching about Jesus. But God would keep him safe *eternally*, bringing him safely to His eternal kingdom. Awesome stuff.

PRAY ABOUT IT

Verse 18 is true for all believers. Read it (out loud if you can) and praise God for its incredible truth.

THE BOTTOM LINE

Christians are safe with the Lord. Eternally.

NEHEMIAH

Big build-up

Remember how God's people kept on getting things wrong? Turning away from Him. Marrying the foreign women around them and worshipping their fake gods. Forgetting how God had rescued them to be His special people.

AWAY FROM HOME

Just as He'd warned them, their rebellion could only end one way, and God always keeps His promises. So He handed His people over to their enemies, and they were taken off into exile in Babylon (modern-day Iraq). But that wasn't the end of the story — remember that God always keeps His promises — and there would be a way back.

RETURN JOURNEY

Sure enough, after 70 years, King Darius lets some of the Jews return, and that's where two guys named Ezra and Nehemiah come in. The events in the book of Nehemiah are closely linked to those in the book of Ezra — they take place straight afterwards.

BUILDING WORK

Ezra is concerned with rebuilding the temple, while Nehemiah has a God-given mission to rebuild the city of Jerusalem. But the big question is: as the city is rebuilt, will the people be reformed?

Will it be a fresh start or the same old story? Will the people return to God or their old ways? Is there any hope? And what about us? Can we change? Or will we keep falling back into those same old sins time after time? Read Nehemiah and see what God has got planned!

263 | City in ruins

The good news: since King Darius had let some of the Jewish people return to Jerusalem, there had been progress. The temple was being rebuilt and things were looking positive. The bad news? Read on...

👁 Read Nehemiah 1 v 1–4

ENGAGE YOUR BRAIN

▶ Where is Nehemiah (v1) and what is his job? (v11)

▶ What news does Nehemiah receive? (v2–3)

▶ What is Nehemiah's reaction?

▶ Why do you think he's so bothered?

After the misery of exile, it looked as though God had forgiven His people and things were looking up. But then it started to fall apart. That's why the reality of the situation in Jerusalem hit Nehemiah so hard. But his first thought was to talk to God about it. Look at what he prays.

👁 Read verses 5–11

▶ What does Nehemiah know about who God is? (v5)

▶ What does he admit about himself and the rest of his people? (v6–7)

▶ What else does he remember about God? (v8–9)

▶ So what does Nehemiah ask? (v10–11)

PRAY ABOUT IT

Do you sometimes find prayer difficult? Try following Nehemiah's example. Thank God for who He is. Say sorry for the ways in which you have sinned. Ask Him to act based on His character and promises.

THE BOTTOM LINE

God always keeps His promises.

264 Nervous questions

Nehemiah was devastated when he heard that God's city, Jerusalem, was lying in ruins. So he pleaded for God's help as he nervously went to ask King Artaxerxes a big favour.

👁 Read Nehemiah 2 v 1–4

ENGAGE YOUR BRAIN

▶ *Why do you think Nehemiah was so scared in verse 2?*

Appearing before the king with a gloomy face was a total no-no. The king's servants were expected to be professionally cheerful.

▶ *Amazingly, what does the king ask? (v4)*

▶ *What is Nehemiah's first response? (v4)*

Nehemiah's quick silent appeal for God's help is often called an "arrow prayer" — a quick shot upwards asking for help. Do you ever do this? When you're facing a difficult decision, awkward conversation, or are asked a tricky question about your faith?

PRAY ABOUT IT

Get into the habit of asking for God's help and power in every part of your life. 1 Peter 5 v 7 reminds us to "cast all your anxiety on him because he cares for you".

👁 Read Nehemiah 2 v 5–10

▶ *What is Nehemiah's reply to the king? (v5)*

▶ *Even more amazingly, how does the king react? (v6–9)*

▶ *Who is really behind all this?*

▶ *How do the enemies of the Jewish people respond to these developments? (v10)*

God answered Nehemiah's prayer brilliantly! But verse 10 hints that Nehemiah might have some enemies when he starts rebuilding Jerusalem. More about that tomorrow…

265 Hope in ruins

So Nehemiah sets off on his mission to inspect the damage in Jerusalem. And yes, things are as bad as he'd feared. But he also knows that God is able to do more than we can possibly ask or imagine.

👁 Read Nehemiah 2 v 11–20

ENGAGE YOUR BRAIN

▶ *How does Nehemiah begin his task? (v11–16)*

▶ *What does he find?*

▶ *Why do you think he's so secretive?*

▶ *What words does he use in verse 17 to describe the current situation?*

▶ *How does he describe God? (v18)*

▶ *How do the people of Jerusalem respond? (v18)*

God prepared the way with the king and now He's clearly behind the people's enthusiasm to start rebuilding. Things are looking up.

▶ *What about Sanballat and his cronies? (v19)*

▶ *What is Nehemiah's comeback to their taunts? (v20)*

GET ON WITH IT

How do you respond when people mock you for being a Christian? Are you as confident in God's grace as Nehemiah was? Can you carry on despite opposition? It's only God's grace and power that will enable us to do so.

PRAY ABOUT IT

Get a bigger picture of God. Read Ephesians 3 v 20–21 and let it shape your prayers today!

THE BOTTOM LINE

God's in control and always wins.

266 | Gate expectations

OK, so it's time to start building, and everyone pitches in!

👁 Skim Nehemiah 3 v 1–32

ENGAGE YOUR BRAIN

▶ *Where did the building work start (see v1, 3, 6 etc)?*

▶ *Why were gates so important to a city?*

As we'll see in the next few chapters, Jerusalem was still surrounded by enemies. Even with the backing of King Artaxerxes, the city needed to be defended.

▶ *How did the people group themselves to start the building work?*
v3:
v7:
v8:
v28:

▶ *What surprising types of people got involved? (v12)*

▶ *Any slackers? (v5)*

GET ON WITH IT

Do you ever think you're too important to do certain tasks? Need to rethink? Remind yourself of Jesus' words in Mark 10 v 42–45.

▶ *So how exactly will you serve God in a new way?*

PRAY ABOUT IT

Christians are heading to another city — a heavenly Jerusalem, which has strong walls and beautiful gates, but these gates are never shut! Read Revelation 21 v 10–27 and thank God that one day all threats, enemies and war will be over and we will live in perfect peace, face to face with our King.

THE BOTTOM LINE

God's people will one day live in perfect security with Him.

267 Prayer in action

After such a great start, trouble is not far behind. Yep, it's Sanballat and co. again.

👁 Read Nehemiah 4 v 1–9

ENGAGE YOUR BRAIN

▶ *How did Sanballat and Tobiah try to discourage God's people?*

▶ *How did Nehemiah react?*

▶ *What exactly did he pray?*

▶ *Why do you think he prayed this?*

Look at what Sanballat and Tobiah are mocking in verse 2 — not just the city but the sacrificial system and the whole worship of God. It's a very dangerous business to mock the living God.

▶ *How did the building work progress despite the mockery? (v6)*

▶ *Had Sanballat's attempts to dishearten them worked? (v6)*

▶ *What tactics do Sanballat and co. resort to next? (v8)*

▶ *And Nehemiah and the Jews' response?*

Pray and act. Prayer doesn't mean we sit back and wait. When people hassle us, we shouldn't let it get in the way of serving God. We've got to carry on living God's way.

THINK IT OVER

How do you react when people mock you or your faith? Do you lose your temper? Do you feel sorry for yourself? The great news is that we can talk to God about our problems and hand them over to Him to deal with them.

PRAY ABOUT IT

What do you need to ask God to enable you to do today? Ask Him and then get on with it!

THE BOTTOM LINE

God's people will face opposition

268 | Prepared for battle

God's people are rebuilding Jerusalem and are about to face more opposition. Will the people start to crack just like the walls (groan)? Not on Nehemiah's watch!

👁 Read Nehemiah 4 v 10–15

ENGAGE YOUR BRAIN

▶ *What problems are the people facing? (v10–13)*

▶ *What is Nehemiah's two-pronged response? (v13–14)*

▶ *Why will it help them to remember who God is?*

▶ *Who wrecked their enemies' plans? (v15)*

👁 Read verses 16–23

▶ *What system does Nehemiah put in place to ensure the building work continues and is protected? (v16–20)*

▶ *What was he confident of? (v20)*

Under huge pressure, the work went on. Starting something is all very well, but keeping going through the tough times until it is finished is what counts. The great news is that whenever life seems too hard to keep going as a Christian, we have God with us on our side, fighting for us!

PRAY ABOUT IT

The Bible says that God's people should always be ready for battle — prepared to fight against the devil's schemes and temptations. Read Ephesians 6 v 10–18 and pray through the armour you need to put on today, remembering that prayer itself is part of our weaponry.

THE BOTTOM LINE

Our God will fight for us.

269 Trouble within

We've seen Nehemiah and his team of builders facing heavy opposition from enemies outside the city. But there were big problems inside the city too.

Read Nehemiah 5 v 1–5

ENGAGE YOUR BRAIN

▶ *What was the problem? (v1–4)*

▶ *What had they resorted to? (v5)*

Shockingly, it was the Jewish officials, placed in charge by Artaxerxes' regime, who were extracting huge amounts of money from their own people in tax.

Read verses 6–13

Your Bible version may say "usury" in verse 7. This means lending money at extortionate interest rates.

▶ *What does Nehemiah accuse the VIPs of? (v7–8)*

▶ *What does he tell them they should do? (v9–11)*

▶ *What happens? (v12–13)*

Nehemiah said God's people shouldn't cheat each other in this way. Instead, they should extend gifts and generosity to the needy.

Read verses 14–19

▶ *How does Nehemiah set an example of how God wants His people to be? (v14–18)*

▶ *Was Nehemiah entitled to money and great food?*

▶ *Why didn't he enforce his rights?*

PRAY ABOUT IT

The whole earth belongs to the Lord and yet He generously gives us life, food, friends, family and salvation. Thank God for His generosity, especially in sending Jesus, who "though he was rich, yet for your sake he became poor, so that you through his poverty might become rich" (2 Corinthians 8 v 9).

THE BOTTOM LINE

God is generous. So we should be generous too.

270 Fighting talk

The work on the wall is going well though not finished yet. But Sanballat, Tobiah and co. are still trying to derail the work and intimidate Nehemiah and God's people.

👁 Read Nehemiah 6 v 1–7

ENGAGE YOUR BRAIN

▶ Where has the work got to? (v1)

▶ What are Sanballat and his cronies up to? (v2)

▶ What is Nehemiah's reply? (v3–4)

▶ How persistent are they?

▶ How do they become sneakier in verses 5–7?

▶ Why might this approach work for them?

Not only is Nehemiah accused (falsely) of treason but it's in an open letter that anyone can read. Sanballat is trying to intimidate and undermine all those working with Nehemiah.

👁 Read verses 8–14

▶ How does Nehemiah respond? (v8)

▶ Who does he turn to? (v9)

▶ What tactic do God's enemies try next? (v10–14)

▶ Does Nehemiah see through them? (v11–13)

GET ON WITH IT

The apostle Peter gives this advice to Christians facing false accusations: "Live such good lives among the pagans that, though they accuse you of doing wrong, they may see your good deeds and glorify God on the day he visits us" (1 Peter 2 v 12).

Ask for God's help to do that in your situation today.

271 Finished!

Have you ever seen a building site in action?
Houses or offices can go up fairly quickly,
but they've got nothing on Nehemiah's gang.

👁 Read Nehemiah 6 v 16–19

ENGAGE YOUR BRAIN

🔸 *How long had the whole project taken? (v15)*

🔸 *What did that show about the whole thing? (v16)*

🔸 *How did it affect the surrounding enemy nations?*

Seven weeks is a seriously impressive timescale for this amount of work. No long tea breaks for Nehemiah's team. They have been motivated and dedicated despite major opposition. Clearly God is the one at work. But it's not all plain sailing.

🔸 *What new problem does Nehemiah face? (v17–19)*

Tobiah is using his family ties to manipulate people within the city. It's a prime example of why marrying outside of God's people was such a bad idea. Keep this in mind; it's going to be a major issue later on in Nehemiah.

👁 Read Nehemiah 7 v 1–3

🔸 *Once the work is complete, are the troubles at an end? (7 v 1–3)*

🔸 *What are the criteria Nehemiah uses to decide who should be in charge of defending the city? (v2)*

PRAY ABOUT IT

Hanani and Hananiah feared the Lord. Proverbs 9 v 10 tells us that: "The fear of the LORD is the beginning of wisdom". Ask God to help you to fear, love and respect Him and value His opinion above anyone else's.

THE BOTTOM LINE

Fear the Lord.

272 | Listed building

The city walls are rebuilt, but Jerusalem is still a bit on the empty side. Time for operation repopulation!

👁 **Skim Nehemiah 7 v 4–73**

ENGAGE YOUR BRAIN

ⓘ What is the situation in verse 4? What does God move Nehemiah to do about it? (v5)

ⓘ Why do you think he starts with those who were first to return?

ⓘ What does that show about their hearts?

ⓘ How does Nehemiah list them? What groupings does he use?

ⓘ What does that show about his concerns (eg: v43, 46)?

ⓘ Why do you think he is particularly concerned about the priests being pure? (v63–65)

One of the big problems before the exile was corrupt worship. So Nehemiah is taking no chances. They're out until they've been properly approved. Urim and Thumin (v65) was a kind of lot-drawing only done by the priests.

ⓘ How do the people contribute towards the building programme? (v70–72)

ⓘ Where do the people settle? (v73)

Jerusalem hasn't been repopulated yet, but a clear record has been established of which of God's people could be part of it. Incidentally, it's the same list as in Ezra chapter 2.

PRAY ABOUT IT

In Revelation 21 v 3 we read about the new Jerusalem, where "God's dwelling place is now among the people, and he will dwell with them. They will be his people, and God himself will be with them and be their God". Thank God for that wonderful promise made possible because of Jesus.

THE BOTTOM LINE

All of God's people get to live in the new Jerusalem!

273 | Psalms: Singing from the depths

Is your life a bit of a rollercoaster? David probably never went to his local Jerusalem theme park for a ride on the "Deadly Corkscrew", but his psalms brilliantly reflect life's highs and lows. Psalm 30 is a great example.

Read Psalm 30 v 1–3

ENGAGE YOUR BRAIN

▶ *What did David do when he was in "the depths"? (v2)*

▶ *How did God respond?*

▶ *Do you pray for healing when you're ill?*

Read verses 4–7

Depending on your Bible version, verse 4 may say "faithful people" or "saints". A saint isn't some totally perfect, golden boy, halo gleaming in the secure knowledge he's never, ever sinned. When the Bible talks about saints, it simply means people who trust in Jesus. Christians.

Saints still mess up and sin, provoking God's anger. What's the good news for them in verse 5?

▶ *What is David's response to God's care? (v6)*

"Rejoicing ... in the morning" (v5). The ultimate "morning" for Christians is eternal life. Even if life on earth is full of weeping, we always have the rejoicing-filled hope of eternal life with God.

Read verses 8–12

▶ *Which characteristics of God give hope in despair?*

▶ *What's happened to David's wailing and mourning?*

Interestingly, God's ultimate purpose in transforming David's grief is to bring glory to Himself.

PRAY ABOUT IT

Think of a seemingly hopeless situation you are going through. Pray about it to God – the great hope-giver, who has transforming power.

MATTHEW

Are you ready?

How do you tend to get ready? Are you a planning-ahead, well-prepared kind of person? Or do you leave things till the last minute?

As we dive back into Matthew's Gospel, picking up the story in chapter 23, we meet a King who is ready — ready to die. Jesus, the all-powerful, eternally-ruling "Son of Man", is in Jerusalem, surrounded by His followers and His opponents.

And He knows that "the Son of Man will be handed over to be crucified" (26 v 2). He knows that it's time for all the Old Testament prophecies about Him to be fulfilled. He knows that it's time to pour out His blood so that His followers can be forgiven (v28). Jesus knows that the moment He was born for, which His life has been preparing for, is about to come — His death. The King is ready to die.

But in His final teachings, we'll see Him getting His followers ready too.

Ready to live. Jesus knows His death will not be the end.

He points us to the day "when the Son of Man comes in his glory, and all the angels with him, [and] he will sit on his glorious throne" (25 v 31). He warns people to be ready for His return: ready to welcome Him and enjoy eternal life with Him. And He tells us how to live in a way which shows we're ready for the day when the King comes again.

So, as we spend time with Jesus in His final few days before death… as we follow Him through His arrest, on to His cross, into His tomb and beyond… as we watch His enemies plot against Him, His friends fail to back Him, and even His Father God completely desert Him… we'll see a King who loves His people so much that He's ready to die for them.

And we'll see Him call us to be ready to live. Get ready to get ready!

274 Rotten religion

One of the shocks of the Gospels is that Jesus and religion just don't get on. In fact, Jesus is about to give the religious leaders of His day both barrels...

👁 Read Matthew 23 v 1–7

The "teachers of the law and the Pharisees" led Israel's religious life (v2). They were the bishops and pastors of their day. Surely they had religion sorted...

ENGAGE YOUR BRAIN

▶ But how does Jesus criticise them? (end of v3, 5)

▶ What do they love most? (v6–7)

THINK ABOUT IT

These guys do a lot of very religious stuff. But it's rotten. Imagine this kind of person was part of your church. What would they be like?

PRAY ABOUT IT

Lord Jesus, help me never to make my religion about me. Help me never to use my Christianity to try to look good in front of other people. Amen.

👁 Read verses 8–12

These leaders loved to have impressive-sounding titles (v7).

Today, they'd want to be addressed as "The Right Very Especially Reverend Dr So-and-So".

▶ What does Jesus say His true followers should not do? (v8–10)

▶ What should their motivation be? (v11)

Spot the difference? These religious leaders want others to look up to them; Jesus' followers are to get on their hands and knees to serve others. That's the point in verse 12. Christians don't need to big themselves up. God will do it for them.

PRAY ABOUT IT

Lord, help me to serve your people as I follow you, and rely on you to give me the glory of eternal life.

275 Pulling no punches

Jesus' words here are as hardcore as you can get. "Woe" is a way of saying "God's condemnation and anger". With that in mind...

👁 Read Matthew 23 v 13–22

ENGAGE YOUR BRAIN

▶ *How many times does Jesus promise "woe" here, and who to?*

▶ *What reasons does He give?*
v13:
v15:
v16–22:

These men are very, very religious. They take it very seriously.

▶ *What are they willing to do in order to convert someone to their way of thinking? (v15)*

▶ *That's evangelism — great! Isn't it? (end of v15)*

THINK ABOUT IT

Here's the sting. It's possible to be religious, hardworking, committed and successful — and at the same time be condemning yourself, and leading others towards hell (v15). It doesn't matter if you really believe something. What matters is believing something real. The road to hell can be a very religious one.

▶ *Re-read verse 10. What is the right way to be religious?*

GET ON WITH IT

In one way, we should be the opposite of the Pharisees.

▶ *How should we act differently from the Pharisees? (v13)*

In another way, we can learn from the Pharisees.

▶ *How far were they willing to go to get just one person to believe what they did? (v15)*

▶ *How does this challenge you?*

THE BOTTOM LINE

You can be very religious and go to hell: make sure you're following Christ into His kingdom.

276 | Good looks

Are you good-looking? Jesus says you won't find the answer in a mirror.

👁 Read Matthew 23 v 23–28

ENGAGE YOUR BRAIN

▶ What do the leaders do? What don't they do? (v23–24)

It's not only giving 1/10th that they are hot on: it's also cleaning anything they eat food from (v25). So Jesus uses a cup and dish as a picture of the religious leaders themselves.

▶ What's the problem? (v25)

▶ What should they be focusing on? (v26)?

▶ How does Jesus' image in verses 27–28 repeat the point He's making?

THINK ABOUT IT

▶ If you were looking at a Pharisee, how good-looking, in religious terms, would they seem?

▶ But Jesus doesn't care about the outside. What does He say really matters?

▶ How would it be possible for you to be good-looking on the outside, and ugly on the inside?

GET ON WITH IT

Look at your heart. Really look hard! Have you asked Jesus to be in charge of it? Have you asked Jesus to take away all the wrong in it? Or are you just looking good at church, on the outside, to hide the fact that there are all kinds of "wickedness" in your heart which you really enjoy and don't want to get rid of?

PRAY ABOUT IT

Ask God to let you see the state of your heart. Ask Him to help you never to cover up an ugly inside, but instead to ask Jesus to deal with it.

THE BOTTOM LINE

The world cares about our outside: Jesus cares about our heart.

277 | Jesus' wings

The "woes" continue. Is there any way these guys can escape hell? Yes! But will they take it?

👁 Read Matthew 23 v 29–36

Israel had a long history of killing God's messengers instead of listening to them (v31). But that was a long time ago — in Jesus' day, the leaders said they would never make that mistake (v30).

But now God's Son had come. And He would send "prophets and wise men and teachers" to Israel (v34), to call God's ancient people to truly know and serve God.

ENGAGE YOUR BRAIN

▶ *How would these religious leaders treat them? (v34)*

PRAY ABOUT IT

It's easy to think how stupid these men were for shutting up Jesus' messengers instead of listening to them. But isn't that exactly what we do whenever we don't bother to read or remember or obey their words in the Bible?

Speak to God now. Admit to Him the times this week you've ignored people He's spoken through in the Bible.

👁 Read verses 37–39

The Jews of Jerusalem deserve "being condemned to hell" (v33).

▶ *But what does Jesus want to do? (v37)*

A hen does this to protect her children from harm. When God's judgment on those who have rejected Him is unleashed, there will only be one safe place: under Jesus' wings. Tragically, these guys didn't want that (v37).

PRAY ABOUT IT

Tell God, for the first or thousandth time, that you're putting yourself under Jesus' protection, to avoid the judgment you deserve and enjoy the eternal life He gives.

304 | Matthew 24 v 1–14

278 The end of the world

**Warning: Matthew 24 is hard.
But it's well worth the effort!**

👁 Read Matthew 24 v 1–3

ENGAGE YOUR BRAIN

🔘 *What does Jesus predict? (v1–2)*

🔘 *What two questions do His
followers ask Him? (v3)*

Verse 3 is the key to the whole
chapter. Jesus is talking about two
events at the same time. One is the
destruction of the temple and the
whole of Jerusalem. This was Jesus'
judgment on Israel for rejecting Him,
and happened in AD 70. The other
is the destruction of the entire world
at "the end of the age". This will
be His judgment on the whole of
humanity, and hasn't happened yet!

What happened to Israel in AD 70
was a catastrophe. But it was just
a picture of God's final judgment.
And as Jesus told His followers how
to live waiting for His judgment of
Israel, He was also telling Christians
now how to live awaiting His final
judgment.

👁 Read verses 4–14

🔘 *What will happen before Jesus
returns? (v4–9)*

🔘 *What will happen within the
Christian community? (v10–12)*

🔘 *So what must we do? (v13–14)*

For people who do that, there will
be rescue from judgment (v13).
For those who keep going with
Jesus, "the end" will in fact be a
beginning, of perfect life in a perfect
world.

GET ON WITH IT

🔘 *How do Jesus' words here help
you keep going when it's hard to
be a Christian?*

THE BOTTOM LINE

"The one who stands firm to the
end will be saved" (v13)

279 Where's the world heading?

**Environmental disaster? Nuclear destruction?
Robots taking over? Aliens landing? Nope...**

👁 Read Matthew 24 v 15–28

ENGAGE YOUR BRAIN

Again, Jesus is mixing details that are only about the fall of Jerusalem (v15–16, 20) with details about the end of the world (v21).

▶ What do His followers need to be particularly careful about? (v23–26)

▶ What will these fakes be able to do? (v24)

If we saw someone who could do this, we'd be very impressed! And we'd probably listen to them — after all, surely someone who can do these amazing feats must be from God?! But Jesus says: "No!" Don't be influenced by someone just because they can do miracles. Check verse 35. What counts more?

GET ON WITH IT

Don't be impressed by powerful teachers, witty speakers, impressive leaders. Be impressed by those who point you to Jesus' eternal words. We don't need to worry that we might miss Jesus' return. It will be totally obvious to absolutely everyone (v27).

👁 Read verses 29–35

▶ What will happen to the creation? (v29) And to Jesus? (v30)

▶ And to "the peoples of the earth" who don't know Jesus? (v30)

▶ And to Christians (the "elect")? (v31)

THINK ABOUT IT

How does all this motivate you to keep living for Jesus today?

THE BOTTOM LINE

When Jesus returns, the world will fall, but His people will be with Him.

280 And then... BANG!

Today is pretty much like yesterday. Tomorrow will probably be the same. The world turns, life continues, nothing much changes... AND THEN BANG!

👁 Read Matthew 24 v 36–44

ENGAGE YOUR BRAIN

▶ *When will Jesus return? (v36)*

Jesus compares the day He comes to the days of Noah (v37).

▶ *What were people doing? (v38)*

▶ *AND THEN BANG! What happened? (v39)*

▶ *So what is Jesus saying about His return? (v40-41)*

The world's destined for destruction (v29). But Jesus will gather His people so they avoid that destruction (v31). One day, everyone will be going about their everyday business, just like the day before, AND THEN BANG! And you don't want to be left behind.

▶ *What's the right response? (v42)*

👁 Read verses 45–51

Jesus is explaining how we know whether we're ready for Him to return to His world. All of us have been given ways to help His people, "the servants" (v45).

▶ *What does Jesus, "the master", want to find us doing when He returns? (v46)*

▶ *What will He then do? (v47)*

Exciting stuff! But if, instead, we live for ourselves, abusing our privileges (v48-49), then we're showing we don't really think Jesus will return (v50). We're not ready. We'll face an eternity outside His kingdom (v51).

THINK ABOUT IT

▶ *Are you ready to welcome Jesus as your Lord and Saviour if it happens today?*

▶ *How will you serve His people while you wait?*

281 Don't be f-oil-ish

The question keeps coming: Are you ready?

👁 Read Matthew 25 v 1–13

ENGAGE YOUR BRAIN

▶ *What's Jesus' point, again? (v13)*

But He's wanting to give a particular warning by telling this parable. The "virgins" (or bridesmaids) have lamps so they can meet the bridegroom, as was traditional.

▶ *What's the only difference between the two kinds of bridesmaids? (v3–4)*

The bridegroom's taking ages to get to the wedding reception, and they all snooze off... (v5). And then suddenly, unexpectedly, he's there (v6)!

▶ *What problem do some of the bridesmaids have? (v8)*

▶ *What do they do?*

▶ *How do the wiser bridesmaids respond? (v9)*

▶ *Where do the bridesmaids who were ready end up?*

▶ *What about those who weren't ready? (v10–13)*

THINK ABOUT IT

The foolish bridesmaids thought they could rely on those around them. But the wiser bridesmaids only had enough oil for themselves. The foolish ones discovered they couldn't rely on anyone else. And they missed out. For virgins/bridesmaids, read "people". For oil, read "faith in Jesus".

▶ *What point is Jesus making?*

GET ON WITH IT

Check that you've got real, personal faith in Jesus. When He returns, it won't be enough to say, "My parents know you, Jesus" or "I go to a church which loves you, Jesus" or "When I was younger I followed you, Jesus".

282 ┆ No time to relax

How do we wait for Jesus' certain return? Put our feet up and relax till He comes? Not exactly...

👁 Read Matthew 25 v 14–30

ENGAGE YOUR BRAIN

This famous parable has often been misunderstood because the original Greek uses "talents" to describe an amount of money. Your Bible version may say "talents" or "bags of gold". Either way, the parable is not about making the most of your talents!

A master's going on a journey (v14)...

▶ *What does he give his servants? (v15)*

▶ *What do the servants do? (v16–18)*

▶ *When the master returns, how does he respond to:*
the first servant? (v21)
the second? (v23)
the third? (v26–30)

The master expected his servants to use what he'd given them — not just to wait.

THINK ABOUT IT

Jesus is the "master". People who call themselves Christians are the "servants". The crucial thing is to realise that "bags of gold/talents" (v15) represent all the circumstances and abilities Jesus has given us.

▶ *Do all Christians have the same circumstances and abilities?*

▶ *How does Jesus want us to use all that He's given us?*

GET ON WITH IT

▶ *Have you ever thought: "If I had the ability or life or time that he/she has got, then I'd serve God — but as it is, I can't?"*

▶ *What does this parable have to say about that attitude?*

▶ *Are there any abilities you have that you use for yourself, but never for Jesus?*

▶ *How will you change?*

283 Be sheepish

As He continues to talk about His return, Jesus takes us into the farmyard.

👁 Read Matthew 25 v 31–46

ENGAGE YOUR BRAIN

We're fast-forwarding to the end of time, "when the Son of Man comes in his glory" (v31). Can you imagine what a sight that will be? No?! Me neither. It'll be more awe-inspiring than anything we've ever seen.

▶ *What will happen to the nations of the world? (v32–33)*

▶ *Where will the "sheep" and "goats" end up? (v34, 41)*

▶ *What makes someone a sheep? (v34–40) And a goat? (v42–44)*

THINK ABOUT IT

As we've seen (24 v 45–51), the way we treat Jesus' people in public shows how we're treating Jesus in our hearts. If someone knows Jesus is their King, they will treat His subjects well. And if you are a subject of King Jesus, how wonderful to see how much He loves you. You're so close to Him that He sees something kind done for you as being done for Him; if something nasty is done to you, He sees it as nastiness towards Him. And one day, He'll give you everything that's His (25 v 34). That's how much He cares about you!

▶ *How should this parable shape your view of your identity?*

▶ *And your church family?*

▶ *And your friends who don't know Jesus as King?*

PRAY ABOUT IT

Thank Jesus for His love and for your inheritance. Ask Him to give you chances to feed His sheep and warn the goats.

THE BOTTOM LINE

You come up with it today!

284 | Beauty in the darkness

Jesus is now just two days from His death. It's going to be an ugly 48 hours: but here we catch a glimpse of beauty.

👁 Read Matthew 26 v 6–13

ENGAGE YOUR BRAIN

▶ *How is the perfume described? (v7, 9)*

▶ *Why do the disciples react as they do? (v8–9)*

▶ *How does Jesus describe it? (v10)*

THINK ABOUT IT

When we give up all we are and all we own for Jesus, the world around us says, "What a waste!" But Jesus Himself says it's "a beautiful thing". And as we honour Jesus, He uses our contribution. We become part of the gospel story, the story of Jesus' death and resurrection and mission throughout the world (v12–13).

GET ON WITH IT

▶ *In what ways are you living in a way Jesus would say is "beautiful"?*

▶ *Are there any areas of life you're holding back from Jesus because they're too precious to you?*

▶ *Will you let Him have them now?*

👁 Read verses 1–5 and 14–16

▶ *What is going on while the woman pours her perfume on Jesus?*

Surrounding that woman's actions, we see plotting and betrayal. This world rejects Jesus. But we don't have to. Be like the woman, not like Judas!

PRAY ABOUT IT

Lord Jesus, Thank you that when I do what I can for you, you notice it, you use it, and you say it's beautiful. In a world that rejects you, help me to give everything I am and have in your service today. Amen.

285 Passover picture

What's the Communion service all about?
What are you meant to think about?
Jesus tells us at the first ever Lord's Supper.

👁 Read Matthew 26 v 17–19

ENGAGE YOUR BRAIN

Matthew tells us it was "the Passover" three times. Passover was the festival where God's people remembered how God had rescued them from slavery in Egypt and brought them into His promised land. He'd told each family He would kill each firstborn son in Egypt — but that they could kill a lamb instead, and not face the same punishment.

👁 Read verses 20–30

As Jesus eats the Passover, He uses the bread as a picture.

▶ *Of what? (v26) What is the wine a picture of? (v27–28)*

▶ *Jesus is talking about His death. What will the pouring out of His blood achieve? (v28)*

▶ *What else is he looking forward to? (v29).*

Until this meal, the Passover had been about remembering the rescue from Egypt through a lamb's blood, and how God brought His people into the promised land. Jesus is saying that from now on the Passover meal (which we call "Communion" or "the Lord's Supper") should be about two events.

▶ *What are they? (v28, 29)*

THINK ABOUT IT

▶ *How do you think the disciples felt as they thought about Jesus' death and His kingdom?*

▶ *How does this passage help us know what we should think, and how we should feel, when we share the Communion meal?*

THE BOTTOM LINE

At Communion, we look back to Jesus' death, and forward to being in His kingdom. Take it seriously!

286 Scattered

The shepherd says to his flock: ewe are going to be feeling sheep-ish...

👁 Read Matthew 26 v 30–35

ENGAGE YOUR BRAIN

▶ *What does Jesus predict? (v31) Why?*

▶ *How does Peter respond to being told he'll abandon Jesus? (v33, 35)*

Even though Jesus tells Peter he won't stand up for Him, Peter's insistent. He's confident. He's up for it. He won't let Jesus down! But Jesus knows Peter better than Peter knows Peter: he *will* let Jesus down.

It sounded pretty depressing. That night, God was going to strike Jesus, the shepherd, and the Christian community would be scattered. It sounded like the end of the story.

▶ *Why wasn't it? (v32)*

There wasn't just hope for Jesus beyond being struck down by God; there was hope for His people too, beyond them deserting Him. They would be together again.

THINK ABOUT IT

It's easy to think that Jesus is quite lucky to have us. That He should be pleased we're on His team. That we can do loads to help Him. But this passage reminds us that Jesus' sheep scatter. Left to ourselves, we'll run away from following Jesus. So what matters is not how we serve Jesus, but how He serves us: not how we live as Christians, but how Christ lived and died and rose again for us.

PRAY ABOUT IT

Thank Jesus that He allowed Himself to be struck for you; and that because He rose again, you'll see Him one day.

Admit the ways in which you "fall away". Acknowledge that, left to yourself, you can't live for Jesus.

Ask for His help now.

1 PETER

Stand firm

Strangers and aliens in a hostile world, they face trial after trial, yet are shielded by an awesome power. Entrusted with a mystery from before all time, they must stand firm as they wait for the return of the king.

No, it's not the latest fantasy epic from Hollywood but reality for the first readers of 1 Peter. And for Christians today too!

SIMON SAYS

1 Peter is a letter written by the apostle (Simon) Peter; you remember him — ex-fisherman, often spoke before he engaged his brain, let Jesus down badly but was forgiven and restored by Him. Peter wrote this letter to a group of Christians scattered all around the Mediterranean and Middle East.

These Christians were (a bit like their Lord) chosen by God but rejected by people. They faced persecution.

They struggled to be holy, just as we do. But, like all who know Jesus, they had a great and inexpressible joy because they knew that they were forgiven and loved by God and that they had a wonderful future awaiting them.

Peter's letter reminds these Christians that living a life trusting Jesus will bring suffering before glory. Pain before gain. He tells believers that they don't belong on this earth — they have a new home to look forward to. And God has made sure they won't miss out when Jesus returns.

As you read 1 Peter, be encouraged to stand firm, and to be thankful for what you have been saved from and excited about what you have been saved for!

287 Perfect strangers

Ever been somewhere you've felt completely out of place in? Like a total stranger? Well, Peter says that Christians are strangers, or exiles, in this world.

👁 Read 1 Peter 1 v 1–2

ENGAGE YOUR BRAIN

▶ *Who is writing the letter and how does he describe himself?*

▶ *What does that mean?*

▶ *Who is he writing to and where are they located?*

These Christians ("God's elect", God's chosen people) were scattered all over the area — probably after persecution. The authorities were trying to crack down on this new religion but the effect was like blowing on a dandelion — the seeds went everywhere and the gospel spread far and wide!

▶ *How do you think being "scattered" must have felt like?*

▶ *How does Peter describe the life of a Christian? (v2)*

In the Old Testament, animal blood could be sprinkled on people to make them clean (or "sanctified")

before God. This picture points us to Jesus, whose death can make people clean in God's sight. Notice that every member of the Trinity is intimately involved in calling someone to belong to God — Father, Son and Spirit (v2).

▶ *How does Peter greet these Christians? (end of v2)*

PRAY ABOUT IT

If we are members of God's family, grace and peace really are ours. Spend some time giving thanks to God for that now.

THE BOTTOM LINE

Christians are strangers in the world… but they are God's chosen people!

288 | A new hope

Peter has hinted at the grace that these (and all) Christians have experienced, but the full reality is eye-poppingly good! Check out what it means to belong to Jesus!

👁 Read 1 Peter 1 v 3–7

ENGAGE YOUR BRAIN

▶ *What has God done for us? (v3–5)*

▶ *What does that mean?*

▶ *What should be our response? (v3, 6)*

▶ *Why can we even rejoice in trials and tough times? (v6–7)*

We don't tend to see much gold-refining going on these days, but when mobile phones are recycled, they are put through something very similar so that the high temperatures melt away the rubbish and only the valuable metals needed to make new parts remain.

TALK IT OVER

Chat with another Christian about verses 6–7. Does it make it easier to know that hard times are being used by God to grow you as a Christian and to bring praise to Jesus? How can you pray that this would be a comfort to you both?

👁 Read verses 8–12

▶ *What deep joy does the Christian have? (v8)*

▶ *What does this emotion assure us of? (v9)*

We can't see Jesus (yet), but Christians believe in Him, love Him, and are filled with joy as they think about the salvation (rescue) that God has achieved for them. Exciting!

PRAY ABOUT IT

Spend some time praising Jesus for who He is and all He has done for you.

THE BOTTOM LINE

Christians have a new birth and a living hope.

289 Look around you

A word to cyclists: looking down may help you avoid stones but OW! not parked cars. A word to Christians: for the full view, look up and ahead as well as back. That's what Peter says.

👁 Read 1 Peter 1 v 13–16

ENGAGE YOUR BRAIN

▶ *How does Peter begin verse 13?*

It's a bit cheesy, but when you see a "therefore" in the Bible, you need to ask what it's there for!

▶ *What has Peter been reminding his readers of in verses 1–12?*

-
-
-
-

▶ *How should Christians be in the present? (v13)*

▶ *What are they to look forward to in the future?*

Bearing in mind all the amazing things God has done for us, we should be fired up to live for Him in the present. And if that wasn't enough, Peter reminds us that a glorious future awaits! So prepare your minds for action!

▶ *How did Christians live before they were saved by Jesus? (v14)*

▶ *How should we live now? (v15)*

▶ *What is our motivation? (v16)*

GET ON WITH IT

A very wise Christian once said: "Be what you are". In Christ we are holy and blameless; we need to start living up to our new identity in Christ. BUT we can only do that in Him — with the help of His Holy Spirit, not just by making a bit more effort…

PRAY ABOUT IT

Ask God to help you to remember His love and to have a mind that is alert and prepared for action. Thank Him that because Jesus is holy, we can be too. And pray for His Holy Spirit to enable you to live for Him.

290 Strange but true

Remember how Peter described his readers back in verse 1? More on what it means to be strangers in this world...

👁 Read 1 Peter 1 v 17–22

ENGAGE YOUR BRAIN

▶ *Who are we trying to please? (v17)*

▶ *How much did it cost God to bring us into His family? (v18–19)*

▶ *How long has God had His rescue plan for? (v20)*

▶ *What has Jesus accomplished for us? (v21)*

▶ *Jesus has brought us into a new family — so how should we now live? (v22)*

GET ON WITH IT

Do you love other Christians? Even the weird or annoying ones? Ask God to change your heart so you start genuinely caring about them today! Talk to or sit with someone at church/youth group/CU because it will encourage them rather than to make you feel comfortable.

👁 Read verses 23–25

▶ *What is it that makes us able to live for ever? (v23–25)*

▶ *What would our natural state be? (v24)*

PRAY ABOUT IT

All people are like grass. We look good for a while but soon wither and die. It's only God's word — the good news about Jesus — that will make us live for ever. Pray for someone you know who is living like grass, that God would give them new birth into a living hope that lasts for ever.

THE BOTTOM LINE

The word of the Lord stands for ever.

291 Milking it

There's another "therefore" at the start of verse 1. So what's it there for?

👁 Read 1 Peter 2 v 1–3

Remind yourself of some of the great things Peter has been talking about in the second half of chapter one. In particular, what is the word of God like and what does it do?

ENGAGE YOUR BRAIN

- *Bearing all that in mind, how does Peter urge these Christians to live? (v1–2)*

- *What are the negative things to stop doing? (v1)*

- *Can you put that in everyday language?*

- *What positive things should they do instead? (v2)*

- *What does that mean?*

THINK IT OVER

How would you describe your attitude to Bible-reading? Remember that God's word saves you and gives you eternal life (1 v 23–25).

- *Do you crave the Bible like a newborn baby desperate for milk? If not, why not?*

- *What is the end goal of feeding on God's word? (end of v2)*

- *What do you think that means?*

- *What does Peter remind us of in verse 3?*

PRAY ABOUT IT

Ask God to give you an appetite for His word. Somebody once said that, unlike eating normal food, the more we "eat" of the Bible, the hungrier we get! We want more and more!

THE BOTTOM LINE

Crave pure spiritual milk.

292 Love/hate relationship

There are some things that people either love or hate —
in the UK it's a spread called Marmite! Sadly, in every
country and throughout history, it's been Jesus. Read on
to see why.

👁 Read 1 Peter 2 v 4–8

ENGAGE YOUR BRAIN

▶ What is Jesus called in verse 4?

▶ What are the two ways He is
described in the rest of verse 4?

▶ What are Christians called in
verse 5? Why?

▶ How does the Old Testament
describe Jesus? (v6) How has this
come true for us? (v7)

▶ What else did the Old Testament
predict? (v7–8) How has that
come true?

The cornerstone is the most
important stone in a building —
absolutely vital. Jesus is either
essential and precious, or rejected
and dangerous. You can't sit on the
fence with Jesus — you're either for
Him or against Him. We will stand
or fall on how we respond to Him.
Have you thanked Him for dying in
your place and acknowledged Him
as Lord of your life?

PRAY ABOUT IT

Pray for people you know who are
currently rejecting Jesus, that they
would see how precious He is and
not stumble.

👁 Read verses 9–12

List the ways Peter describes
Christians in verses 9–10.

•

•

•

•

Take some time to let these things
sink in. Thank God for them.

▶ So what does all this mean for
us? (v11–12)

THE BOTTOM LINE

You are a part of a chosen people.

293 | God's the boss

Christians don't belong in this world any more. We're strangers here, waiting for our new home with God. So, let's give up school, college, work. Ignore authority, drop out, enjoy our freedom, right? Not quite...

👁 Read 1 Peter 2 v 13–17

ENGAGE YOUR BRAIN

▶ *What should Christians do? (v13–14)*

▶ *For what reason? (v13)*

▶ *Why does God want us to behave in this way? (v15)*

TALK IT OVER

Do you think it's always right to submit to our governments and authorities (police, teachers, parents etc)? Are there any exceptions? Chat with a Christian friend about this.

ENGAGE YOUR BRAIN

▶ *How does Peter describe us? (v16)*

Whether you were a slave back in Peter's day or have the most tyrannical boss (or parents!) today, Christians are truly free. We are free from sin and its consequences,

thanks to the death and resurrection of Jesus. BUT, notice that Peter says we shouldn't use our freedom to "get away with" anything now. Our lives should show we serve God rather than ourselves.

PRAY ABOUT IT

We can't do this on our own! It's hard to show respect for unfair teachers, corrupt politicians and our parents sometimes. But Jesus did it. Ask for the help of His Holy Spirit today.

▶ *How does Peter sum up this section? What are our duties to each of the people listed? (v17)*

GET ON WITH IT

How can you love other Christians, show honour to those in authority and, most importantly, fear (respect and serve) God today?

294 | Suffering servant

However tough you have it, you're probably not living the life of a first-century slave...

👁 Read 1 Peter 2 v 18–25

ENGAGE YOUR BRAIN

▶ What is the surprise in verse 18?

▶ Why is it good to submit to and respect even harsh masters? (v19–21)

God is pleased with the heart attitude that seeks to do good even while being treated badly. But more than that, it's God's own attitude (v21).

▶ Whose example are we to follow? (v21)

▶ What did He do that we can follow? (v23)

▶ What did He do that He alone could do? (v24)

▶ Why should we follow Jesus?

PRAY ABOUT IT

Thank God for the wonderful news of verse 24. Thank Him for the comfort and reassurance of verse 25.

Ask for the strength to be able to do good even when you're treated badly, remembering what Jesus did for you.

GET ON WITH IT

Learn 1 Peter 2 v 24 off by heart — you might be able to use it to explain to someone what Jesus has done.

THE BOTTOM LINE

Christ suffered for you.

295 Job: Why me?

The story so far: Satan claimed that Job only served God because he had an easy life. Yet with his family, wealth and health taken from him, Job still didn't turn against God. But he didn't understand why he was suffering.

👁 Read Job 22 v 1–11

ENGAGE YOUR BRAIN

▶ What point was Eliphaz making? (v2–3)

▶ What did he accuse Job of? (v4–9)

Eliphaz started out by gently trying to persuade Job to turn back to God (chapter 4). But now he was resorting to vicious lies. Job lived for God. None of these accusations were true. When reasoning fails, people often resort to spreading nasty rumours and lies about Christians.

👁 Read verses 12–20

Eliphaz was saying: *God is above everything, so how can humans stand up to Him? Job, you're just like the sinners who think God can't harm them. But now God's punishing them.* Yep, Eliphaz is talking garbage again.

👁 Read verses 21–30

▶ What steps should someone take if they want to turn back to God?
v21:
v22:
v27:

▶ What does Eliphaz claim will happen? (v23, 25, 28)

Eliphaz is right that sinners need to turn back to God and obey Him. But he's wrong to say that people who turn to God will have all their wishes granted. And he's also wrong to assume that Job needs to turn back to God. Job may be gloomy, but he has never turned his back on God.

PRAY ABOUT IT

Ask God, by His Holy Spirit, to help you stand firm against opposition. Even when people spread lies about you. Ask God to help you continue to honour Him with your life.

296 Distant deity

"If only I could talk to God face to face."
"God seems so far away."
"God is terrifying and has a cruel side."
Can you identify with any of those thoughts?

👁 Read Job 23 v 1–7

ENGAGE YOUR BRAIN

▶ *What's Job complaining about? (v2–3)*

▶ *What does he want to do? (v4–5)*

Job can't understand why he's suffering so much even though he's always lived for God. He just wants the chance to explain things to God, so that the Lord might end Job's suffering. Do you ever feel like that? That if only you could explain things to God, He might make everything better?

👁 Read verses 8–17

▶ *What's the problem? (v8–9)*

▶ *What else is getting Job down? (v13–14) How does he feel about it? (v15–17)*

▶ *Yet what hope does he hold on to? (v10)*

God seems so distant. And so terrifying.

THINK IT OVER

Can you understand how Job feels? God seems so far away from you? It seems impossible to talk to Him? Most people feel like that sometimes. But God doesn't leave His people! God always knows what His people are doing. He's always with them, even when it doesn't feel like it.

PRAY ABOUT IT

Because of Jesus, you can go to God and tell Him exactly how you feel. Just pour it out to God: He's listening. He knows all about you, and cares for you. Talk to Him now.

THE BOTTOM LINE

God's not far away — He's with you and wants to listen to you.

297 God's greatness

Eliphaz, Bildad and Zophar have been harrassing Job for ages — telling him how sinful he is. But they've run out of steam. One final blast from Bildad is met by sarcasm from Job.

👁 Read Job 25 v 1–6

ENGAGE YOUR BRAIN

▷ *How would you sum up Bildad's opinion of God? (v2–3)*

▷ *And what about humans? (v6)*

We're all pathetic compared to God. None of us can stand before God and claim innocence. The great news for Christians is that Jesus stands before God in our place. Because of Jesus, we can be right with God.

👁 Read Job 26 v 1–14

▷ *How would you describe Job's reply to Bildad? (v1–4)*

▷ *What about Job's description of God? (v5–14)*

This is a powerful picture of God. He's so mighty. Nothing is out of His control. No other powers (such as the beasts in verses 12–13) are a match for God. We can clearly see that God is powerful and wise, yet our understanding barely scratches the surface of how great God is (v14)

👁 Skim-read Job 27 v 1–23

▷ *Despite his suffering, has Job turned against God? (v2–4)*

▷ *How does God deal with those who reject Him? (v13–23)*

THINK IT OVER

▷ *What's your opinion of God? How would you describe Him?*

▷ *Why should you live God's way rather than your own way?*

▷ *How are you living at the moment?*

PRAY ABOUT IT

Spend time praising God for His wisdom and power. Thank Him for loving pathetic humans like us. Ask Him to help you devote yourself to Him and not turn away from Him.

298 Treasure hunt

Are you ready for a break from all the misery of Job? Well, chapter 28 plunges down into the depths again. But not the depths of depression — we're going down to the very depths of the earth in search of great treasure.

◉ Read Job 28 v 1–19

ENGAGE YOUR BRAIN

▷ *How much trouble do people go to, to find silver, gold and precious stone? (v1–11)*

▷ *What treasure is greater? (v12)*

▷ *But what's the problem? (v13)*

Job tells us that true, godly wisdom is more precious than gold, silver or expensive jewels (v15–19). We should chase after it much more than any earthly possessions.

◉ Read verses 20–28

▷ *Who alone knows how to get truly wise?*

▷ *How does God define wisdom and understanding? (v28)*

We can't expect to find wisdom by ourselves. Wisdom comes from God — only God can give it to us. Being truly wise means "fearing the Lord". It means knowing how weak and sinful we are and how great and holy God is. It means giving God the respect, honour and love He deserves. That's true wisdom!

It also means turning our backs on evil. If we love and respect God, then we'll want to stop doing things that anger Him. We'll want to stop living our way and start living God's way.

PRAY ABOUT IT

Ask God to make you truly wise. Pray that you'll fear Him and live for Him, with the help of the Holy Spirit. Ask Him to help you to shun evil — pray about specific sins you struggle with.

And pray all these things for at least three other Christians you know.

299 Job the defendant

Job is in court, trying to prove that he's a good man who serves the Lord. He's about to sum up his case and try to prove his innocence to God.

👁 Skim-read Job 29 v 1–25

ENGAGE YOUR BRAIN

▶ What was Job's life like before he lost everything?

▶ What did people think of him?

▶ Who was responsible for it all? (v2–5)

When life is going well for us, God is often forgotten. We should take a leaf out of Job's book and give God the glory when things are going well.

👁 Skim-read Job 30 v 1–31

▶ What is Job's life like now?

▶ How do people treat him?

▶ Who does Job say is behind his suffering? (v11, 19–23)

👁 Skim-read Job 31 v 1–40

▶ How many different sins does Job list?

▶ How many does he say he's committed?

▶ What does Job want from God?

Job says that he's always obeyed God, so he can't understand why he's suffering. But God isn't punishing him for anything. Sometimes people just have a tough time. We can't explain it. We can only ask God to help us.

PRAY ABOUT IT

It's impossible for us to live perfect lives. We'll sometimes mess up. But we can say sorry to God, pick ourselves up and start living His way again. Say sorry to God for some of the bad things you've done this week. Ask Him to help you to start living His way again. And remember to thank Him for the good things in your life.

300 Eli-who?

Eliphaz, Bildad and Zophar have finally given up trying to persuade Job that he's suffering as punishment for sinning. Quiet at last! Er, no. Young Elihu is next to arrive and he has loads to get off his chest.

👁 Read Job 32 v 1–5

ENGAGE YOUR BRAIN

🔟 *Why was Elihu angry with Job? (v2)*

🔟 *Why was he angry with Job's friends? (v3)*

In verses 6–22, Elihu says he'd kept quiet so far because he was younger than the others. And because he wanted to hear Job's defence. Now he can't keep quiet!

👁 Read Job 33 v 1–13

Job couldn't understand why he was suffering. He thought he was innocent, so he asked God for answers. Elihu said Job had no right to argue with God, who's so much greater than him.

👁 Read verses 14–22

🔟 *How did Elihu claim God gets people to turn back to Him? v15–18: v19–22:*

God does use many different ways to speak to people and warn them about their sin. In the Bible, we sometimes see God using visions or even illness, pain and disasters to call people back to Him.

Elihu was talking about falling into a dark pit. To die without knowing God is like falling into a disgusting pit that no one can ever get out of. But God gives us loads of warnings! The Bible is packed with warnings telling us that we need to turn away from our sinful lives and start living God's way. He even sent Jesus to rescue us.

PRAY ABOUT IT

Is there anything you want to talk to God about today?

301 Big rant

Know anyone who just doesn't stop talking? Well, Elihu is one of those people. He's let himself get worked up and now he's overflowing with anger. Brace yourself as we dip into parts of his long rant against Job.

👁 Read Job 34 v 10–15, 21–30

▶ What truth about God does Elihu mention in verses 10–15?

▶ Does God act fairly or unfairly? (v21–28)

Elihu is right that God is always fair. But he's wrong that God always punishes the wicked in this life. God will punish sin on Judgment Day, even though some sinners seem to go unpunished in this life.

👁 Read Job 35 v 9–16

▶ Why does Elihu think God remains silent? (v10–13)

▶ So what does Elihu think of Job? (v14–16)

Elihu is wrong that God only hears us when our motives are totally pure or when there's no sin in our hearts. If that was always true, no one could ever know God's rescue. We all deserve punishment. Yet God still sent Jesus to rescue sinners like us.

👁 Read Job 37 v 14–24

▶ What point does Elihu make in verses 14–19?

▶ What's Elihu's summary of his long argument? (v21–24)

Elihu's long-winded rant is a mixed bag. There are some great truths about God but there's plenty of nonsense too. And, like the other three ranters, he's completely wrong about Job.

Some people give us great advice and teach us about God. Others will mislead us and fill our minds with untruths. And some do a bit of both. We have to test what people say against God's word. If it's in line with the Bible, it's good. If it disagrees with God's word, it's rubbish.

PRAY ABOUT IT

Talk to God about anything He's challenged you with today.

Tomorrow: God speaks.

302 : God speaks

For the last 35 chapters, Job and his friends have been chatting (well, arguing), trying to work out why God let Job suffer so much. But now a storm is brewing, and God is going to speak.

👁 Read Job 38 v 1–15

ENGAGE YOUR BRAIN

▶ What does God think of Job's anger? (v2)

▶ What are the answers to God's questions?
v4:
v8:
v12–13:

Job had dared to question God's actions, without even beginning to understand God! Job wasn't around when God created the world. So there's no chance he could understand how everything is controlled.

👁 Read verses 16–30

▶ What else does Job not understand?
v17:
v18:
v19:
v22–30:

God is awesome! He can do anything, go anywhere and He understands everything. Of course Job can't do what God can!

👁 Read verses 31–38

Job had to be humbled and realise he is very small compared with God! It's easy to blame God. But we know zilch compared to God, so we need to listen to what He tells us in the Bible.

PRAY ABOUT IT

Thank God that even though He's so big and powerful, He loves you! Ask Him to help you shut up and listen.

THE BOTTOM LINE

Shut up and listen to God.

303 Creature comfort

Job wants to know why he's suffering so much. He wants answers from God. So why is God talking about lions, goats and donkeys?

⊙ Read Job 38 v 39 – 39 v 12

ENGAGE YOUR BRAIN

▶ *Can Job provide food for lions and ravens or understand how animals give birth?*

▶ *What are the answers to God's other questions?*
v5:
v9–10:

⊙ Read Job 39 v 13–30

▶ *What's God's opinion of the ostrich? (v13–18)*

▶ *What are the answers to the questions in verses 19, 20, 26, 27?*

God must have a sense of humour — He created the ostrich! He also gave it amazing speed. And He made horses so impressive and fearless. The incredible flight and hunting skills of birds of prey are all down to God. Through this speech, God is reminding Job how powerful, wise and impressive He is.

How can mere humans like Job, and ourselves, think we have the right to argue with God? We can't possibly hope to understand Him. And yet we sometimes act as if we know better than God. Crazy. God doesn't need to defend Himself or explain why suffering happens. He's the Creator of the universe. We must bow down before Him and accept that His plans are always best.

THINK IT OVER

▶ *How has Job helped change your view of God?*

▶ *How do you need to treat Him differently?*

PRAY ABOUT IT

Think of what impresses you in God's creation. Which creatures remind you of how great our Creator God is? Spend time praising God for these things.

304 Job silenced

Are you a big talker or a good listener? Job had said plenty about how fed up he was and how God had no reason to make him suffer. Now it's God's turn to question Job.

👁 Read Job 40 v 1–5

ENGAGE YOUR BRAIN

▶ What had Job's attitude been towards God? (v2)

▶ How did it change? (v3–5)

Job has no more arguments left. He realises how small and feeble he is compared to God. So he stops himself saying anything else — he knows he's already said too much. That's a big change in Job's attitude.

👁 Read verses 6–14

Job, a mere, ordinary, sinful man had dared to doubt God's fairness. It's almost funny that ordinary people like us dare to question the great, holy, perfect, powerful, infinitely wise God!

It's good to ask big questions and wonder why bad things happen. But don't make the mistake of blaming God. We might not understand why bad stuff happens, but we can be confident that God is always fair and His plans are perfect.

👁 Read verses 15–24

No one is sure if Behemoth is a hippo or an elephant or a brontosaurus. But we do know that it's one of the most impressive creatures God created (v19) and that only God can tame it! How can weak little humans like us dare to challenge and accuse our all-powerful God? We should bow down and worship Him!

PRAY ABOUT IT

Do that right now as you pray to our astonishing, perfect, all-powerful Creator God.

305 Simply the beast

God is still speaking to Job. It's probably not the response he was expecting, but it's had a huge impact on Job. God finishes off His speech with a long poem about another terrifying beast.

👁 Read Job 41 v 1–34

ENGAGE YOUR BRAIN

▶ *Could Job control this monster?*

▶ *If no one can tame this beast, what does it tell us about God, who can? (v10–11)*

Some people think this terrifying animal is a sea monster or giant crocodile. Others think it symbolises God's enemy, Satan. If humans can't control this beast, how can we expect to stand against God or make claims against Him?

God's response to Job's questions has been surprising. He hasn't explained Job's suffering at all. Instead, He showed Job His great wisdom, so Job couldn't claim God didn't know what He was doing. God showed Job His justice — so Job couldn't say God was unfair by letting him suffer. God showed His immense power — so Job couldn't claim God wasn't able to carry out His will. God is in control.

👁 Read Job 42 v 1–6

▶ *What has Job realised about…*
God?
himself?
his suffering?

In chapters 1–2, we saw that sin was not the cause of Job's suffering. All along, Job claimed his innocence. He questioned God but never turned away from Him. So why repent? (v6)

Well, Job's just had a staggering personal encounter with God. Job now realises his arrogance at expecting an answer from God — as if God was accountable to him! Job sees that he doesn't know God as well as he should, hence his response.

PRAY ABOUT IT

Thank God that He's in control of everything. Pray that your attitude to Him and to suffering would be right. Pray that you'll know Him better.

306 Happily ever after

Well done for staying the course. We've reached the end of 42 chapters of suffering, questioning and confusion. Along the way we've learned about ourselves and about our remarkable God. And there's even a happy ending...

👁 Read Job 42 v 7–9

ENGAGE YOUR BRAIN

▶ Why was God angry with Job's friends?

▶ What were they required to do?

▶ What does God call Job, 4 times?

It's official — the things these guys have said about God were not true. Yet God gave them a chance to be forgiven and He accepted Job's prayers for them. God is so forgiving. He always gives us the chance to turn away from our sinful ways and turn back to Him! During all his suffering, Job never turned away from God. God knew that Job still served Him with his whole life.

THINK IT OVER

Could God call you His servant, living to please Him instead of just yourself? Will you tell God how sorry you are for disobeying Him and start living His way again?

👁 Read verses 10–17

▶ How did Job's new wealth compare with before? (Job 1 v 3)

▶ What else did God do for Job?

When Job had his family, possessions and health taken away from him, his friends said God was punishing him. He must have done a terrible sin. But God let everyone know this wasn't true by giving Job so many blessings. God showed that He loved Job and was pleased that Job hadn't turned away from Him.

God loves His children. Sometimes they go through times of suffering, but God never leaves them. And one day He will give them the best blessing ever – a perfect life with Him.

PRAY ABOUT IT

Talk to God about issues, questions, confessions, challenges and praise that have come from reading the book of Job.

307 Nehemiah: Big build-up

Jerusalem's walls have been rebuilt. Now on to the issue of rebuilding and reforming the lives of God's people. Will the damage be as quick and easy to repair?

👁 Read Nehemiah 8 v 1–12

ENGAGE YOUR BRAIN

The real work begins with the reading and hearing of God's word.

▶ *Who gets to listen? (v2–3)*

▶ *How long does it last?*

▶ *How would you describe the people's attitude? (v3, 5, 6)*

▶ *How does Ezra ensure everyone understands what is being read? (v7–8)*

▶ *How many times does the word "understand" appear in these verses?*

Good system. Everyone hears God's word together, and then smaller groups really dig deeper, making sure they understand it. Does your church do that?

GET ON WITH IT

Are you part of a small group (CU, youth group, home group, Bible study) that really gets involved with understanding God's word and applying it to your life? If not, is there one you could join?

▶ *Why do you think the people responded to the reading of the Law in the way they did? (v9)*

▶ *What are they encouraged to do instead? (v10–12)*

▶ *Why?*

PRAY ABOUT IT

God's word can often make us sad as we see our sin more clearly, but it also shows us how wonderful God is. Spend some time now celebrating how great our God is.

308 Branching out

There was plenty to discover in God's long-neglected Law. And one of the first things the people did was to celebrate a festival. With some DIY thrown in too.

👁 Read Nehemiah 8 v 13–18

ENGAGE YOUR BRAIN

▶ *What did the people discover (or rediscover) in the Book of the Law? (v14–15)*

The Festival of Booths/Shelters was when everyone camped out for a week to remember how they lived when God rescued them from Egypt (way back in the book of Exodus). Now that the people had returned from exile in Babylon, it was time to thank God in a big way again.

▶ *How wholeheartedly did the people celebrate? (v17)*

▶ *What was the focus of their joy? (v18)*

▶ *Does it look as if the people are changing for the better?*

It must have been an amazing sight! Everyone built these wooden shelters and lived in them for a week. They continued listening to Ezra reading God's word and they held a great feast, celebrating God's goodness to them. They really wanted to start living God's way again. Obeying Him.

GET ON WITH IT

▶ *How can you take God's word more seriously?*

▶ *Which of God's commands do you tend to ignore?*

▶ *What will you do to sort that out?*

PRAY ABOUT IT

Ask God to help you dig deeper into the Bible, learning from Him. And talk to Him about the teaching that you find hardest to obey.

309 | History lesson

Party's over. The people gather again to hear God's word, but this time the mood is definitely more sombre.

👁 **Read Nehemiah 9 v 1–21**

ENGAGE YOUR BRAIN

▶ *What are the people wearing? (v1)*

▶ *What do you think that signifies?*

▶ *What do they do? (v2–3)*

▶ *What has God done for the Israelites so far in history?*
v6:
v7–8:
v9–12:
v13–14:
v15:
v17, 19:
v20–21:

▶ *What word would you use to describe the Israelites in these verses? How about God?*

As we'll see in the next part of chapter 9, the people's consistent unfaithfulness is met by God's consistent faithfulness. Our sin is met by God's grace.

THINK IT OVER

▶ *How much did the Israelites have to thank God for?*

▶ *How about us?*

▶ *But how do we usually respond to God?*

PRAY ABOUT IT

Think over the last week, or even the last 24 hours. Spend some time now talking to Him about the times you've failed to go His way, and thank Him for His great mercy in Jesus Christ.

THE BOTTOM LINE

God is good; we reject Him, but still He shows mercy.

310 | God is great

The sorry story goes on. Yet more grace from God is thrown back in His face by His ungrateful people.

👁 Read Nehemiah 9 v 22–37

ENGAGE YOUR BRAIN

▶ What had God done for His people?
v22–25:
v27b:
v28b:
v30–31:

▶ How did the people respond? (v26, 28–30)

▶ How does verse 33 sum up all that took place in Israel's history?

▶ What have the people realised by this point?

▶ Do you think they will change?

▶ Why / why not?

▶ How does verse 26 point to the worst thing God's people will do in the future?

▶ What words are used to describe God throughout chapter 9?

God acts faithfully, while we do wrong. The worst thing human beings ever did was to murder God's Son. But, incredibly, God used that very act to bring about forgiveness and reconciliation for His enemies. God is so gracious and merciful!

PRAY ABOUT IT

Think about the blessings God has given you. Check out Ephesians 1 v 3–14 if you need ideas. Thank Him that all of these blessings come because of what Jesus did, not because of what you have done (or failed to do)!

THE BOTTOM LINE

God is faithful; we are not.

311 Promising future

It's a serious business making promises to God, but that's what the people decide to do. But what exactly are they promising?

👁 Read Nehemiah 9 v 38–10 v 39

ENGAGE YOUR BRAIN

▶ What did the people decide to do? (9 v 38)

▶ Who is included in this oath? (10 v 1–28)

▶ What will happen to them if they fail to keep their oath? (v29)

▶ Do you think they will succeed, based on their track record?

▶ What are the three key elements of their oath?
v30:
v31:
v39:

▶ Why do you think those three things are so important?

▶ What does "not neglecting the house of God" involve? (v32–39)

Keeping away from the surrounding nations in marriage, keeping the Sabbath free from trading and money-making, and making sure they don't neglect the temple were all things they'd got wrong in the past. But why were they so important? They all boil down to putting God first — not romance, money or self-centredness.

PRAY ABOUT IT

▶ How are you at putting God first?

▶ Is your boyfriend/girlfriend, job, party lifestyle or academic success more important to you?

▶ How do you spend most of your time? Money? Thoughts?

Talk to God about that now and ask Him to show you how amazing Jesus is so that you love Him above everything else.

THE BOTTOM LINE

Put God first.

312 | On the move

Remember Operation Repopulation back in chapter 7? Well, it's about to kick in properly. Not much point in having a rebuilt city with no one living there!

👁 Read Nehemiah 11 v 1–2

ENGAGE YOUR BRAIN

🔘 *How do the people decide who is to live in Jerusalem? (v1)*

🔘 *How many people will be chosen? (v1) Sound familiar?*

The idea of giving a tenth of something to the Lord (or in this case "the holy city") is called a tithe. It was a way of reminding the people that everything they had, even themselves, belonged to the Lord, and so they would give part of it back to Him.

GET ON WITH IT

The New Testament doesn't tell us we have to give 10% of our time or money to God — instead it tells us to be generous. How can you remind yourself that everything you have is a gift from God by giving generously of both yourself and what you have today?

👁 Skim through verses 3–36

🔘 *Why do you think it's important to have these lists of names?*

🔘 *Where do Judah and Perez (v4) crop up again? (Hint: see Matthew 1 v 3 and 16.)*

🔘 *The city is rebuilt. Does it look as though the people are reformed?*

PRAY ABOUT IT

There is a story behind all these names — God is still keeping His promises to His people. Thank God that His rescue in Jesus was planned before the foundation of the world.

313 Celebration nation

Party time! The walls are up; the people have moved in; everything is looking great! Time to dedicate the walls. And yes, there's another list, but stick with it! It's worth it.

👁 Read Nehemiah 12 v 1–30

The priests and Levites looked after God's temple, offered sacrifices to Him, taught God's Law to the people and led them in worshipping God. The Lord had chosen them to do important stuff — so they got their own list!

ENGAGE YOUR BRAIN

▶ *What did they do here? (v24, 27, 30)*

▶ *Who had originally arranged this method of praising God? (v24)*

▶ *Does it look as if the people of God are back to the glory days of David and Solomon's kingship?*

▶ *Why is it so important that the priests, the people and the city are pure? (v30)*

▶ *Can you remember how God's people are made pure? (eg: Numbers 19 v 1–10)*

It's looking promising, but as we'll see in the very next chapter, these positive signs are short-lived.

PRAY ABOUT IT

The people of God had to be purified from sin again and again. Thank God that in Jesus we have a great High Priest who has purified us from sin and is sitting at God's right hand (Hebrews 1 v 3).

THE BOTTOM LINE

One day God's people and God's city will be totally free from sin. Thanks to Jesus.

314 Praise party

It's a major celebration — two choirs and bands circling the city walls in opposite directions, then arriving at the temple for a huge praise party.

👁 Read Nehemiah 12 v 31–43

ENGAGE YOUR BRAIN

▶ What was the purpose of the two choirs? (v31)

▶ What instruments did they have?

▶ Who was in charge of each choir? (v36, 38)

▶ Where did they stop? (v39)

▶ What happened in the temple? (v43)

▶ Why?

▶ How big were the celebrations? (v43)

Remember how pitiful things looked back in chapter 1 v 3? Now there was definitely cause for rejoicing and God had clearly been at work in all the construction work, even in the face of enemy opposition.

PRAY ABOUT IT

When you pray, do you take time to thank God for all he's done? Or does it turn into a shopping list of all your needs and worries?

God tells us to cast all our anxieties on Him, so it's not wrong to pray about those things, but sometimes it's good just to spend time thanking and praising Him.

▶ Why not do that right now?

THE BOTTOM LINE

God is worthy of our praise.

315 Time to change

The Israelites have been marching around Jerusalem, singing and praising God in one massive celebration. They wanted to serve God all the time, but realised that they'd have to make some changes to the way they lived.

👁 Read Nehemiah 12 v 44–47

ENGAGE YOUR BRAIN

- ▶ Who is provided for? (v44)

- ▶ What do the Israelites do to make sure God's praise continues to be sung? (v46-47)

- ▶ Who contributes? (v47)

👁 Read Nehemiah 13 v 1–3

- ▶ What issue does the reading of the Law highlight? (v1)

- ▶ Is this just xenophobia (fear of foreigners) or is there a good reason? (v2)

- ▶ Do the people obey God's word? (v3)

Remember those big three areas the people made oaths about in chapter 10? Keeping away from the surrounding nations in marriage, keeping the Sabbath free from trading and money-making, and making sure they don't neglect the temple. So far it looks as if they're standing by their promises.

THINK IT OVER

Is your faith sometimes all talk and no action? James says: "Faith without deeds is dead" (James 2 v 26). He doesn't mean that doing good things can save us, but if our so-called faith doesn't change the way we live, it was never real to begin with.

PRAY ABOUT IT

Talk to God about how you can put your faith into action this week.

THE BOTTOM LINE

Worship God in word and deed.

316 Trouble in store

**After such a great celebration comes the fallout.
The city is rebuilt but the people haven't changed.**

👁 Read Nehemiah 13 v 4–14

ENGAGE YOUR BRAIN

▶ Why is Eliashib not a great choice to put in charge of the temple storerooms? (v4)

▶ Remember Tobiah? Look back at 6 v 17–19.

▶ What had Eliashib done for Tobiah? (13 v 5) Good idea?

▶ Why was Nehemiah out of the loop? (v6)

▶ What does he do when he finds out? (v7–9)

▶ What else has gone wrong during Nehemiah's absence? (v10)

▶ How does Nehemiah sort the problem out? (v11–13)

▶ What does Nehemiah say to God in response to all of this? (v14)

It hadn't taken long for God's people to go back to their old ways, forgetting God. And there's worse to come. Poor Nehemiah must have felt all his hard work was for nothing, but instead of indulging in self-pity he turns to God. It is God's assessment of our lives that matters.

PRAY ABOUT IT

Ask God to help you to live all out for Him, and for His opinion to be the one that matters most to you.

THE BOTTOM LINE

God's assessment of our lives is the only one that matters.

317 Trouble and strife

As the book of Nehemiah reaches it's climax, things have gone from bad to worse. The city is rebuilt but the people are not reformed. They have fallen back into the same old sins. Is there any hope at all?

👁 Read Nehemiah 13 v 15–31

ENGAGE YOUR BRAIN

- ▶ What is going wrong in v 15–16?

- ▶ Why is this such an issue? (v18)

- ▶ What practical steps does Nehemiah take? (v19–22)

- ▶ What's the other problem? (v23)?

- ▶ What has this led to? (v24) Why is this an issue? (v26)

Half-Israelite children, who don't speak the language and with one parent who worships a fake god, can't grow up learning about God.

GET ON WITH IT

- ▶ Know a Christian who is dating a non-Christian? Yourself?

- ▶ What does this passage suggest?

ENGAGE YOUR BRAIN

- ▶ Why is verse 28 the icing on this rotten cake?

- ▶ What did Nehemiah do? (v25, v28, v30–31)

- ▶ Do you think this worked in the long term?

- ▶ Why do you think Nehemiah repeatedly cries out to God for mercy? (v22, 29, 31)

Despite a short-lived return to following the Law and reinstatement of temple worship the way David and Solomon had set it up, the same sins are tripping Israel up once more.

PRAY ABOUT IT

Thank God that we aren't saved by turning over a new leaf or trying our hardest. Jesus lived the perfect life and died our sinful death so we could truly change from the heart.

THE BOTTOM LINE

If anyone is in Christ, they are a new creation.

318 | 1 Peter: Pain before gain

Today we return to Peter's first letter and a controversial subject — wives and husbands. As you read Peter's controversial words, remember that it's Jesus we are following.

👁 Read 1 Peter 3 v 1–2

ENGAGE YOUR BRAIN

- ▶ What does the "in the same way" refer back to? (end of chapter 2.)

- ▶ What is the possible result of this submission?

In the ancient world — and in some places today — you couldn't choose who you married. Some Christian women were in the difficult position of being married to a non-believer, or may have become Christians after their marriage. Either way (just like slaves with harsh masters) their Christ-like behaviour could win over their husband for Christ.

PRAY ABOUT IT

Pray for someone you know who is a Christian married to a non-Christian or who is the only Christian in their family. Ask God to help them to be Christ-like in their behaviour so that they might draw attention to Jesus.

👁 Read 1 Peter 3 v 3–7

- ▶ What is the best way to be beautiful? (v3–4)

- ▶ How did Sarah honour God? (v6)

- ▶ Why might Christian wives be tempted to be afraid? (v6)

- ▶ What instructions does Peter give to Christian husbands? (v7)

- ▶ How would this have been against the culture of the time?

Men and women are both heirs of the gift of eternal life, so they're of equal worth in God's sight. BUT Peter says they need to show respect for one another in different ways. Both in Christ-like submission and in Christ-like care, consideration and respect.

THE BOTTOM LINE

Honour God by your behaviour.

319 | Living in harmony

Our behaviour isn't just a way to communicate Christ to others; it's what God has called us to be like. Christianity isn't a hobby, it's a way of life.

👁 Read 1 Peter 3 v 8–9

GET ON WITH IT

▶ *Who do you need to live more harmoniously with?*

▶ *Who will you be more sympathetic towards?*

▶ *Which Christians can you show brotherly/sisterly love to?*

▶ *When do you find it hard to be compassionate or humble?*

▶ *With the Holy Spirit's help, what do you need to do about that?*

▶ *Who do you like to insult or backstab?*

▶ *How will you be a blessing to them?*

👁 Read verses 10–12

▶ *What's the warning in these verses?*

▶ *What's the encouragement?*

Peter is quoting Psalm 34. These verses were originally written to Old Testament believers — they are NOT saying that the way to get God to listen to you is to be good! The "righteous" in that psalm are not the morally good but those who "take refuge in the Lord" (Psalm 34 v 8) — people who turn to Him for help and mercy.

PRAY ABOUT IT

Ask for God's help to keep walking in His ways, to turn from evil and to do good. Pray about your answers to the earlier questions.

320 Stand up, speak out

It's often pretty scary being pointed out as a Christian, and as for telling (sometimes hostile) people why you are a Christian — eeek!

👁 Read 1 Peter 3 v 13–16

ENGAGE YOUR BRAIN

▶ *What might these Christians be worried about? (v13)*

▶ *What's the encouragement (v14)?*

▶ *Why shouldn't Christians fear the world around us?*

▶ *What changes our perspective? (v15)*

We might face mockery or social exclusion for being known as a Christian. Peter's first readers (and many Christians around the world) could face loss of income, physical attack or even death for following Christ. But we're not to fear these things; we're to fear God (2 v 17). And Peter reminds us that if we suffer for doing good, we're blessed by Him.

▶ *Instead of being frightened, what should we do? (3 v 15) How? (v15–16)*

▶ *What will the outcome be?*

TALK IT OVER

Chat with another Christian about how you can explain your beliefs. Do you find it scary? Then pray together that you won't fear people, but God. Do you tend to get argumentative or pushy when trying to show how Christianity is the truth? Then pray together for a spirit of gentleness and respect. Remember that Christ is Lord and ask for the courage to show and tell that.

PRAY ABOUT IT

Pray that you would see Christ as He really is — Lord of everything — and that you wouldn't be scared to be known as His follower.

THE BOTTOM LINE

In your heart, set apart Christ as Lord.

321 Christ's perfect example

Suffering and Jesus — two themes that Peter returns to again and again.

👁 Read 1 Peter 3 v 17–22

ENGAGE YOUR BRAIN

▶ What does Peter remind us of again in verse 17?

▶ Who does he point us to again and why? (v18)

▶ Why was Jesus' death far from pointless? (v18)

GET ON WITH IT

Learn 1 Peter 3 v 18 — it's a wonderful explanation of the amazing swap that took place at the cross.

Verses 19–22 have caused many people to scratch their heads over the years — what exactly is Peter referring to? We'll start with what is clear!

▶ According to verse 20, how did most people respond to God in the days of Noah (and now!)?

▶ Who was saved and how?

▶ What truth does baptism remind us of? (v21)

▶ What is it that saves us? (v21–22)

▶ What are we reminded about Jesus? (v22)

PRAY ABOUT IT

Ask God to help you pass the message of verse 18 on to those who are currently rejecting their Creator. Thank Him that if we trust in Jesus, we can be washed clean inside, just as baptism makes us clean outside.

THE BOTTOM LINE

Jesus died for your sins, to bring you to God.

322 Living for God

Suffering. It's not exactly appealing, is it? But, as Peter reminds us, it's the sign of a serious Christian.

👁 Read 1 Peter 4 v 1–7

ENGAGE YOUR BRAIN

▶ *What's the "therefore" there for? What has chapter 3 been reminding us about?*

▶ *Which attitude of Christ's are we to imitate? (4v1)*

▶ *What are we living for? (v2)*

▶ *If we are not living for God, what are we living for? (v2)*

▶ *What does this look like in practice? Try putting verse 3 into everyday language.*

▶ *What will be the outcome of not joining in? (v4)*

Have you ever experienced this? Being mocked or excluded for going God's way can feel pretty miserable.

▶ *How is verse 5 an encouragement to Christians who are persecuted for their changed behaviour?*

GET ON WITH IT

We will all have to give an account to God for the life we've lived. The good news is that we can have Jesus' perfect record because He paid all our debts on the cross. Can you share this with someone today?

PRAY ABOUT IT

Read verse 7. How will remembering this help you to pray? What sort of things can you be praying about from the previous verses? Do it!

THE BOTTOM LINE

Live for Jesus; He died for you.

323 Love above all

Love one another; so simple yet so difficult. Jesus said it was the second most important commandment and a sign of being one of His followers.

👁 Read 1 Peter 4 v 8–11

ENGAGE YOUR BRAIN

- ▶ *Why is loving each other so important? (v8)*

- ▶ *What might this look like in practice? (v9–10)*

Ever grumble about having to hang out with people at church who are a bit weird? Or being made to welcome new people at youth group instead of chatting to your friends? Loving each other is often inconvenient, but it's what Jesus wants us to do. It also helps us to forgive people when they do us wrong (v8).

God gives all Christians different gifts.

- ▶ *What are these gifts for? (v10)*

- ▶ *What does Peter remind us that we are administering (sharing) or being stewards of?*

- ▶ *What should be the end result? (v11)*

So whether you're good at music, make a mean cappuccino, can stack and put away 100 chairs in ten minutes or can lead a great Bible study, remember that it's not about you. You're here to serve others in God's strength so that He gets the glory. Got it?

PRAY ABOUT IT

Thank God for His grace to you — shared with you by other people who teach and serve you at church. (Why not thank them too?) Ask for God's strength to serve others and to glorify Him.

THE BOTTOM LINE

Above all, love one another deeply.

324 Painful reading

Peter keeps reminding us that the Christian life involves suffering. But is it really worth it?

👁 Read 1 Peter 4 v 12–19

ENGAGE YOUR BRAIN

▶ What might our reaction to suffering be? (v12)

▶ But how should we respond to suffering?

▶ What does Peter remind us of? (v14)

▶ How might we be tempted to feel when suffering? (v16)

▶ What does Peter say we should do instead?

THINK IT OVER

Can you think of examples in the media recently where someone has suffered for being a Christian? Can you think of any examples in your own life?

▶ What does Peter call us in verse 17?

▶ How does that make you feel?

▶ If things are tough now for Christians, how much tougher will they ultimately be for others? (v17–18)

▶ What is Peter's encouragement to his readers and us in verse 19?

▶ How does Peter describe God?

PRAY ABOUT IT

God is faithful — we follow a suffering Saviour, and although we will face trouble, we are part of His family and more blessed than we can imagine. Spend some time now praising and thanking God that you belong to Him.

325 Relationship advice

More about our relationships with other Christians and our relationship with God, as Peter gets towards the end of his great letter.

Read 1 Peter 5 v 1–4

ENGAGE YOUR BRAIN

▶ Who does Peter address first of all? (v1–4)

▶ What word does he use to sum up the way they should lead God's people? (v2)

▶ What are the dos and don'ts in verses 2–3?

▶ Who is the Chief Shepherd? (v4)

▶ What should ultimately motivate Christian leaders? (v4)

PRAY ABOUT IT

Pray for your church leaders / youth leaders, that they would have these characteristics and that they would receive the crown of glory when Jesus returns.

Read verses 5–7

▶ Who does Peter advise next? (v5)

▶ What does he tell them to do? (v5)

Whether you're overseeing other people or submitting to another's lead, humility is the key. If you find yourself thinking you're more important than another Christian, you shouldn't be in leadership.

▶ How does God react to the proud? (v5)

▶ Who determines our worth and status? (v6)

▶ So how should we respond to Him and why? (v6–7)

PRAY ABOUT IT

Verse 7 — do it now.

THE BOTTOM LINE

Humble yourself, so that God may lift you up.

326 In conclusion...

Closing words now — the things Peter really wants his original readers (and us) to hang onto.

👁 Read 1 Peter 5 v 8–11

▶ What two things does Peter tell us to be in verse 8?

▶ Why do we need to be on our guard?

▶ What will encourage us to stand firm in the faith? (v9)

▶ How might the devil use suffering or persecution to tempt us away from our faith?

▶ Who is really in control? (v10)

▶ How will He help us? (v10)

A wise Christian minister once said: "Suffering can make you bitter or it can make you better". Get your head round how God can use suffering and persecution for our good BEFORE it happens, so that you don't fall apart when it inevitably comes.

👁 Read verses 12–14

▶ How does Peter sum up the message of his letter in verse 12?

▶ How does Peter describe Silas and Mark?

Mark wasn't biologically related to Peter, but Peter treated him like a son. This is the guy who wrote Mark's Gospel, which appears to be largely based on Peter's testimony.

▶ What is Peter's final blessing to those who are in Christ? (v14)

PRAY ABOUT IT

Pain before gain. Suffering before glory. The Christian life will be tough. But God won't forget that He's called you to share in His eternal glory. Think how 1 Peter has prepared you to keep going as a Christian. Thank God for this letter. And ask for His help not to give up.

327 Matthew: Are you ready?

We're back in Matthew, near the end of Jesus' life. Before you read this next section, remember that this really happened. It really happened to the Son of God. Don't just read the words — feel the emotions.

👁 Read Matthew 26 v 36–44

ENGAGE YOUR BRAIN

▶ How is Jesus feeling? (v37–38)

▶ What does He ask His Father God to do? (v39)

The cup is a picture of God's wrath — His right anger at, and punishment of, sin. To be given this cup is to experience God's judgment. That's what Jesus knows is going to happen to Him as He dies on the cross. Remember that Jesus has never done anything wrong. God has no reason to be angry with Him.

▶ What is amazing about what Jesus says in verse 42?

It's incredible that Jesus would take God's punishment in His friends' place. Especially when we see what His friends are like…

▶ What does Jesus ask them to do for Him? (v38, 41)

▶ How do they react? (v40, 43)

THINK ABOUT IT

Have you realised how awful the cross was for Jesus? He'd been loved by His Father for all eternity; on the cross, He knew only His Father's anger.

Have you realised that He did this for you? You deserve God's wrath, but Jesus drank your cup.

Have you realised how undeserving you are? You let down Jesus all the time (we all do). He knew that, and still He died for you. Astonishing.

PRAY ABOUT IT

How can you not thank Jesus for all of this?

THE BOTTOM LINE

Jesus drank the horrific cup of God's wrath — for you.

328 Who's in control?

**Does Jesus tell you what your life should be like?
Or do you tell Him?**

👁 Read Matthew 26 v 45–50

Again, it looks on the surface as if everything's out of Jesus' control. And yet it's Jesus who gives Judas permission to betray Him (v50).

👁 Read verses 51–56

ENGAGE YOUR BRAIN

▶ *Draw the scene (it doesn't need to be a masterpiece!):*

▶ *What is Jesus' priority? (v54, 56)*

▶ *What is the disciples' priority…
in verse 51?
at the end of verse 56?*

Jesus could whistle up an army of angels (v53)! But He doesn't. His plan is not to win a military victory but to defeat death on the cross, just as the prophets predicted in the Old Testament. The disciples don't trust or like Jesus' plan. When He won't fit in with what they want to do, they abandon Him.

THINK ABOUT IT

We all either fit in with Jesus' plan for our lives, even when that's hard — or we try to make Jesus fit in with our plans, and forget about Him when He won't.

When have you done hard things for Jesus in the last month? Praise God and be encouraged!

How have you decided to follow your own plan, and turned your back on Jesus when it's hard? Be challenged and ask God for help!

THE BOTTOM LINE

Follow Jesus' plan, not your own, even when it's hard.

329 Who's on trial?

Judas is guilty of betrayal. The disciples are guilty of desertion. Next, it's Jesus on trial. Or is it? As you read, picture the scene in your head and feel the tension of the conversation.

👁 Read Matthew 26 v 57–64

ENGAGE YOUR BRAIN

▶ *How fair is Jesus' trial? (v59–60)*

Notice that Jesus doesn't answer the crooked judges about the fake evidence (v63). The chief priests are getting nowhere… so the high priest gets right to the heart of the issue.

▶ *What does he challenge Jesus to do? (v63)*

▶ *How does Jesus answer? What does He add? (v64)*

Jesus is guilty of one thing: being the Son of God. And as He stands on trial, He points forward to another trial, when everyone, including His enemies, will see Him "coming on the clouds of heaven".

👁 Read verses 65–68

▶ *What does the high priest find Jesus guilty of?*

▶ *What sentence do they pass? (v66)*

THINK ABOUT IT

The world still puts Jesus on trial today. It pre-judges Jesus, refuses to listen to Him, and then dismisses Him as a fake. But one day He will judge the world. And the world will have nothing to say (see Romans 3 v 19).

▶ *How does this encourage you to keep following Jesus in a world that rejects Him?*

GET ON WITH IT

Jesus told the truth about Himself even when on trial for His life. In what situations can you stand up for the truth about Him, even when that risks rejection, unpopularity or even physical harm? Ask God to give you the courage to actually do this.

330 Denied

As Jesus stands in the courtroom, facing death, another man is put on trial just outside.

👁 Read Matthew 26 v 57–58

ENGAGE YOUR BRAIN

▶ *Where is Peter as Jesus' trial begins? (v58)*

👁 Read verses 69–75

Three times Peter is given a chance to stand up for the truth about Jesus.

▶ *What does he do with those chances? (v70, 72, 74)*

▶ *Who is interrogating him? (v69, 71, 73)*

As Jesus stands up to the most important priest in the whole nation, Peter caves in to some bystanders. Pathetic!

But unsurprising, because Jesus had said this would happen. He knew Peter, and He knew Peter was flawed and would disown Him (v34).

▶ *When the cock crows, what does Peter remember? (v74–75)*

▶ *How does he react when he realises what he's done?*

GET ON WITH IT

We're all Peters. We all fail to stand up for Jesus. We all fail to be loyal to Him in what we say and how we live.

But do we all react like Peter? He "wept bitterly". He was honest about himself and what he'd done. He didn't make excuses. He didn't convince himself it didn't matter.

He wept.

And the question is: when we let Jesus down, does it affect us as deeply?

PRAY ABOUT IT

Admit to Jesus the ways in which you've denied Him. Feel the pain of letting Him down. Then thank Him that He knows all your flaws, and that He still died for you.

331　Dead end or happy end?

Yesterday we saw Peter in tears when he realised he'd let Jesus down. Today we focus on someone who had even more of a reason for feeling rotten and pathetic.

👁 Read Matthew 27 v 1-4

ENGAGE YOUR BRAIN

Jesus has now been condemned to death (v1–2).

▶ How does Judas, "who had betrayed him", feel about this? (v3)

▶ What does he do, and why? (v3–4)

Judas regrets his sin. He confesses his sin. He tries to make up for his sin.

👁 Read verses 5–10

▶ What does Judas end up doing? (v5)

Judas was really sorry, just as Peter was. Peter went on to be one of Jesus' main men, preaching the gospel and setting up churches. So why isn't there a happy end to Judas' story? It's because he hasn't done one crucial thing. Let's listen in to Peter preaching, later on, in Acts.

👁 Read Acts 3 v 19-21

▶ What does Peter tell people to do? (v19)

▶ What will then happen to their sins? (v19)

Judas knew he'd sinned — but he didn't look to Jesus to wipe them out for him. Instead he tried to make up for them. But he couldn't. And he ended up dead.

Feeling bad about sin, confessing it, and trying to repair the damage is no use if we don't also turn to Jesus as Lord, and ask Him to be our Saviour.

PRAY ABOUT IT

Do you need to "repent and turn to God" and ask him to "wipe out" a particular sin?

332 | God's King? Kill him!

It's one of the most stupid decisions ever. Looking at Jesus and saying: "Kill Him". Why did they do it?

👁 Read Matthew 27 v 11–31

ENGAGE YOUR BRAIN

Three sets of people send "the king of the Jews" (v11) to the cross.

The chief priests stand next to Pilate, the Roman governor, accusing Jesus (v12).

▶ *Why? (v18)*

They need Jesus out of the way so that they can keep their power.

The people

▶ *What does Pilate ask? (v17)*

▶ *What's the sensible answer?*

▶ *Why do they crucify Jesus? (v20)*

The governor

▶ *How does Pilate's wife describe Jesus? (v19) But what does Pilate do? (v26)*

Why? Because he's afraid of an uproar (v24). Pilate does what's easiest, not what's right. He's a coward.

THINK ABOUT IT

We don't shout "Crucify him!" But we do live as though Jesus doesn't exist and isn't King — we sin. And we do it for the same reasons…

When do you reject Jesus as your King because:

• you want to be in charge, not Him?

• you listen to those around you, not Him?

• you choose what's easiest, rather than obeying Him?

THE BOTTOM LINE

Sin is stupid. These people chose not to let God's loving King be part of their lives — and chose to set loose a murderer (Luke 23 v 19). Sin means turning away from the perfect King, choosing to mess things up. Stupid.

333 Defeated man, or Lord?

Who died on the cross? OK, clearly it was Jesus, but who was He, really? Jesus' followers called Him "Lord". Yet many people who saw Jesus die thought He was pathetic: just a defeated man.

👁 Read Matthew 27 v 32–44

ENGAGE YOUR BRAIN

Really try to picture the scene.

▶ *What do people walking past say to Jesus? (v40)*

▶ *What would make them believe Jesus is the "Son of God"?*

▶ *What do the religious leaders say about Jesus? (v42–43)*

▶ *What would make them believe Jesus is God's King?*

But Jesus stays hanging from the cross. And these people look at Him and say: *He can't be the Son of God.*

But they've misunderstood. It's because of who Jesus is that He stays on the cross. If He hadn't been God's Son, He'd never have let Himself be killed without a fight. If He hadn't been God's King, He wouldn't be dying to save people from God's punishment: eternal death.

👁 Read Matthew 27 v 54

▶ *What do the Roman soldiers say about Jesus?*

As Jesus dies on the cross, these men look at Him and say: *He's clearly the Son of God. He is the Lord.*

THINK ABOUT IT

▶ *When you look at Jesus on the cross, do you see a defeated man or do you see your Lord?*

PRAY ABOUT IT

Thank Jesus that, although He could have easily saved Himself from the cross, He chose not to. Thank Him for deciding to go through all this so that you don't have to.

THE BOTTOM LINE

Jesus isn't defeated — He's our Lord.

334 | The big question

**People sometimes ask "Why did Jesus die?"
Actually, He tells us Himself.**

👁 Read Matthew 27 v 45–46

ENGAGE YOUR BRAIN

The "sixth hour" (v45, ESV) is midday.

▶ *What's strange about what
happens in verse 45?*

Centuries before, God had warned
this would be a sign of His anger
(Amos 8 v 9). Of course God was
furious — His Son was being killed!
But the great surprise of the cross is
who He was angry with…

▶ *What did Jesus shout? (Mt 27v46)*

"Forsaken" means "abandoned" or
"deserted".

▶ *What is the dying Son of God
saying about His relationship with
His Father?*

The punishment of complete
separation from the loving God,
from all joy and hope, should be
falling on the mocking people and
gloating leaders. Instead, it's falling
on God's perfect, innocent Son.

👁 Read verses 47–50

As He explained why He was dying,
Jesus mentioned Eli — God (v46).
But people didn't bother to listen
carefully. They thought He'd said
Elijah (v47). So they completely failed
to understand why Jesus died.

People still do that today. They don't
listen to God's Son explaining that
His death is the only way they can
avoid God's punishment of being
abandoned by Him for ever.

▶ *Are you listening?*

PRAY ABOUT IT

The punishment should have fallen
on me and you. Instead, it fell on
Jesus. He offers to take your place.
Have you ever asked Him to do this
for you? If not, what's stopping you?
If you have, when was the last time
you actually thanked Him properly?
Do it now!

335 Can people live with God?

You probably don't ask this very often! But it's of eternal importance. If we can't survive in God's presence, we face an eternity cut off from Him and all good things.

ANSWER ONE

👁 Read Genesis 3 v 22–24

The first people had disobeyed God, and thought they could "know" (means "decide") good and evil for themselves. They were trying to become like God, making the rules themselves. That's sin.

▶ *What could humans no longer do? (v22–23)*

▶ *Why? (v24)*

So, can people live with God? NO.

ANSWER TWO

1,500 years before Jesus, God told His people that He'd live among them in the tabernacle. In the centre of this tent was where God dwelled — the "ark". And God told the people to put a curtain around it.

👁 Read Exodus 26 v 31–33

▶ *How does this link to Genesis 3?*

The curtain represented the separation between perfect God and sinful people. Can people live with God? NO.

ANSWER THREE

Eventually, the curtain got moved into the temple.

👁 Read Matthew 27 v 50–56

▶ *As Jesus died, what happened? (v51)*

▶ *What does this show is the great achievement of Jesus' death?*

PRAY ABOUT IT

Thank Jesus that He died for your sin and removed the barrier so you can live with God. Ask Him to give you certainty that you're headed for perfect eternity in God's presence.

THE BOTTOM LINE

Can people live with God? YES.

336 | A real follower

Today's verses show us one way to see whether or not we're true disciples of Jesus, the crucified King.

👁 Read Matthew 27 v 57–61

ENGAGE YOUR BRAIN

▶ What does verse 57 tell us about Joseph?

▶ What does he do? (v58–60)

Remember that the last thing Pilate did was to have Jesus tortured and killed.

▶ How is Joseph taking a huge risk in verse 58, do you think?

▶ How is Joseph giving something up for Jesus in verses 59–60?

Remember who Joseph's doing all this for — a corpse! Jesus is dead! Surely risking everything for (and giving everything to) Jesus can't do any good now... yet Joseph still does it.

And in the end, Joseph has the great privilege of his tomb being the place where Jesus rose from the dead. But he doesn't know that as he speaks to Pilate, or lays Jesus' body to rest.

▶ How is Joseph an example of how a true follower of Jesus acts?

GET ON WITH IT

▶ What risks can you take to stand up for Jesus this week?

▶ What things can you give to serving Jesus this week: Some money? Some time? Some talents? Some words?

👁 Read verses 62–66

The religious leaders wanted to completely crush the "Jesus cult". Instead, they made it certain that, when Jesus' body disappeared from the tomb, it was impossible that His disciples had stolen it.

THE BOTTOM LINE

True Jesus-followers risk everything, and give everything, to Him.

337 Jesus is risen – so what?

Ever seen a sports team snatch victory from the jaws of defeat? Or a film where all seems lost but then the hero makes a spectacular comeback? Today we see the greatest victory — the most amazing comeback — of all time.

👁 Read Matthew 28 v 1–7

ENGAGE YOUR BRAIN

- ▶ Sum up in a sentence what happens in verses 1-4.

- ▶ Why is Jesus' dead body not in the tomb? (v6)

- ▶ Who had predicted this would happen? (v6)

- ▶ How do you think you'd have felt if you'd been with the women?

- ▶ What does the resurrection show about Jesus' promises?

👁 Read verses 8–10

- ▶ How are the women feeling? (v8)

- ▶ How do they react to meeting the risen Jesus? (v9)

- ▶ What does He tell them to do? (v10)

GET ON WITH IT

- ▶ How do verses 8–10 show us what the right reactions to Jesus' resurrection are?
  v8:
  v9:

- ▶ How can you do each of these things this week?

PRAY ABOUT IT

Thank God that Jesus rose from the dead and that everything He says is true. Thank Him that you can rely completely on Him.

THE BOTTOM LINE

Jesus is risen. This should give us great joy. We should live for Jesus and tell other people about Him.

338 Killing the truth

Someone you were involved in killing has come back to life. What do you do?!

👁 Read Matthew 28 v 11–15

ENGAGE YOUR BRAIN

The chief priests had Jesus executed. Now it seems He's come back to life. Here's their choice: admit they were wrong and take Jesus seriously, or keep ignoring reality.

▶ *What choice do the religious leaders take? (v12–14)*

These are professional soldiers — they would never all have fallen asleep (v13)! Ever since that day, no one's come up with a convincing explanation of what happened at Jesus' tomb — apart from that He is the Son of God, risen from the dead.

TALK ABOUT IT

▶ *What reasons do people give for not believing Jesus rose from the dead? Can you answer them?*

If you're not too confident, get together with some Christian friends and practise talking about why you believe in the resurrection. The chief priests chose to ignore reality and make up a story. But not everyone reacted like that to the crime of killing Jesus…

👁 Read Acts 2 v 22–23, 37–41

These men realise they've done something terrible in killing Jesus (v23). They know they need to change (v37). 3,000 of them stop opposing Jesus, and instead accept Him as Lord and Saviour (v38, 41).

GET ON WITH IT

It's the same today. People hear that they've rejected the risen Jesus, God's Son, and are in trouble. Lots keep ignoring reality. But some realise their sin, and accept Jesus as their Lord and Saviour.

▶ *Who could you talk to about the risen Jesus today?*

339 | What Jesus deserves

Why should Christians tell other people about Jesus? It can be so difficult, cause us hassle, and leave people thinking we're crazy. Why bother? Well, here's one big reason, straight from the lips of Christ Himself...

👁 Read Matthew 28 v 16–20

ENGAGE YOUR BRAIN

▶ *Where do the disciples go, and who do they meet? (v16–17)*

This shouldn't have surprised them. Jesus had told the women this would happen (v10) — and, as we've seen, what Jesus says will happen always happens.

▶ *What does Jesus claim? (v18)*

▶ *So how does Jesus want His followers to respond? (v19–20)*

Because of who Jesus is — the crucified, risen Lord, in charge of absolutely everything — He deserves all people to love Him and respect Him. If we understand who Jesus is, we'll love and respect Him so much that we'll tell others about Him. Because we'll want Him to enjoy their love and respect, too. Jesus is Lord — THEREFORE we should tell others about Him. But doing this is hard!

That's why the last sentence of Matthew's Gospel is fantastic!

Jesus doesn't just send us to tell people about Him — He goes with us as we do it. Awesome.

GET ON WITH IT

▶ *Who are you going to try to tell about how great Jesus is?*

If you find yourself not really wanting to — remember that Jesus is amazing and deserves their love and respect.

PRAY ABOUT IT

Pray for those people now. Thank Jesus that He's with you. Ask Him to give you courage to talk about Him.

THE BOTTOM LINE

Jesus deserves love and respect — THEREFORE tell others about Him.

JONAH

Stormy waters

You probably know the story of Jonah. He's the one who was swallowed by a whale. It's a big fish, actually...

But Jonah isn't about the big fish.

And although the book is called Jonah, he isn't even the main character. As with every book in the Bible, it's all about God. He's the hero, and it's God's character that we really need to pay attention to.

As a prophet, it was Jonah's job to bring God's word, His message, to others. Jonah lived in Israel nearly 800 years before Jesus. His usual target audience was the Israelites — God's chosen people.

Through Jonah, Israel had seen God keep His promise to them by restoring the land that had been taken from them. Jonah was probably happy living in Israel, delivering such a positive message from God.

However, God's plan extended way beyond Israel to Nineveh and the rest of the world. The problem was that Israel (and Jonah) didn't want others to benefit from God's love in the same way that they had. And especially not their enemies! In their minds, the Lord was *their* God and no one else's.

Thankfully, God didn't exactly agree, and His mission (to show all people their need for His rescue) was not about to be scuppered by an unwilling prophet. Can you sense a storm brewing?

340 Runaway prophet

How good are you at taking orders?
Are you obedient or rebellious?
What about when the orders are from God?

👁 Read Jonah 1 v 1–3

ENGAGE YOUR BRAIN

▶ *What did God want Jonah to do?*

▶ *Why? (v2)*

▶ *What was Jonah's response? (v3)*

Nineveh was an important city in Assyria, a nation who rejected God and fought the Israelites. The people of Nineveh needed to hear God's message and turn to Him.

But Jonah wouldn't take God's message to Nineveh. Instead, he ran away to Tarshish — which was probably in what is now Spain. It was in the opposite direction from Nineveh.

Later on (Jonah 4 v 2), we're told why Jonah didn't want to go. But we're still left thinking: *"How can Jonah run away from God???"* The temptation is to think Jonah is a bit crazy… surely we'd never disobey a direct command from God?

THINK IT OVER

Yet, if you're honest, are there some commands in the Bible that you don't pay much attention to? What about honouring your parents, loving your enemies or not wanting other people's stuff?

PRAY ABOUT IT

Ask God to help you obey Him in every part of your life — your thoughts, words and actions — no matter how difficult it might be.

Quickly write a list of areas where you don't obey God. Spend time praying about each of them, saying sorry and asking God's help.

THE BOTTOM LINE

Obey the Lord; don't run away from Him.

341 Nowhere to run

**We've seen how Jonah responded to God —
he ran away! But how will God respond to
Jonah's rebellion?**

👁 Read Jonah 1 v 4–10

ENGAGE YOUR BRAIN

▶ *Did God let Jonah get his own
way? What did God do?*

▶ *How did Jonah react? (v5, 9)*

Jonah gives us the ultimate
definition of *stubborn*: he runs
away from the Lord, sleeps through
a storm sent by God, and totally
ignores the captain's plea to ask God
to spare them! And then he has the
nerve to say he worships God (v9)!
But Jonah wasn't worshipping God
in the way he lived.

GET ON WITH IT

What specific changes can you make
so that you're worshipping God in
the way you live?

👁 Read verses 11–17

▶ *Did Jonah turn back to God and
repent?*

▶ *What did the sailors recognise
about God? (v14)*

▶ *How do we see that God's in
complete control? (v13, 15, 17)*

We're not told whether Jonah
turned back to God at this stage.
What is absolutely certain is that
God was in total control. His original
plan for Jonah hadn't changed.
Despite Jonah's disobedience, God
rescued him with a huge fish. He
showed great mercy to Jonah, giving
him so many extra chances!

PRAY ABOUT IT

Ask God to help you to live a life
with Him in charge. Glance back
at GET ON WITH IT and pray about
those things.

THE BOTTOM LINE

God's in charge, whether we like it
or not.

342 Nowhere to hide

It's a pretty strange place to find yourself, in a fish's stomach... Now we find out just how and why that happened, and notice a big change in our man Jonah.

👁 Read Jonah 2 v 1–10

▶ *What happened to Jonah? (v3, 5)*

▶ *What was his response? (v2, 7)*

▶ *And how did God respond to Jonah's prayers? (v2, 6, 10)*

Finally! Jonah did what he should have done ages ago — he called out to God. Amazingly, the Lord still showed patience with Jonah after his repeated disobedience.

▶ *What word does Jonah use to sum this up in verse 8?*

Grace (some Bible versions have "love" or "steadfast love") is when God gives us far more than we deserve. In fact, we deserve the opposite. Jonah realised that he didn't deserve God's grace, yet he also realised that salvation (rescue) only comes from the Lord (v8–9).

Sadly, many people worship other things in their lives (money, relationships, sport, image, good grades etc) instead of accepting God's grace and rescue from sin, and putting Him first.

SHARE IT

Verse 8 is as true for your friends as it was for Jonah, so why don't you plan how you can tell a friend about the grace, love and rescue that we can have through Jesus?

PRAY ABOUT IT

Thank God that He does answer people who call out to be rescued. Pray for a non-Christian friend, that they would experience God's grace, love, and the rescue and forgiveness of Jesus.

THE BOTTOM LINE

"Those who cling to worthless idols turn away from God's love for them ... Salvation comes from the Lord." (Jonah 2 v 8-9)

343 Second chance

After running away and refusing to take God's message to Nineveh, Jonah was given a second chance.

👁 Read Jonah 3 v 1–4

ENGAGE YOUR BRAIN

▶ *How is Jonah's response different this time?*

▶ *What was God's message to Nineveh? (v4)*

God hates sin and will punish all those who rebel against Him. The future looked bleak for Nineveh.

👁 Read verses 5–9

▶ *How did the Ninevites respond to Jonah's terrifying news?*

▶ *What hope did they have? (v9)*

The people of Nineveh realised that God Himself was speaking to them. They stopped eating, gave up their sinful ways and pleaded with God to forgive them. They realised they had sinned against God and deserved to be destroyed by Him. They asked God to forgive them and they turned away from their evil ways. Turning *away* from sin and turning *to* God is repentance. It's how you become a Christian.

▶ *Know anyone who needs to do that? Maybe yourself?*

👁 Read verse 10

God will punish and destroy evil. But He's also a God of incredible love. Here, He forgave the Ninevites. And God offers forgiveness to anyone who turns from their evil ways and trusts in Jesus' death in their place.

SHARE IT

Who can you tell about God's anger against sin and His offer of forgiveness?

PRAY ABOUT IT

Thank God for His compassion, especially to you. Pray for His compassion on friends/family who don't yet live for Him.

344 | All inclusive

God showed amazing compassion and didn't destroy Nineveh. Imagine the parties in Nineveh! And the relief. Everyone was happy. Well, not quite everyone...

👁 Read Jonah 4 v 1–3

ENGAGE YOUR BRAIN

▶ Why was Jonah angry and why had he run away earlier? (v2)

▶ How do you feel about Jonah's anger?

Jonah saw everything from his own point of view, not God's. He hated the idea of the Ninevites turning to God. They were Israel's enemies — surely they should be destroyed, not forgiven.

👁 Read verse 4

▶ What's the right answer to God's question?

▶ Why?

Jonah seems to have forgotten that he had run away and refused to obey God. He had deserved to be destroyed. But when he cried out to the Lord, God rescued him! And God showed the same compassion to the people of Nineveh when they cried out to be rescued from destruction. God is compassionate, fair, and consistent. God always gets it right!

Jonah didn't seem to understand that God cares for all people, not just the Israelites. That's one of the big messages from this book (and the whole Bible): God wants *everyone* to turn to Him and find forgiveness.

GET ON WITH IT

If God cares for everyone, how should this affect the way you view other people? What about those people you can't stand? What do you need to change?

PRAY ABOUT IT

Ask God to help you see people the way He does. And to make your priorities the same as His.

345 Vine whine

Jonah: God, you're so loving, I knew you'd forgive the Ninevites. It's so annoying!
God: Have you any right to be angry, Jonah?

👁 Read Jonah 4 v 5–9

ENGAGE YOUR BRAIN

▶ *What was Jonah hoping would happen to Nineveh? (v5)*

▶ *Did Jonah deserve the vine? (v6)*

▶ *So, was his answer to God's question true? (v9)*

It's easy to think we deserve things from God. We don't. At all. Yet God does so much for us anyway, because of His great love for us.

👁 Read verses 10–11

▶ *How are God's priorities and Jonah's priorities different?*

▶ *So what's the answer to God's question at the end of verse 11?*

Jonah didn't deserve the vine and he had no right to be angry about it dying. 120,000 people were far more important than a desert plant! Even though they were enemies of the Israelites, God still showed great love for the people of Nineveh.

TALK IT THROUGH

We've seen how God's priorities are very different from Jonah's, and probably ours. Talk with a friend about how your youth group or church can reach those who, like the Ninevites, haven't heard about God's judgment, love and compassion.

PRAY ABOUT IT

Thank God for His plan for people to know Him. Thank Him for sending Jesus to make this possible. Ask God to help you warn people of His judgment and tell them about His amazing love.

346 Psalms: Stress and rescue

The pressure's on. No one's offering to help. It's totally unfair. What's your next move? (a) Panic? (b) Give up and get out? (c) Lash out at the nearest target? (d) Other. Check out David's coping mechanism below.

👁 Read Psalm 31 v 1–20

ENGAGE YOUR BRAIN

▶ *How does David describe his trouble? (v4, 11-13)*

▶ *What is it about God that gives David hope of rescue? (v3, 19–20)*

When it seems as if the world is your enemy, God's word can strengthen you like nothing else. It reminds us that God has come through for generations of believers before and He's not about to change.

THINK IT OVER

Ever experienced God's help in a crisis? Make this memory a reason to trust Him the next time trouble comes.

▶ *In his prayer, what words show how David is strengthened?*
v1:
v5:
v6:
v14:

👁 Read verses 21–24

Rounding off his story of stress and rescue, David gives us a two-word action plan. *Be strong* (v24). See the invisible. Hebrews says, "Faith is confidence in what we hope for and assurance about what we do not see" (Hebrews 11 v 1). If we can stay confident in God, even if everything looks desperate, we're learning to be strong in the Lord.

PRAY ABOUT IT

What sort of stress is heading your way? Tell God about it, and then ask His help not to panic or lash out.

GET ON WITH IT

Know anyone who might identify with David's troubles? Get in touch today and point them to Psalm 31. It might be the boost they need to keep hanging on.

ESTHER

God's beauty queen

"There I was, on the beach in Spain, and who taps me on the shoulder? Sally from next door! What a coincidence!" Ever wondered why things happen the way they do? Ever been baffled at God's ways? Ever been amazed at seemingly chance occurrences that have transformed situations?

The book of Esther is full of "coincidences". Esther's twisty-turny story not only tells us *what* is happening but gives us some huge clues as to *why* it's happening.

In 539 BC, God enabled His people (the Jews) to return to Jerusalem after the punishment of being exiled far from home. Just as He had promised in Ezekiel! Some did return (see Ezra and Nehemiah), but others remained, scattered across the Persian Empire.

Pretty girl **Esther** was one of them. So was her cousin **Mordecai**. They lived under the rule of Persian King **Xerxes**, his wife **Vashti** and the soon-to-be-appointed prime minister, **Haman**. By now it was the mid-fifth century BC.

This book, Esther, will help us understand God better — His greatness, His plans and the way He works. And so Esther will help us live that bit better for Christ. Get ready — coincidences are about to happen.

Vashti vanishes

Are you ready for a tale of mystery and intrigue with lots of cliffhangers? Well, the story opens with a lavish party in the court of Xerxes, king of all Persia.

👁 **Read Esther 1 v 1–9**

ENGAGE YOUR BRAIN

▶ How powerful was Xerxes? (v1)

▶ What were the signs of his wealth and extravagance?
v4:
v6:
v7–8:
v9:

👁 **Read verses 10–22**

▶ What was Xerxes' drunken command? (v11)

▶ What surprise did he get? (v12)

▶ How did he react? (v12–13)

▶ What decision was made? (v19)

▶ Why? (v19–21)

Xerxes was drunk and showing off. He wanted everyone to see how gorgeous his queen was. Understandably, she didn't want to be gawped at by the king's drunken mates. Xerxes' furious temper kicked in and the rest is history. His drunkenness, pride and anger led to bad decisions and divorce.

GET ON WITH IT

▶ Ever had your decisions clouded by alcohol?

▶ Ever done something rash when you were angry?

▶ What do you need to say sorry to God about?

▶ And what relationships do you need to mend that were broken in a rash moment?

Talk to God about your answers.

THE BOTTOM LINE

Anger and alcohol can get the better of us.

348 | Beauty contest

King Xerxes has dumped his beautiful wife and wants a new queen. What could all this possibly have to do with God and His people?

👁 Read Esther 2 v 1–11

ENGAGE YOUR BRAIN

▶ *What was the queen-finding plan? (v2–4)*

▶ *What coincidences followed? (v5–9)*

▶ *What was Esther's secret? (v5, 10)*

Imagine Esther's mixed feelings when she was chosen as a possible future queen. She would get to live in the king's palace but she would have to leave Mordecai and pretend not to be one of God's people, the Israelites.

It seems unlikely that God would be working through a beauty contest. But He often uses the least likely things and most surprising people in His perfect plans.

👁 Read verses 12–20

▶ *What was in store for the girls in the king's harem? (v12–14)*

▶ *What was special about Esther? (v16–17)*

▶ *So what happened? (v17–18)*

Esther's life would change loads as queen. But she wouldn't forget cousin Mordecai and the way he'd taught her to live. She may be queen now, but she was still one of God's special people — a Jew.

THINK IT OVER

▶ *What talent (likely or unlikely!) has God given you the ability to do?*

▶ *How can you use this gift to serve God?*

PRAY ABOUT IT

Thank God that He's in control. Ask Him to use your abilities in His great plans.

349 | The plot thickens

The twisty-turny tale of Esther continues to twist and turn today. We'll uncover two plots: one to murder the king and one to wipe out a whole people.

👁 Read Esther 2 v 21–23

ENGAGE YOUR BRAIN

▶ What did Mordecai discover? (v21)

▶ What did he do about it? (v22)

▶ What happened? (v23)

Yet another "coincidence" in Esther's story. This little incident will have significance later in the story.

👁 Read Esther 3 v 1–15

▶ Who became a big shot? (v1)

▶ Who refused to bow down to him? (v2)

▶ Why do you think he refused?

▶ What was Haman's shocking reaction? (v5–6)

▶ What law did Haman persuade King Xerxes to make? (v13)

▶ How long before it would happen? (v12, 13)

Haman wasn't satisfied with the idea of killing Mordecai, he wanted to wipe out all of God's people, the Jews. Notice he didn't mention them by name to the king (v8), so he could sneak through his murderous plot.

In countries such as North Korea, Sudan, Syria and Pakistan, Christians are still attacked and even killed. And even if you don't face death for being a Christian, you can expect people to treat you badly for following Jesus.

PRAY ABOUT IT

Pray for Christians in countries where people are imprisoned, attacked or killed for loving Jesus. Ask God to give them the courage to keep living His way, so that many people turn to Jesus in those countries.

350 | Getting the sack(cloth)

Esther's cousin Mordecai refused to bow down to powerful Haman. So Haman persuaded King Xerxes to issue a decree that all Jews in the kingdom would be slaughtered at the end of the year. Genocide.

Read Esther 4 v 1–8

ENGAGE YOUR BRAIN

▶ *How did Mordecai and the Jews respond to the news? (v1–3)*

▶ *What did Mordecai want Esther to do? (v8)*

People wore sackcloth and ashes to show they were massively upset. Sackcloth was made of rough goats' hair. Ashes were the black bits left after a fire. Uncomfortable stuff! But there was hope for God's people. Mordecai realised that God had put someone in a position to help them.

Read verses 9–17

▶ *Why didn't Esther want to approach the king? (v11)*

▶ *What did Mordecai say?*
v13:
v14:

▶ *What was Esther's answer and what did she request? (v16)*

Esther was worried she'd be killed for just approaching the king. But Mordecai knew she'd been made queen for a reason and there was nothing to lose. Eventually, Esther agreed and asked that all the Jews go without food for three days to pray for her.

GET ON WITH IT

Sometimes, fear can lead us to do nothing rather than take a risk for God. For example, chickening out of telling friends about Jesus' impact on your life. But really, what do you have to lose? Take a leaf out of Esther's book, take a chance and ask Christian friends to pray for you.

PRAY ABOUT IT

Ask God to help you serve Him in the situation He's put you in. Ask Him for courage to do what you know you should do. Then ask friends to pray for you.

351 Dinner invitation

Tense stuff. Esther, Mordecai and the Jews in Susa went without food and prayed their sandals off (4 v 15–17). But would Esther chicken out? Would Haman succeed? Would God's people be wiped from the map? Would Esther die?

👁 Read Esther 5 v 1–8

ENGAGE YOUR BRAIN

▶ What was the first positive sign for Esther? (v2)

▶ And the second? (v3)

▶ What did Esther request? (v4)

▶ When her chance came, what did she ask for? (v8)

What suspense! Esther has had two opportunities to beg for her people's lives, but so far she's just handed out dinner invitations! What will happen?

👁 Read verses 9–14

▶ What was Haman's view of himself? (v11)

▶ What did he think of Esther's invitation? (v12)

▶ What made him furious? (v9, 13)

▶ So what did he do? (v14)

Everything's in the balance for God's people. The king has ordered all Jews to be put to death. Their hope now rests on Queen Esther's shoulders. But so far, she hasn't got around to even telling King Xerxes that she's a Jew. Things are not looking good. And now Haman has set up a huge pole (NIV) (or "gallows", ESV) to impale Mordecai on.

Only God can bring rescue to such a hopeless situation. All humans are in a desperate situation — sinful and awaiting God's death sentence. But God Himself has arranged for the rescue — Jesus alone can save us from the death sentence.

PRAY ABOUT IT

Talk to God about anything tough you're facing at the moment. Thank Him for His power and His compassion. Thank Him for the rescue He offers though Jesus.

352 Robe reversal

Haman's feeling smug because he's the king's favourite. Everything seems to be going well for him — and he's soon going to kill his enemy Mordecai and all the Jews. But one sleepless night was about to change everything.

👁 Read Esther 6 v 1–9

ENGAGE YOUR BRAIN

▶ What did Xerxes discover in the history book? (v2–3)

▶ What did Haman think the king wanted to do? (v6)

▶ So what did he suggest? (v7–9)

So far, Haman's hopes were high. He thought Xerxes was going to honour him, not Mordecai! If the king was ready to do all this for Haman, then Mordecai's death was a small thing to ask for! But God was turning Haman's plans inside out.

👁 Read verses 10–14

▶ What was the twist in the tale for Haman? (v10)

▶ What did he have to do for his hated enemy? (v11)

▶ How did it affect Haman? (v12)

▶ What did his wife and advisers tell him? (v13)

▶ What would happen next? (v14)

Loads more "coincidences" today. God was at work behind the scenes. Just at the right time, God reminded King Xerxes of what Mordecai had done for him. Haman thought he would get revenge on Mordecai, but he had his hopes dashed by God's perfect timing. Amazing.

PRAY ABOUT IT

Have little coincidences ever caused things to work out just right for you? Thank God for any times you've seen Him use "coincidences" to work out His perfect plan in your life.

353 The big banquet

Oh, the unbearable tension. What would happen at Esther's banquet? Would Mordecai be killed? Would Esther ask the BIG question? Would God's people survive? Who needs soaps when you've got this nail-biting drama?

👁 Read Esther 7 v 1–10

ENGAGE YOUR BRAIN

▶ *What did the king ask Esther yet again? (v2) How did she answer this time? (v3–4)*

▶ *Who was revealed as the villain of the story? (v6)*

▶ *How did the king respond? (v7)*

▶ *How about Haman? (v7) How did he make things even worse for himself? (v8)*

▶ *What was ironic about his fate? (v9–10)*

Once again, the whole story is turned on its head. Haman seemed to be flavour of the month and was close to wiping out his enemy Mordecai and all of the Jews in the kingdom. But Esther finally admitted her Jewish roots in a moving speech. King Xerxes was furious he'd been tricked into ordering the extermination of his wife's people, so Haman would pay for his plotting. Egotistical Haman had hoped to impale Mordecai on the huge pole he had set up. Instead, it was his own body that hung from a great height.

GET ON WITH IT

Proverbs 26 v 27 fits perfectly. Check it out and then memorise it.

THINK IT OVER

▶ *Ever plan to bring someone down?*

▶ *Is there someone you deliberately hurt?*

PRAY ABOUT IT

Talk to God about these things. Ask Him to help you make peace with your enemies. Or family who wind you up until you treat them badly.

Haman was dead. But the law to kill all the Jews still stood. And Xerxes *never* changed his laws.

354 | Celebration nation

Haman is dead. Esther and Mordecai are safe. But there's a problem. The law to destroy all the Jews still stands. And King Xerxes isn't allowed to change his laws.

👁 Read Esther 8 v 1–8

ENGAGE YOUR BRAIN

▷ *What did King Xerxes do for Esther? (v1)*

▷ *And for Mordecai? (v2)*

▷ *What did Esther again beg the king for? (v3–6)*

▷ *What was the problem? (end of v8)*

Xerxes had ordered that all the Jews be slaughtered on the thirteenth day of the twelfth month. This law couldn't be changed. But another law could be made…

👁 Read verses 9–17

▷ *What new law was passed? (v11–12)*

▷ *How did the Jews react? (v16–17)*

▷ *How did it affect other people? (end of v17)*

The law to attack the Jews still stood, but now they could defend themselves. And only their enemies would attack them, not everyone, as King Xerxes was now on their side. All of this led to more people joining God's people, the Jews (v17).

They weren't safe yet, but the Jews certainly thought everything would be OK (v16). So they celebrated something that hadn't yet happened. We can do the same. God has promised to rescue His people. This life will be hard for Christians, but one day Jesus will return and gather His followers for a perfect eternity. That's worth celebrating!

PRAY ABOUT IT

Spend time thanking God for some of His promises that have yet to be fulfilled. And think how you can share your joy over a brilliant future promised by God.

355 Day of destruction

The time has come — it's destroy or be destroyed. What would happen on the 13th day of the 12th month? Execution of God's people? Or them beating up the rest?

👁 Read Esther 9 v 1–10

ENGAGE YOUR BRAIN

▷ *What did happen? (v1–2)*

▷ *What did politicians do? (v3)*

▷ *How had life changed for Mordecai? (v4)*

▷ *What happened to the enemies of God's people? (v5–10)*

👁 Read verses 11–17

▷ *What extra request did Esther make? (v13)*

▷ *What fact is repeated in verses 10, 15 and 16?*

▷ *What happened after all the fighting? (v17)*

It was a day drenched in blood. 75,000 people were killed. Horrific. But this was God's day of punishment for everyone who had been against His people. That's why the Jews had to kill so many.

God was protecting His people and punishing His enemies. Maybe that explains why Esther asked for another day to kill more of their enemies.

A day is coming when God will fight against everyone who is still on the wrong side. Everyone who has not trusted in Jesus to save them will be punished. And all of God's people will be rescued from sin and death. No more sadness or pain.

PRAY ABOUT IT

Think of five people you know who are God's enemies. People who hate Christianity, or maybe are positive about it but won't accept Jesus as their King. Ask God to bring about an incredible U-turn in their lives.

356 | Party!

God's people, the Jews, didn't get wiped out! In fact, their enemies were the ones who suffered. Time for a party!

👁 Read Esther 9 v 18–32

ENGAGE YOUR BRAIN

▶ What did Mordecai make sure happened? (v20–22)

▶ Why was it called Purim (the **pur** was a lot/dice thing)? (v23–26)

▶ What did they do at Purim? (v22, 27–28)

The Jews' happiness bubbled over to others. They had been rescued from their enemies, and they showed their thanks to God in a practical way by giving to other people. They didn't celebrate this occasion just once, but every year. Esther and Mordecai made sure that God's people would never forget God's goodness to them.

👁 Read Esther 10 v 1–3

▶ How would you describe Mordecai's status?

▶ Why was he so popular?

Well, that's the Esther story. A miraculous reversal of situations, celebrated with a festival. At the beginning, Esther was an unknown, pretty Jewish girl, stuck in a foreign country. At the end, she's the powerful queen of Persia, who helped save God's people. At the start, Mordecai was a hated Jew who was going to be killed. Now he's Prime Minister. The second most powerful man in the country.

God isn't mentioned in the book of Esther, but He's clearly behind the scenes for His people and for His own glory. In Esther's pages we glimpse God's character, His promises, His power and His providence.

PRAY ABOUT IT

Thank God that He rescues His people. Thank Him that He's in control of everything. Ask Him to help you to serve Him and serve His people.

357 | Psalms: Cover it or confess it

"I will" — two tiny words. But in a wedding ceremony they represent a big change in two people's lives. In Psalm 32, David's choice brings about a transformation that's even more dramatic!

👁 Read Psalm 32 v 1–11

ENGAGE YOUR BRAIN

▶ *How does David describe the experience of keeping his sins hidden? (v3–4) And of being forgiven? (v1–2, 10)*

Verse 5 describes the two options with sin. Cover it or confess it. And the choice we make shapes the whole of our lives… it all changes when we own up to God.

▶ *What does running from God feel like? (v9)*

▶ *What else does God do for those who stop hiding? (v8-10)*

THINK IT THROUGH

Attempting to keep secrets from God has to be the most pointless plan imaginable. Not only can it not be done (Hebrews 4 v 13), the only person we're hurting is ourselves. And the alternative is so much better!

GET ON WITH IT

1. Make a list of as many sins as you can remember committing. It's not a test of your ability to remember, but about being honest with God. All of your thoughts and attitudes, words and desires. Get it all out of your system.

2. On top of your confessions write Psalm 32 v 1.

3. Act out verse 11 in a way that suits you. Do a little jig of celebration. Or whatever God's forgiveness stirs you to do!

THE BOTTOM LINE

Read 1 John 1 v 7

God is offering us more than a quick fix for guilt issues. He invites us to walk in an everyday friendship, characterised by honesty and purity. Now that's what I call *"Blessed"*!

2 PETER

Think straight, stand firm

How do you wake up your brain in the morning? Coffee? Cold shower? Cereal? The message of 2 Peter is to switch your brain on. Urgently. Because Christians need to think straight.

Peter was one of Jesus Christ's closest friends (and the writer of 1 Peter, which we looked at earlier this issue). He was also an "apostle" — someone who saw Jesus after He rose from the dead and received personal instructions from Him. The apostles' mission was to tell people what they'd seen Jesus do and had heard Him say.

Peter was writing to Christian friends. He wanted them to get their brains into gear: to think straight. To think about what they'd already heard about Jesus from the apostles — so they knew what it meant to live as Christians. Peter wanted them to deepen their understanding of what they already knew.

Peter was worried about false teachers, who called themselves Christians but were spreading dangerously wrong ideas about Christ. They were making these believers doubt what Peter had said about Jesus, and so doubt whether God had really rescued them through Jesus' death or not.

Peter wanted his friends to think straight to stand firm. To tune their brains in to what they already knew so they wouldn't be fooled by false teachers.

So, get your double-strength coffee or whatever you need... and stay tuned. Christians need to think straight to stand firm.

358 Everything we need

This may not be the traditional way to begin a letter, but it's a brilliant one. Peter hits us with top truths right from the start.

Read 2 Peter 1 v 1–2

ENGAGE YOUR BRAIN

▷ *What does Peter call himself?*

▷ *How does he describe the people he's writing to? (v1)*

▷ *What can Christians have because of Jesus? (v2)*

Peter humbly calls himself a servant of Jesus. And also an apostle — one sent out by Jesus to tell others about Him. Peter wants to restore his friends' confidence in what God has done for them. They were being tempted by false teachers not to believe what he'd told them.

Read verses 3–4

▷ *What else has God given Christians?*

-
-
-

Through Jesus, God gives us everything we need to live for Him. He has called Christians to serve Him and gives them the ability to do it. God has promised us perfect eternal life and, even now, lives in us through His Holy Spirit.

Good, eh? From first to last, our Christian faith depends on God, not us; He's the source of our faith, our motivation and the spiritual strength and ability we need to keep going.

PRAY ABOUT IT

Spend longer in prayer today. Take your time working your way through today's verses, using them to help you thank God for all He's done for you and continues to do for you.

THE BOTTOM LINE

God gives us everything we need.

359 Keep on running

Peter's friends are in a marathon — the Christian life. They began when they became Christians; the finish line is heaven. Peter wants his readers to break the tape having run a good race.

👁 Read 2 Peter 1 v 5–11

Being sure of what God's done, through Jesus' death and resurrection, we should work hard at living for Jesus. As with invitations to some parties, there's a dress code for heaven. It's *holiness*.

ENGAGE YOUR BRAIN

▶ *What qualities does Peter say Christians should have?*

-
-
-
-
-
-

▶ *What will Christian runners avoid if they have these things? (v8)*

▶ *What kind of athletes are they if they don't have them? (v9)*

GET ON WITH IT

▶ *Which of these qualities do you need to work on most?*

▶ *How can you do that?*

Peter wants his readers to finish the race strongly (v10–11). The "election" in verse 10 isn't political: it means that God has chosen people who will live with Him for ever. Peter doesn't want His readers to be smug, but to work hard at being Christians.

▶ *What great thing will happen to them if they run well? (v11)*

PRAY ABOUT IT

Thank God for giving us all we need to finish the Christian race. And for endless forgiveness that helps us to get up when we fall down and to carry on running. Ask God to help you live out the qualities listed in verses 5–7.

360 | Refreshing your memory

Peter's worried that his readers will be deflected from the gospel by people spreading lies about Jesus. So now he tells us how to think straight about who's right about God.

👁 Read 2 Peter 1 v 12–15

ENGAGE YOUR BRAIN

▷ Any idea what the "things" are that Peter refers to in verse 12? (See v1–11)

▷ What is Peter determined to do before he dies? (v13–15)

Peter knows he's going to die soon — and after he's gone, he wants his friends to think straight. To remember Jesus' rescue (v11). And to stand firm in their faith (v12). But why should we listen to Peter?

👁 Read verses 16–18

▷ So why should we listen to Peter and the other apostles? (v16)

Christianity is based on what eye-witnesses saw and heard. The apostles saw it all themselves, so what they've written (the New Testament) is reliable.

▷ How does this give you confidence when people say your faith is a load of rubbish?

👁 Read verses 19–21

▷ What should we do with the Old Testament ("prophetic message")? (v19) Why? (v20–21)

So Jesus' rescue through His death is a historical event — Old Testament prophets predicted it and the New Testament apostles proclaimed it.

THINK IT OVER

How will this knowledge help you think straight and keep going as a Christian?

PRAY ABOUT IT

Thank God that the Bible is Him speaking directly to us. Pray that you will learn from it, remember it and grow in your faith.

361 Religious conmen

Fake life-insurance policies end in tears because they don't deliver what they promise. But (eternal) life insurance offered by Peter and the apostles does deliver because they're telling the truth — as we saw last time.

In chapter 2, Peter warns against conmen — and tells us what happens to people who offer false hope.

👁 Read 2 Peter 2 v 1–3

ENGAGE YOUR BRAIN

▶ *How are Peter's readers in the same situation as God's Old Testament people? (v1)*

▶ *What's the sad truth? (v2)*

People will always be gullible and truth will remain under threat. These conmen denied "the sovereign Lord who bought them". That's Jesus, who bought them with His life when He paid for their sins on the cross. These conmen called themselves Christians, but had turned their backs on Jesus. They were in it for the money.

👁 Read verses 4–10

The destruction of the world by the flood and the rescue of Noah, the burning of Sodom, and the rescue of Lot all happened in Old Testament times. But what have they got to do with these religious conmen?

▶ *How does the Old Testament show what will happen to such conmen? (v9–10)*

False teachers can be subtle and not always easy to spot. But the con is revealed when someone contradicts what the Bible says about Jesus. God will punish such conmen. And He'll rescue His faithful people (v9).

PRAY ABOUT IT

Ask God to help you to know the Bible better so you'll be more able to think straight and stand firm for Jesus.

362 Washed pigs

Peter's warning his friends about religious conmen — false teachers who lead people away from Christ. Peter has strong words for those kinds of people.

👁 Read 2 Peter 2 v 10–16

ENGAGE YOUR BRAIN

▷ Do these false teachers know what they're talking about? (v12)

▷ How are they described? (v13–15)

▷ What will happen to them? (v12–13)

Here's another way to spot false teachers — if someone's behaviour is clearly immoral, then their teaching probably isn't too great either.

👁 Read verses 17–22

▷ How do false teachers con people?
v18:
v19:

▷ Why is an anti-God lifestyle not a life of freedom? (v19)

▷ What does Peter say about such conmen in verses 20–22?

A washed pig going back to the mud — no fundamental change has occurred. True believers in God can be identified: they don't return, like conmen, to a filthy lifestyle.

SHARE IT

How will you answer people who say: "Forget old-fashioned morality, no sex before marriage etc. So what if it's in the Bible? Real Christianity is about freeing the spirit"?

PRAY ABOUT IT

Think straight, or you'll be sucked into a wrong lifestyle. Ask God to help you not to get conned into doubting the message of the Bible. Or conned into thinking that being free is doing what feels good at the time.

THE BOTTOM LINE

To obey God is to be really free.

363 Jesus — the return

Ever get teased for your faith in Jesus? Peter says Christians will be taunted by unbelievers and made to question their beliefs. So think straight and stand firm.

👁 Read 2 Peter 3 v 1–2

ENGAGE YOUR BRAIN

▶ *Why did Peter write his two letters? (v1)*

▶ *In the face of false teaching, what must his friends do? (v2)*

👁 Read verses 3–7

▶ *What do people try to make Christians doubt? (v4)*

▶ *What have they forgotten? (v5–6)*

▶ *And what will happen when Jesus returns? (v7)*

The "last days" (v3) means the time between Jesus' return to heaven in 1st-century AD and His second coming in the future. Peter's friends lived in the last days, and so do we.

People will mock us and try to make us doubt that Jesus will return. But God's word is a guarantee that it will happen. We can see from the Bible that God always keeps His promises.

Jesus WILL return and take His people to a perfect new life.

👁 Read verses 8–9

▶ *Why is Jesus delaying His return?*

THINK IT OVER

"Repentance" (v9) = turning to Christ; becoming a Christian.

▶ *What would have happened to you if Jesus had returned before you became a Christian?*

▶ *What will happen to your friends if they don't become Christians before Jesus returns?*

PRAY ABOUT IT

Thank God that He's delaying the second coming so that people have a chance to turn to Jesus. Thank Him that you had that chance. Pray for friends who don't know Jesus yet.

364 Wait, watch

Listen up. Peter's got more to say on Jesus' return — and how Christians should live while we wait.

👁 Read 2 Peter 3 v 10–14

ENGAGE YOUR BRAIN

▶ *In what way will Jesus' return be like a burglary? (v10)*

▶ *What will happen to the universe when Jesus returns? (v10, 12)*

▶ *Will that be the end of everything? (v13)*

When the world ends, Christians are going to get a new home of righteousness — a great place with no selfishness, depression or death. A place where we'll be overcome by how great and loving God is. A place to get excited about.

▶ *So what should Christians do while we wait for this? (v11–12)*

▶ *What should we aim for?*

▶ *What do you think that means exactly?*

Peter says: "Make every effort". He doesn't say we'll always succeed at being blameless (obviously!). But he is saying don't aim for second best. Don't be half-hearted. Be in training when Jesus comes again.

GET ON WITH IT

▶ *How do you shape up alongside verse 14?*

▶ *What do you need to work on for starters?*

PRAY ABOUT IT

Thank God that Jesus will return one day and that believers can look forward to a perfect new world. Ask Him to help you live for Him as you wait excitedly.

THE BOTTOM LINE

Make every effort to be found spotless, blameless and at peace with Him.

365 Ready, steady, grow

Peter signs off now with a few reminders, warnings, encouragements and even some name-dropping. Ask God to speak to you through 2 Peter one more time.

👁 Read 2 Peter 3 v 15–16

ENGAGE YOUR BRAIN

▶ *What are Peter and Paul agreed on? (v15, and see v9)*

OK, so Peter didn't always find Paul easy to understand (neither will we at times!). But Paul's letters are important — God is the driving force behind them, speaking to us.

▶ *Instead, how do the conmen treat Paul's letters? (v16)*

👁 Read verses 17–18

These verses sum up Peter's letter. Try to put them into your own words:

Peter says: *Don't get taken in by religious conmen and false teachers. Instead, grow in your faith.*

The way to grow is:

1. Remember that God's forgiveness and love are always there for us because of Jesus (that's *grace*, v18).

2. Know more and more about what it means to obey Jesus in our daily lives (that's *knowledge*, v18).

GET ON WITH IT

What exactly can you do to…
remember?
know more?
obey?

PRAY ABOUT IT

Ask God to help you do this daily. And thank Him for 2 Peter.

Oh, and remember: think straight and stand firm.

What is the Bible?

One of the main ambitions of *Engage 365* is to encourage you to dive into God's word. So here are four major truths about the Bible and how they affect the way we study it.

1. THE BIBLE IS FROM GOD

Paul tells us that the Bible is "God-breathed" (2 Timothy 3 v 16–17) — it comes directly from God. Behind the human writers, He is the ultimate author. When we read the Bible, we're reading God's words to us! And Paul tells us we should use God's words to teach us, train us and challenge us, so that we can serve God with our lives.

2. THE BIBLE IS TRUE

One of the amazing things about God is that He doesn't lie (Titus 1 v 2). He doesn't make mistakes either, because He knows everything there is to know. If the Bible is God's word, then it follows that the Bible doesn't lie or make mistakes. We can trust everything the Bible says. It will never mislead us. The word of God is the strongest foundation that you can build your life on.

3. WHAT GOD SAYS GOES

Another vital truth to remember as we read the Bible is this: what God says goes. He is the supreme Lord and King of the universe. He is the one in charge. Christians want to live with God in charge of their lives, and in practice that means obeying God's word. As we read the Bible, we should expect to find God saying things we don't like or find difficult (2 Timothy 3 v 16). We should expect to be corrected and trained in living God's right way. You might find it helpful to use the sides of the *Engage 365* pages, or a separate notebook, to jot down what God is teaching you.

4. GOD GIVES US HELP

We're not left alone with God's huge book! The Holy Spirit helps Christians understand the Bible (1 Corinthians 2 v 9–13). Someone who isn't a Christian won't be able to fully understand the Bible, because they don't have the Spirit helping them (1 Corinthians 2 v 14). We should be wary of the "expert" on TV or the latest controversial book about Christianity. It's easy to bow to what seems to be impressive knowledge, but if they haven't got the Spirit of God working in them, then they haven't a hope of grasping the Bible's message. However, Christians can understand the Bible for themselves, since all Christians have the Spirit. All God's children have access to God's truth.

We need to remember that we depend on God to help us understand His word and His ways (2 Timothy 2 v 7). We can't do it alone, so we must ask for God's help. Pray before you open the Bible. Pray when you get stuck and don't understand stuff. Pray when you do understand it — and say thank you!

SO, WHAT IS THE BIBLE?

▶ *The Bible is God's word direct from God to us. It is relevant today as God speaks into our lives.*

▶ *The Bible is totally true and trustworthy.*

▶ *So we must obey it — what God says goes.*

▶ *We're not on our own — the Holy Spirit helps us understand God's word and apply it to our lives.*

What's the point?

Do you ever read a Bible passage and think "What is the point of that?" It's a good question to ask.

WRITING WITH PURPOSE

It sounds obvious when you say it, but the Bible authors wrote their books with a particular purpose in mind. They weren't just scribbling down random things that popped into their heads. We know that, because they often tell us what their aim is.

For instance, near the end of his Gospel, John says: "Jesus performed many other signs in the presence of his disciples, which are not recorded in this book. But these are written that you may believe that Jesus is the Messiah, the Son of God, and that by believing you may have life in his name" (John 20 v 30–31).

There are loads of things that John could have told us about Jesus but hasn't. He has selected his material with the specific aim of showing us that Jesus is the Messiah/Christ, the Son of God, so that we will come to believe in Him and so have eternal life.

Since the writers of the Bible were inspired by God (2 Timothy 3 v 16), their purpose is God's purpose. This means that one of the most helpful questions we can ever ask is "Why did the author write this?"

IT'S OBVIOUS

Sometimes the author bluntly tells us why he is writing his book, in what's sometimes called the "purpose statement". We've already seen one from John's Gospel. Now check out these two:

Luke 1 v 1–4
1 John 5 v 13

SEARCHING FOR CLUES

But what about Bible books that don't obviously state their purpose? Here are a few tips.

1. Get to know the book
Nothing beats reading the whole book several times. Becoming familiar

with a Bible book helps you to notice themes running through it and to work out the writer's purpose.

2. Ask key questions

These questions are especially helpful if you're reading a New Testament letter (like 1 Timothy) or an Old Testament prophet (like Habakkuk). You might need to grab a study Bible or a commentary to find the answers.

▶ *Who is writing and who's he writing to?*

▶ *What is the situation of the author and the original readers?*

▶ *Are there any problems the author says need to be dealt with?*

▶ *Are there any repeated themes, or a single idea that holds everything together?*

3. What's in and what's out?

"Narrative" books are ones that talk us through historical events (like Genesis or Acts). In these books, you can get an idea of the author's purpose from what he chooses to put in and what he leaves out of his account. Sometimes the author hits the accelerator pedal and covers someone's whole life in two verses; at other times he slows down and gives us a few hours in great detail. We should be asking, "Why do we hear so much about this and so little about that?"

In this article, we've shown you the very best tool for understanding the Bible. Whenever you read a Bible passage, ask: "What's the author's purpose for writing this?", "What are the big themes?", "What is the author trying to do?"

In other words, what's the point?

(The ideas on pages 396–399 are taken from *Dig Deeper* by Nigel Beynon and Andrew Sach, published by IVP.)

thegoodbook
COMPANY

BIBLICAL | RELEVANT | ACCESSIBLE

At The Good Book Company, we are dedicated to helping Christians and local churches grow. We believe that God's growth process always starts with hearing clearly what he has said to us through his timeless word—the Bible.

Ever since we opened our doors in 1991, we have been striving to produce Bible-based resources that bring glory to God. We have grown to become an international provider of user-friendly resources to the Christian community, with believers of all backgrounds and denominations using our books, Bible studies, devotionals, evangelistic resources, and DVD-based courses.

We want to equip ordinary Christians to live for Christ day by day, and churches to grow in their knowledge of God, their love for one another, and the effectiveness of their outreach.

Call us for a discussion of your needs or visit one of our local websites for more information on the resources and services we provide.

Your friends at The Good Book Company

thegoodbook.com | thegoodbook.co.uk
thegoodbook.com.au | thegoodbook.co.nz
thegoodbook.co.in